Queer Youth in the Province of the "Severely Normal"

Sexuality Studies Series

This series focuses on original, provocative, scholarly research examining from a range of perspectives the complexity of human sexual practice, identity, community, and desire. Books in the series explore how sexuality interacts with other aspects of society, such as law, education, feminism, racial diversity, the family, policing, sport, government, religion, mass media, medicine, and employment. The series provides a broad public venue for nurturing debate, cultivating talent, and expanding knowledge of human sexual expression, past and present.

Previous volumes in the series are:
Masculinities without Men? Female Masculinity in Twentieth-Century Fictions
    by Jean Bobby Noble
Every Inch a Woman: Phallic Possession, Femininity, and the Text
    by Carellin Brooks

Gloria Filax

Queer Youth in the Province
of the "Severely Normal"

UBCPress · Vancouver · Toronto

15 14 13 12 11 10 09 08 07 06   5 4 3 2 1

Printed in Canada on acid-free paper.

Library and Archives Canada Cataloguing in Publication

Filax, Gloria, 1951-
  Queer youth in the province of the "severely normal" / Gloria Filax.

(Sexuality studies series 1706-9947)
Includes bibliographical references and index.
ISBN-13: 978-0-7748-1245-0
ISBN-10: 0-7748-1245-1

  1. Gay youth – Alberta – History – 20th century. 2. Gay youth – Government policy – Alberta – 20th century. 3. Homophobia – Alberta – 20th century. 4. Homophobia – Press coverage – Alberta – History – 20th century. I. Title. II. Series.

HQ76.3.C32A43 2006   306.76′0835′097123   C2006-901123-0

Canadä

UBC Press gratefully acknowledges the financial support for our publishing program of the Government of Canada through the Book Publishing Industry Development Program (BPIDP), and of the Canada Council for the Arts, and the British Columbia Arts Council.

This book has been published with the help of a grant from Athabasca University.

Printed and bound in Canada by Friesens
Set in Stone by Artegraphica Design Co. Ltd.
Copy editor: Joanne Richardson
Proofreader: Dianne Tiefensee

UBC Press
The University of British Columbia
2029 West Mall
Vancouver, BC V6T 1Z2
604-822-5959 / Fax: 604-822-6083
www.ubcpress.ca

For Debra and Ryan

Contents

Acknowledgments

This book would not have been possible without the young people who so earnestly shared their experiences about living in Alberta in the 1990s. I am very grateful to them for amiably giving me their time as they negotiated a socially volatile time for queer people in Alberta.

I feel very fortunate that UBC Press was willing to take on this book and in so doing honour the courage and vitality of queer youth in Alberta, the province of the "severely normal." Special thanks to Jean Wilson, Associate Director, Editorial at the press, for believing in the merit of the book and for soliciting financial support when it appeared that, despite favourable reviews, the book might not be published due to diminished support from granting bodies for publication of scholarly books.

I am grateful to the Social Sciences and Humanities Research Council and the University of Alberta for help with funding my work from which this manuscript emerged. I am also indebted to Athabasca University, my employer, for heeding Jean Wilson's calls for help to support the publication of this book.

A heartfelt thanks is also extended to those friends and family, especially Elaine and Ryan, who recognized and supported my joys and struggles living and researching as a queer person in Alberta during the very tumultuous 1990s.

My eternal love goes to my life partner Debra Shogan for her unwavering support and assistance. Without Debra, I would be a very sad person and this manuscript would never have made it into print.

Introduction

Rudolf, one of Alberta's queer youth, wrote the following:

I hated junior high. Even though I had not admitted to myself that I was gay until grade nine it seems that everyone else figured it out before me and then discriminated against me. I found a poem that I wrote around that time. It's not that good a poem because it was written by a thirteen-year-old, but it explains how I felt.

Discrimination

The hatred of differences within humans.
A terrible crime when committed.
A serious problem of the human race,
caused when two different individuals conflict.

One – a poor soul whose disturbed and troubled state receives little sympathy.
One – an inventor of mistreatment whose own ideas of superiority have been passed down from
his or
her forebearers.
Discrimination.
When committed, it causes great pain.

Discrimination.
The problem revolves around opinions of others.
Why does it happen?
Everyone is and deserves the same.
Why must it happen?
Why?
It is horrible!

Discrimination.

A problem that must be stopped.

Discrimination.

One of the factors that helped to create our sick and toxic society.

Discrimination.

A part of the predicament in which our world is.

Discrimination.

Almost unsolvable.

Discrimination is.

This book is an account of how queer youth in Alberta in the 1990s negotiated expert, legal, and popular discourses about sexuality, many of which overwhelmingly denied the value of their lives. Alberta is still the only Canadian province distinguished by state-sanctioned homophobia. Yet Alberta is also the home of some important initiatives with respect to queer youth in schools, such as the Calgary Board of Education's "An Action Plan for Gay/Lesbian/Bisexual Youth and Staff Safety" (1996). And, of course, most young people in Alberta have access to popular culture that extends well beyond the provincial boundaries through television, movies, videos, the Internet, books, and magazines, all of which provide a range of representations of queer people.

I am interested in how youth identities are constructed through dominant and often competing discourses about youth, sexuality, and gender, and how queer youth living in Alberta in the 1990s negotiated the contradictions of these discourses. In part, this is a project of "surfacing" what Foucault (1979, 81) refers to as "subjugated knowledges" in order to demonstrate that queer youth are indeed present in Alberta.

The 1990s in Alberta, Canada, were marked by active provincial government contestation of the legal rights of sexual minority citizens; this was juxtaposed with expanding lesbian and gay rights at the federal level. In Canada, federal and provincial governments are both interdependent and autonomous. Provincial governments provide local, regional representation from a provincial capital city, while the federal government, located in Ottawa, represents the Canadian state. While Canadian law is based on a British parliamentary system, the adoption of the Charter of Right and Freedoms in 1982 made Canada into a more hybrid legal culture with an American type of constitutionally entrenched bill of rights (Stychin 1995). Provincial human rights codes were to be realigned with the new federal charter, but a grey area relating to protections for sexual minority Canadians allowed for exclusion within both federal and provincial codes. A series of court challenges taken to the Supreme Court of Canada resulted in inclusion of protections for gays and lesbians in the existing charter (Yogis, Duplak, and Trainor 1996). The province of Alberta remains unique in the Canadian mosaic of ten provinces and three territories for its continued refusal to realign its human rights code or to extend human rights protections by reading homosexuality as a protected category into the provincial human rights code.[1] Provincial premier Ralph Klein has defended this position by indicating that "severely normal" Albertans do not support such measures.[2]

It is worth noting that Alberta is an oil-rich province whose dominant identity and brand of politics is informed by a frontier mentality that focuses on rugged individualism entwined with an ethos that insists that Albertans are misunderstood by an eastern, centrist, urbane, large, and biased federal government. While the content of debates within federal politics shifts, in the minds of many Albertans regional-federal friction is serious enough to surface and to justify calls for western separatism – a desire to pull away from "nanny state politics," which, among other things, are thought to include human rights codes. As well, Alberta's historical legacy includes a brand of religious conservatism – Christian fundamentalism – that shares a thirty-five-year history with Alberta's Social Credit Party, which was in power from 1932 to 1968.[3] Christian fundamentalism, although reduced to minority status in the province, continues to co-exist alongside the fiscal conservatism of the newer provincial Progressive Conservative party, which came to power in 1968 and continues to govern to this day.[4] The struggle over human rights protections for lesbians and gays is one of a series of struggles produced by the contradictions between the interdependence/ autonomy of the regional-provincial government in relation to Canadian federalism.[5] This struggle also concerns determining what constitutes a proper, "normal" Alberta identity and who rightfully belongs within the Alberta community/mosaic.

During the 1990s Alberta was the home of the widely circulated *Alberta Report*, a weekly magazine that, in almost every issue, represented gays and lesbians as disgusting deviants.[6] *Alberta Report* had a considerable impact on the discussion regarding who constitutes a legitimate Albertan. While in many ways a fiscally marginal magazine, *Alberta Report* had a significant impact on discourses about social values. It was regularly engaged in its letters page by university presidents, academics, politicians, and other prominent citizens (Fraser, 21 October 1996, 3; Grundy, 28 October 1996, 3). Copies of *Alberta Report* were often provided free of charge to schools, libraries, and many businesses. As well as being a ubiquitous presence in Alberta, remarkably, *Alberta Report* had the most complete and comprehensive coverage of queer issues in the province during the 1990s. Unlike the mainstream media, *Alberta Report* took (the perceived threat of) sexual minority peoples seriously. From a few articles in 1992, representations of homosexuality rise to a crescendo of hatred in a series of frenzied diatribes that occurred leading up to, during, and immediately following the Supreme Court decision on *Vriend*. Studying queer issues as they are presented in this magazine, which I do in the final chapter of *Queer Youth*, offers a unique understanding of both mainstream and queer culture and politics in 1990s Alberta.

A Note on Queer

Despite its use as a pejorative to refer to sexual minority people, "queer" has been reclaimed both as a political strategy and as a method of inquiry. "Queer" gained intellectual capital at a conference theorizing lesbian and gay sexualities held at the University of California, Santa Cruz, in February 1990. The conference was based on the premise that homosexuality is no longer defined either by opposition to or homology with a dominant, stable form of sexuality (heterosexuality) or as merely transgressive or deviant in relation to a proper or natural sexuality. Participants were invited to reconceptualize male and female homosexualities as social and cultural forms in their own right, even if undercoded and dependent upon more established forms of sexuality. As such, "queer" suggests both a rupture in and the continuity of lesbian and gay identities.

"To queer," as a political strategy and as a method of inquiry, is to problematize identity categories by exposing how the assumptions upon which they are based are normalizing, reifying, homogenizing, naturalizing, and totalizing. Queering of sexuality, then, can and is performed not only by anyone in the street, the cabaret, the legislature, or the academy who refuses to take seriously the straight-gay binary but also by those who disrupt notions of stable gay and lesbian identities. When "lesbian" and "gay," as identity categories, are regarded as opposites to "heterosexual," the effect is not only to fix a notion of a normal sexuality within a two-sex, two-gender, one-sexual orientation system but also to set the characteristics of the "deviant" homosexual. To queer is to expose the assumption that gender, chromosomal sex, sexuality, and sexual desire cohere and that once one has information about one of these, it is possible to know with certainty about the rest (Jagose 1996, 3). To queer is to see heterosexuality not as the original, or that from which homosexuality deviates, but, rather, to see hetero- and homosexuality as mutually productive of one another. This is why Sedgwick (1990, 1) argues that not only do the social consequences of the hetero-homo divide affect "a small, distinct, relatively fixed homosexual minority" but that they are also of "continuing, determinative importance in the lives of people across the spectrum of sexualities."

To queer is to notice, call into question, and refuse heterosexuality as the natural foundation of social institutions. As Warner (1994b, xiii) writes, "realization that themes of homophobia and heterosexism may be read in almost any document of our culture means that we are only beginning to have an idea of how widespread those institutions and accounts are." Because heteronormativity permeates all social institutions (family, religion, work, leisure, law, education), challenging or queering this order has the effect of challenging common sense ideology pertaining to what it means to be a human being.

Used as an adjective, as in queer research, queer youth, or queer researcher, "queer" suggests that the person or the work takes seriously the project of noticing, questioning, and refusing how the notion of "the normal" is produced (Shogan 1999). I refer to the young people in this study as queer youth rather than as sexual minority or gay and lesbian youth because, by virtue of responding to my advertisements, these young people indicated that they questioned and refused how they had been categorized in mainstream Alberta. While many of them did not have the language to signify that they refused the categorizations that fix sexual minority people as deviant and shameful, their boldness in meeting with me to tell their stories in the face of adversity is significant enough for me to see them as queer.

While this work would not have been possible without assuming the position of queer researcher (noticing, questioning, and refusing assumptions of heteronormativity), this is not without its risks. As David Halperin (1995, 138) indicates, queer researchers are often placed in a double bind in which they risk not being heard because of their perceived deviance: "And if to speak as a gay man [queer] about a topic that directly implicates one's own interests is already to surrender a sizable share of one's claims to be heard, listened to, and taken seriously, then to speak not as the designated representative of a subcultural minority but as a dedicated critic of heterosexual presumption is surely to put the remaining share of one's credibility at risk."

The double bind here involves writing from within a heteronormalized culture in which the queer researcher is both the subject of what she writes and the objectified deviant. To refuse to be designated as representative token, while insisting on one's status as a critic of heteronormative culture, risks undermining one's authority as a researcher. The question at its most basic is whether one can be queer and scholarly at the same time. Disallowing the critical queer scholar to function within an authorized category assumes the same logic that de-authorizes, de-legitimizes, and silences social deviants. The "truth" of "deviant" existence is accomplished through the use of objectifying and pathologizing terms. Thus the conundrum of the queer researcher is "the inescapably vexed, treacherous, and volatile politics of any attempt ... to write about the meaning of a socially deviant life" (Halperin 1995, 134).

The Research

Immersion in queer culture is difficult when there is no geographic place that one can locate as "queer." Unlike Spradley's (1979) homeless men, who can be located as a group within particular geographic places in inner city areas and streets, queer people are dispersed and yet everywhere. Nor are queer people contained by race, class, gender, religion, age, physicality, or nation. Warner (1994b, xxv) writes that notions of community and culture are, in fact, problematic for queer people: "Much of lesbian and gay history is about noncommunity, and ... dispersal rather than localization continues to be definitive of queer self-understanding." Adam (1996, 121) refers to this as a colony away from an original homeland, likening it to a diasporic community. However, unlike Jewish peoples, for example, queer people have no collective homeland from which we have been dispersed. Dispersal, non-community, and lack of home are some of the defining features of queer living, often especially so for queer youth. The location of queer people – the diasporic space – is often the closet. Even though I was interested in how these queer youth negotiated their school lives, I did not engage in participant observation in their schools because most of them occupied a diasporic space there, and my presence would have threatened it.

It was possible, however, to use participant observation as a method of examining heteronormative culture (i.e., that from which queer people are dispersed) and, in particular, the ways in which that culture structures life for queer youth in and out of the closet. I was, then, in the unique place of being an ethnographer in the classical sense. I was permitted the peculiar advantage of observing heteronormative culture from the vantage point of a queer person. I was an outsider, a traditional ethnographer, in this hetero-normative world: "a stranger in a strange land." Ethnographic methods did allow me to explore queer culture, and, in particular, ethnographic inter-views provided a way for me to do an in-depth exploration as an insider of a culture without a place.

In the fall of 1997 I began advertising in alternative presses – Edmonton's *Times.10, Womonspace,* and Calgary's *Outlooks* – for queer youth to contact me if they were interested in telling me about their experiences as a queer young person living in Alberta. I was particularly interested in their experi-ences in school. I also attended meetings of queer youth groups in Edmonton and Calgary, where I invited members to participate in the research. The first contact came via mail in late September; others followed by phone and e-mail. I arranged to meet each person for coffee so that we could get to know one another and to ensure that the relationship would be sustainable for at least two two-hour sessions. Several potential subjects did not show up for our arranged coffee, and several others decided not to participate. Half of those who continued with the project were from Calgary or Edmonton, Alberta's two major cities. Of the twelve participants, only three were female (in both Calgary and Edmonton, there were fewer girls than boys participating in youth groups).

One youth decided to communicate via e-mail while the rest met with me on at least two occasions. The Edmonton interviews were conducted in offices and coffee shops around Edmonton. The Calgary interviews were more difficult. The first set included a coffee shop and the University of

Calgary campus. The second set was conducted at the local AIDS network office, and the third was conducted at the International Hotel. If the lobby staff thought anything about the series of young men passing through my hotel room, each for approximately an hour and a half, no one said anything to me. I met each young man in the lobby, and after the interview I escorted him back there, where I would meet the next one – six in a row on one weekend.

During the interviews each young person told a story about his or her life in Alberta. Important as this was, however, my responsibility to these young people involved more than telling their stories. I also felt the need to show that, while many of them had been victimized, they were not victims. Many of them expected that I would take their stories and "do something" (Virginia, 1998; Jack, 1998; Oscar, 1998). They wanted me to put pressure on educational institutions and government to change things so that what had happened to them wouldn't happen to others. This was a lot to expect from a research project, particularly one located in Alberta, with its particular brand of homophobic inertia. But, then, as Jagose (1996, 111) indicates, when it comes to attaining political goals, it is "far from clear that writing a paper, or developing an analytical framework, is any less effective than various other gestures."

Understanding Discourse

My project is to show how the various dominant discourses about gender, sexuality, and youth that circulated in expert, legal, and popular forms were negotiated by queer youth living in Alberta in the 1990s. A discourse is a regulated system of knowledge (in this case, knowledge about gender, sexuality, and youth) supported by social institutions, which constrain what can be spoken, how it may be spoken about, and who can speak it. Discourses produce positions from which people can speak as well as related social practices. In Chapter 1, for example, I am interested in how gender discourses work to keep intact the assumption that there is a coherency between sexed bodies, behaviour, and sexual desire and practice; in Chapter 2 I explore how mainstream youth studies assume the heterosexual subject; in Chapter 3 I look at how Canadian legal discourses have produced sexual minority legal status; and in Chapter 4 I address how ultra-conservative popular discourses, such as that produced by *Alberta Report*, actively work to produce what can legitimately be said about "the homosexual."

Since I focus on dominant notions of what counts as gender, sexuality, and youth, my concern is to make apparent the prominent features of these discourses rather than to systematically document singular examples of them. This is particularly so in Chapter 3, where my project is to outline the features of legal discourse in Canada that facilitated what can be said about who counts as a sexual minority. This discourse analysis contrasts with a traditional historical approach to the material, which might, for example, document all the legal cases pertaining to sexual minority issues.

For a number of reasons I do not present the stories of Alberta's queer youth as a coherent whole. Since I wanted to make sense of these stories in relation to expert and popular discourses, I present the interview material intertextually. As well, a coherent, linear presentation of the youth stories would assume that the experiences they recount are somehow straight-forwardly accessible and knowable. They are not.

I pursue a number of writing strategies in this book. Theoretical, legal, and expert accounts take up a disproportionate portion of the chapters in relation to the voices of the youth. This is in order to demonstrate the relent-lessness and heaviness of the discourses that these young people must ne-gotiate. In the first three chapters the voices of queer youth are juxtaposed with academic discourses that purport either to be about young people or to shape the world in which they live. In Chapter 4 these voices are placed in relation to accounts from the *Alberta Report*, the weekly magazine that devoted itself to documenting events and decisions related to the lives of queer people in Alberta.

As well, the juxtaposition of voices "queers" expert and popular discourses that so unproblematically fix identities, such as "girl," "boy," "youth," "homo-sexual," and "expert." In some cases these categories are called into ques-tion when what the youth have to say contradicts what expert discourses say about gender, youth, and sexuality. In other cases, the youth voices disrupt these categories by substantiating research that has not countenanced their existence. In Chapter 4 queer youth voices resist and expose the mean-spiritedness of the representations of queer people in *Alberta Report*.

In all four chapters it has been important to me to represent the stories of these young people as more than "painful stories of subjection and pathos" (Britzman 1995, 68). It would have been easy to yield to the statistics on suicide and stories of harassment and abuse and to describe how these ac-counts constitute the stories of these young people's lives. However, as the youth voices in *Queer Youth* convey, their lives are not consumed by pathos.

Eve Sedgwick's *The Epistemology of the Closet* (1990) is based on a number of axioms, the first of which is that people are different from each other. She observes that "it is astonishing how few respectable conceptual tools we have for dealing with this self-evident fact" (22-3). By situating the voices of the youth in this text in the way that I do, I hope to demonstrate that, even though these people have faced common difficulties as queer youth, they do differ from one another. Each has a personal life history, differently intersected by religion, family, race, class, gender, physicality, ethnicity, and a range of other differences. The fragments of their voices are intended to disrupt closure or certainty and to represent the partiality of lives that refuse to be trapped in totalizing academic and popular discourses. By offering partial stories and fragmented voices, I resist fixing their identities and, instead, insist on constant and ongoing identity formation. Refusing to fix either them or their experiences is the very least that I can do for the queer youth who shared some parts of their lives with me so that this book might be written.

Organization of *Queer Youth*

Chapter 1, "Gendering: Troubled Theories, Troubling Identities," explores how discourses of gender and sexuality affect gender non-conformist children and youth. The existence of experts (amounting to an industry) to contend with gender non-conformity is an effect of the cultural imperative that physicality must cohere with expected social behaviours and that these, in turn, must line up with sexual desire and sexual practice. The stories of queer youth expose not only how bodies, behaviour, desire, and sexual practice align in a number of different combinations but also the desperation of a culture that would consent to behaviour modification, surgery, and, in extreme cases, death to achieve conformity.

In Chapter 2, "Production and Consumption of Youth Identities: Understanding Youth in the Context of Youth Studies and Popular Culture," I examine how social science research has produced the category "youth" and how queer youth negotiate the subject positions constrained by this category.

Chapter 3, "The Social-Legal Production of Sexual Minorities in Canada," explores how legal discourse has produced what can be said about sexual minority status in Canada and how, in doing so, it has positioned what counts as an illegitimate sexual minority. I look at how Bill C-23 and other laws and legal decisions maintain a notion of who counts as "normal" and "abnormal" members of a community, even as legal possibilities are opened up for sexual minorities. Also, in looking at three cases that focus on teachers and three stories drawn from ethnographic interviews with queer youth, I examine how legal discourse has affected education in Canada.

In Chapter 4, "Queer Identities and Strange Representations in the Province of the Severely Normal," I identify some of the discourses about homosexuality and gender that circulated in Alberta from 1992 to 1998. I do this by examining representations of homosexuality espoused in *Alberta Report*, by elected officials, and by other citizens in the province. In this way I highlight the culture of moral panic around homosexuality in Alberta that confronted the province's queer youth.

Queer Youth in the Province of the "Severely Normal"

1
Gendering: Troubled Theories, Troubling Identities

> Identity is not as transparent or unproblematic as we think. Perhaps instead of thinking of identity as an already accomplished fact, which the new cultural practices then represent, we should think, instead, of identity as a "production," which is never complete, always in process, and always constituted within, not outside representation. This view problematises the very authority and authenticity to which the term "cultural identity" lays claim.
>
> – Stuart Hall, *Cultural Representations and Signifying Practices*

Humans are born into a world with already existing notions of what it means to be embodied as male or female. As philosopher Marilyn Frye (1983, 22) writes, "We are socially and communicatively helpless if we do not know the sex of everybody we have anything to do with." Since, in most cultures, it is inappropriate to show one's genitalia in order to assist communication and other social interaction, pronouncement of sex is made through clothing, comportment, gestures, adornment, speech, and other behavioural manifestations. Together these behavioural markers are often referred to as gender.

While what counts as proper gender behaviour fluctuates with trends in popular culture, what does not change is the conviction that there are but two acceptable ways to display gender and that these reflect that there are but two sexes. Moreover, these two sexes are assumed to be complementary: bodies of one type not only manifest behaviours associated with that body type but they also desire and engage in sexual relations with other bodies that are thought to complement them sexually and behaviourally. This story of biological determinism that links sex, gender, sexual desire, and practice is the dominant gender discourse within our culture.

So important is the story about the coherence of bodies, behaviour, sexual desire, and practice that if someone's body does not line up with gender behaviour (or sexual desire and practice), there are elaborate mechanisms to intervene, correct, and in many cases punish those who do not conform. I elaborate on some of these interventions later in the chapter. Here, however, it helps to recall what Michel Foucault (1979) had to say about disciplines, examination, conformity, and normalization.

Gender can be thought of in much the same way as Foucault thought of disciplines (Shogan 1999). Disciplines establish standards of achievement, behaviour, or performance for specified tasks in relation to the physical and social spaces within which these occur. Everyone engaged in or by a discipline is measured in relation to these standards and ranked in relation to each other. In education, for example, teachers and other specialists assess students' abilities or behaviours. As "experts" they observe and judge students in relation to the standards established for a particular subject matter. Their observations and judgments are part of an examination process that produces information about an individual's placement in relation to established standards and in relation to others. This information makes it possible to isolate individuals so that their weaknesses can be corrected. Participants are subjected to interventions designed by teachers in order to close the gap between the deficient skill or behaviour and that imposed by the standard. As Foucault (1979, 172) indicates, examinations make it possible "to know them; to alter them."

The examination is also central in influencing people to conform to gender standards and norms. The experts in the case of gender are ubiquitous: family, friends, church leaders, and teachers who observe and judge gendered behaviour and intervene with rewards and punishments to exact conformity. There are also credentialed experts who, when consulted, use institutional authority to utilize sophisticated techniques of behaviour modification to normalize behaviour. In education each student becomes more like other students as deviations from the standard are corrected and an individual's behaviour or skills come closer to what is required. Through repeated interventions everyone is moved closer to the standard, or norm. Likewise, repetition of behaviour and skills of gender comes to consolidate and to solidify notions of normal, "real" gender.

An effect of the examination is the production of information about how participants behave or perform in relation to standards and how they respond to corrective measures. This information contributes to the body of knowledge of the discipline and serves to reposition what counts as standard behaviours or skills. Knowledge about individuals in relation to standards is also produced when participants are required to talk about their experiences. In what Foucault refers to as the confessional, participants tell, or perhaps write, their experiences and an authority records the information along with his or her expert interpretation of it. This is followed by an intervention "in order to judge, punish, forgive, console, and reconcile ... and [to] ... produce ... intrinsic modifications in the person who articulate[d] it (Foucault 1980b, 61-2).

In Volume 1 of *The History of Sexuality* Foucault outlines how, through the confessional, sexuality has become identified with the whole truth about a person and therefore occupies a strategic site for the regulation of individuals and populations. Implicit in this is the assumption that individuals attain self-knowledge by confessing to experts who interpret their confession for them. It is also assumed that it is possible to improve the confessor by interventions designed to bring her/him closer to disciplinary standards. Later I discuss the process of labelling an individual as having a "gender identity disorder." This labelling is the result of observing and judging the individual in relation to gender norms, but it is also the result of having the person talk to an expert who interprets this information according to the standards of the American Psychological Association's *Diagnostic and Statistical Manual of Mental and Physical Disorders-IV* (*DSM-IV*). Experts label those who confess that they are not able to meet the standards of normalized gender as "disordered" (*DSM-IV* 1994, 246). When interventions are successful, normalization is the result. Experts often perform these interventions but so does everyone else since we must know another's sex to be able to socially interact and communicate. "In a society of normalization" (Foucault 1980b, 107), we are all disciplinarians (Bartky 1990). Normalization is an effect of the "constant pressure to conform to the same model, so that they might all be ... like one another" (Foucault 1979, 182).

As a discipline, gender is embodied, not easily thrown off, even when one understands that it is a cultural story. The disciplinary embodiment of gender makes gender feel "natural" to most people. Consequently, the prevailing story that gender entails a coherence of bodies, behaviour, desire, and practice persists despite influential work by some theorists of gender who have attempted to disrupt the assumption that behaviour naturally follows from bodies. Among these are psychoanalyst Sigmund Freud (1856-1939) and early feminists such as Simone de Beauvoir (1908-86). Freud was one of the first theorists to understand gender to be constructed through a long and conflict-ridden process rather than to be fixed by nature. Language was central for Freud, and in one of his early works, published in 1891, the human mind is defined as a "succession of inscriptions of signs" (Weeks 1985, 129). Over decades Freud implicitly worked out the precarious but complex construction of adult masculinity and, to a lesser extent, femininity. His early, critical displacement of biology in the formation of gender and sexuality was an insight that was before its time and was of great importance to later understandings of gender, sex, and sexuality (Weeks 1985).

The key moment for Freud is the Oedipus complex, a time in adolescent development during which boys desire their mothers and hate their fathers. The crisis arising from this complex is acted out through a boy's rivalry with the father for the mother and his terror of psychic (not physical) castration as a punishment. Freud contended that homosexuality was not a simple gender switch because many male "inverts" retain masculine dispositions. He hypothesized that, rather than being absolutely masculine or feminine, humans are bisexual, with masculine and feminine characteristics coexisting in everyone. He further worked out, through his famous "Wolf Man" case, that the Oedipus complex was underpinned by a pre-Oedipal narcissistic masculinity. This involved, among other things, desire for the father and jealousy of the mother. Clinical evidence to support a pre-Oedipal "femininity" in boys as a result of identification with and jealousy of the mother followed in the 1920s and 1930s as others took up Freud's theories.

For Freud, wishes and desires are central to the human experience of satisfaction, and these are linked to memory traces of previous experiences of satisfaction that are fulfilled through reproducing them. As well, Freud developed a structure of personality that included the unconscious, formed in relation to the Oedipal crisis by internalizing parental prohibitions that judge, censor, and present ideals as well as by a prompt to break the law. Through this structure of personality, Freud postulated the displacement of a unitary human consciousness. In other words, for Freud, "to be human is to be divided" (Weeks 1985, 131). Just as important, Freud theorized that the internalization of prohibitions occurred through a mechanism he called "repression," which is directed against sexual desires in particular. Thus, for Freud, sexual desires and sexuality have a crucial role in psychical conflict and, therefore, in personality. Significantly, Freud saw the super-ego as gendered (Connell 1995) even though his ideas regarding masculinity and femininity were unproblematized. While Freudian theory is radical in some important ways, Freud spent most of his life backing away from the radical potential in his earlier work and was unable to escape from the hegemony of dominant gender discourse. A dichotomous gender system remained intact as the ideal to be attained through the process of becoming an adult. Gender is regarded by many developmental and educational psychologists as "the outward manifestation and expression of maleness or femaleness in a social setting" (Rice 1999, 167).

This conflation of sex and gender was called into question with second wave feminism. Philosopher Simone de Beauvoir's (1973, 301) aphorism, "one is not born a woman, but, rather, becomes one," provided an impetus for other thinkers to imagine that biology and behaviour are not inextricably linked, that a female body could be masculine and a male body could be feminine. A more contemporary rendering that posits sex as biological and gender as social is reflected as "a more general term encompassing all social relations that separate people into differentiated gendered statuses" (Lorber 1994, 3). Lorber continues: "I see gender as an institution that establishes patterns of expectations for individuals, orders the social processes of everyday life, is built into the major social organizations of society, such as the economy, ideology, the family, and politics, and is also an entity in and of itself" (1).

Despite this insight, considerable feminist work has proceeded as though gender is tied to sex. There is an acknowledgment that sex is "the biological status of being male or female," while gender, in contrast, refers to the "social categories of male and female" (Arnett 2000, 130); however, the assumption persists that females are aligned with femininity, even if what counts as femininity changes socially and historically. This is why a book like Judith Halberstam's *Female Masculinity* (1998) is rare in feminist scholarship. Moreover, the separation of sex and gender by many contemporary feminists still takes for granted a two-sex, two-gender system and assumes that bodies, by virtue of being in the realm of the biological, are not affected by the social.

Poststructural and queer feminist theorists have taken another look at this assumed split between the biological and the social and have argued that what is understood as a sexed body is produced by what is understood about gender. Prominent among these is Judith Butler. Like biological determinists, Butler argues that sex and gender are indistinguishable. However, unlike, biological determinists, who think that physicality and behaviour can be reduced to sex, Butler thinks that physicality and behaviour are both manifestations of gender.

For Butler (1990, 139), gender is a *"corporeal style,* an act ... which is both intentional and performative, where *"performative"* suggests a dramatic and contingent construction of meaning" (emphasis in original). Following Foucault's lead on how discipline is embodied, Butler argues that gender is a process of repetitive, performative acts. What comes to count as a male or a female sexed body is a result of repetitive performances of gendered gestures, movements, and comportment. "What I would propose ... is a return to the notion of matter, not as a site or surface but as *a process of materialization that stabilizes over time to* produce the effect of boundary, fixity, and surface we call matter" (Butler 1993, 10, emphasis in original). Gendered performances establish the boundaries of what are regarded as sexed bodies; hence Butler's assertion that gender and sex are not distinct categories.

Playing with the double meaning of "materialize" and "matter," Butler (1993, 23) argues that, although bodies are material, it is important to notice which bodies "come to matter" in a culture. "To 'concede' the undeniability of 'sex' or its materiality, is always to concede some version of 'sex,' some formation of 'materiality' ... What will and will not be included within the boundaries of 'sex' will be set by a more or less tacit operation of exclusion" (10-11).

While Butler (1990, 76) makes a claim for the universality of gendering processes, she also makes clear that this does not mean that gender "operates in the same way or that it determines social life in some unilateral way cross-culturally." Rather, gender "operates as a dominant framework within which social relations take place" (76) but resists universalizing claims because "distinct articulations of gender asymmetry" operate "in different cultural contexts" (35). Within a particular cultural context what counts as proper gender performance becomes the normalized version of gender for that culture.

Gender performances produce not only what come to count as sexed bodies but also notions of what sexual practices are appropriate to these sexed bodies. The dominant discourse, which indicates that one can read gender and sexual practice from sex, posits everyone as either heterosexually male or female. Like the gender dichotomy that only countenances males and females, sexuality is limited to the hetero and the homo. As Eve Sedgwick (1990, 8) writes:

> It is a rather amazing fact that, of the very many dimensions along which the genital activity of one person can be differentiated from that of another (dimensions that include preference for certain acts, certain zones or sensations, certain physical types, a certain frequency, certain symbolic investments, certain relations of age or power, a certain species, a certain number of participants, etc. etc. etc.), precisely one, the gender of object choice, emerged from the turn of the century, and has remained, as the dimension denoted by the now ubiquitous category of "sexual orientation."

While gender as a *"regulated process of repetition"* (Butler 1990, 144, emphasis in original) is materialized in bodies, gender is not the only way that bodies are materialized. Gender articulates with multiple, competing, contradictory bodily demands and, hence, is open to intervention and resignification (33). Indeed, as Butler indicates, gender necessarily fails: "To be a good mother, to be a heterosexually desirable object, to be a fit worker, in sum, to signify a multiplicity of guarantees in response to a variety of different demands all at once ... produces the possibility of a complex reconfiguration and redeployment" (145). It is because of the necessary failure of gender that there is an opportunity to vary its expected repetitions and, as a consequence, push the boundaries of what counts as sexed bodies, sexual practice, and desire. There is, however, also a price to be paid for failure to meet gendered expectations, even when such failures are inevitable. These are the punishing, interventionist effects of a culture that demands gender conformity.

Gender Identity Disorder

> It is my belief that by looking at what society pathologizes, we can see the clearest common denominator of what society demands of those of us who wish to be considered normal. It is also my belief that, although most children do not undergo formal gender training to the extremes ... almost every child receives this training informally, often at the hands of the most liberal of parents and teachers.
>
> – Phyllis Burke, *Gender Shock:*
> *Exploding the Myths of Male and Female*

In Volume 1 of *The History of Sexuality* Foucault used the term *scientia sexualis* to refer to a systematic discourse in which the confession is transformed into science. *Scientia sexualis* focuses on the "rigorous analysis of every thought and action ... related to pleasure ... which supposedly holds the key to individual mental and physical health and to social well-being" (Dreyfus and Rabinow 1983, 176). Medicine, psychiatry, and pedagogy produced sexual norms against which experts were able to identify the hysterical woman, the masturbating child, and the sexual pervert. Scientific discourses of "sexual perversion" produced "the homosexual" as a species (Foucault 1980b, 43). Through the confessional technology of *scientia sexualis* sexual behaviour was classified as normal or pathological, and "once a diagnosis of perversion was scientifically established, corrective technologies ... could and must be applied" (Dreyfus and Rabinow 1983, 173).

In the latter part of the twentieth century *scientia sexualis* has produced an extensive codification of sexual disorders that are published alongside other "disorders" in the *Diagnostic and Statistical Manual of Mental Disorders*. The *DSM* initially listed homosexuality as a category of mental illness. In 1973, with increasing pressure from lesbians, gays, and others, mental health practitioners sought to eliminate homosexuality as a mental illness. In 1980 homosexuality was removed as a category of mental illness from the *DSM* (Burke 1996, 27). However, with the removal of homosexuality came a new category – "gender identity disorder." As indicated earlier, gender identity disorder (GID) in childhood is regarded as a "pathology involving the Core Gender Identity ... consistent with one's biological sex" (Sedgwick 1993,

158). The notion of GID relies on the gender-constructivist research of John Money and Robert Stoller, so that "the *de*pathologization of an atypical sexual object-choice [is] yoked to the *new* pathologization of an atypical gender identification" (Sedgwick 1993, 158, emphasis in original). The effect is to produce ever-younger cases of psychopathology, which, although this is not explicitly stated, are linked to the risk of adult homosexuality. The following excerpt from the *DSM-IV* desk version is the product of the logic of dominant gender discourse, which has the effect of producing gender pathologized bodies.

A. A strong and persistent cross-gender identification (not merely a desire for any perceived cultural advantages of being the other sex). In children, the disturbance is manifested by four (or more) of the following:

   (1) repeatedly stated desire to be, or insistence that he or she is, the other sex
   (2) in boys, preference for cross-dressing or simulating female attire; in girls, insistence on wearing only stereotypical masculine clothing
   (3) strong and persistent preferences for cross-sex roles in make-believe play or persistent fantasies of being the other sex
   (4) strong preference for playmates of the other sex.

   In adolescents and adults, the disturbance is manifested by symptoms such as a stated desire to be the other sex, frequent passing as the other sex, desire to live or be treated as the other sex, or the conviction that he or she has the typical feelings and reactions of the other sex.

B. Persistent discomfort with his or her sex or sense of inappropriateness in the gender role of that sex.

   In children, the disturbance is manifested by any of the following: in boys, assertion that his penis or testes are disgusting or will disappear or assertion that it would be better not to have a penis, or aversion toward rough-and-tumble play and rejection of male stereotypical toys, games, and activities; in girls, rejection of urinating in a sitting position, assertion that she has or will grow a penis, or assertion that she does not want to grow breasts or menstruate, or marked aversion toward normative feminine clothing.

   In adolescents and adults, the disturbance is manifested by symptoms such as preoccupation with getting rid of primary and secondary sex characteristics (e.g., request for hormones, surgery, or other procedures to physically alter sexual characteristics to simulate the other sex) or belief that he or she was born the wrong sex.

C. The disturbance is not concurrent with a physical inter-sex condition.

D. The disturbance causes clinically significant distress or impairment in social, occupational, or other important areas of functioning. (*DSM-IV* 1994, 246-8)

Gender identity disorder is a relatively unknown category to those who do not work within clinical psychology and psychiatry. Yet Canada is home to the largest GID institute in North America: the Clarke Institute in Toronto. Every major city in Canada has its own clinic, usually attached to a large teaching hospital. According to freelance researcher Phyllis Burke (1996), GID is a large and ever-expanding field of both psychiatric and psychological clinical practice. These clinics inform the narratives of many queer youth and function as context for the youth interviewed for *Queer Youth*. Before I get to their stories, however, I describe some of the "cases" that Burke uncovered in her work. She tells the stories of children forced by parents and teachers to conform to gender standards.

Becky
Seven-year-old Becky was identified by experts as having "female sexual identity disturbance" (Burke 1996, 5), which became manifest as "deviant gender behaviour" (Rekers and Mead 1979). What did Becky do to be pathologized in this way? According to Burke (1996, 5): "Becky liked to stomp around with her pants tucked into her cowboy boots, and she refused to wear dresses. She liked basketball and climbing ... She likes to play with her toy walkie-talkies, rifle, dart game and marbles. She stood with her hands on her hips, fingers facing forward. She swung her arms, and took big, surefooted strides when she walked."

The "cure" for Becky's "disorder" consisted of 102 sessions of behaviour modification in the clinic and ninety-six sessions in her bedroom, including a bug-in-her-ear device through which she was instructed about proper play with toys. She was rewarded for playing with "feminine sex-typed" toys and behaviour and for rejecting "masculine sex-typed" toys and behaviour. The year was 1978 and Becky's treatment was under the auspices of a new federally funded US program. Toys played with, assertiveness, rough-and-tumble play, confidence, and defiance combined with a lack of interest in appearance and typical girl behaviour and toys are, according to *DSM-IV,* hallmarks of female gender dysphoria. A telling infraction was the refusal to wear dresses (Burke 1996; Scholinski 1997).

As Burke (1996, 19) indicates, "rather than being 'cured,' constant monitoring destroyed Becky's self-esteem. Becky's desires and feelings had been worn down, split off from her everyday world, only to become hidden within a secret and shamed place inside her. Becky valiantly strove for acceptance and to do what was necessary in the face of overwhelming odds. She wanted to earn back love, and if that meant choosing the pots and pans over the soft-ball mitt, so be it."

Rekers, Becky's psychiatrist, has stated that gender identity disorder can be determined by comparing a child with same-sex, same-aged peers in athletic skills such as throwing a ball and percentage of baskets made from the free throw line. As Burke (1996, 205) comments, "I ... hate to think that a child's diagnosis of mental health ... depend[s] on basketball shots made, or not made, from the free throw line." Rekers still works in the area of GID and has written articles on identification, assessment, and treatment of childhood gender problems; rationale for intervention in childhood gender problems; and descriptions of clinical and therapeutic interventions spanning the 1970s through to the 1990s (Rekers and Lovaas 1974b; Rekers and Mead 1979; Rekers and Morey 1990; Rekers, Rosen, and Morey 1992; Rekers, Sanders, and Strauss 1981). His contribution to *scientia sexualis* has guided the work of hundreds of workers in both research and clinical practice, and it has earned tens of thousands of dollars that have been put towards funding research and clinical initiatives (Burke 1996).

Kraig

At age five, Kraig, an anatomically normal male, became part of the Feminine Project at the University of California, Los Angeles (UCLA). This project was advertised widely in schools as well as on local television shows because it required a ready pool of feminine boys. Kraig had the misfortune of having his mother watch a television show in which a colleague of Rekers, Richard Green (1987), explained the phenomenon of the effeminate boy and how the UCLA project might help him. Another man on the show explained that playing with dolls turns a boy into an adult homosexual. Kraig's mother became alarmed and began a year-long battle to convince Kraig's father that their son needed treatment. Finally, after an incident in which Kraig was putting his little sister's clothing on her stuffed animal, Kraig's father became angry, spanked him, and agreed that he needed therapy. Kraig's treatment began with a genital exam to ensure that he was unambiguously a biological male. Next, Kraig was sent to Rekers to begin his ten-month behavioural program. He was included in the GID because he "continually displayed pronounced feminine mannerisms, gestures, and gait, as well as exaggerated feminine inflection and feminine content of speech. He had a remarkable ability to mimic all the subtle feminine behaviors of an adult woman ... He appeared to be very skilled at manipulating [his mother] to satisfy his feminine interests" (Burke 1996, 35).

Because of these baseline behaviours Kraig was believed to be at risk not only for "adult transsexualism, transvestism and some forms of homosexuality" but also for "depression, arrest, trial and imprisonment in association with his possible future as a transsexual" (Burke 1996, 34). Further reasons postulated for Kraig's treatment were that his playmates would scorn him and that it would be easier to change the child than the society (Rekers and Lovaas 1974). Kraig's diagnosis was also based on his parents remembering that he once wore a shirt on his head, pretending he had long hair, and that he engaged in some mop and towel play. One night he wore his father's T-shirt to bed and, upon catching his reflection in a mirror, decided he was wearing a dress. These occasions were taken as evidence that Kraig cross-dressed. Mostly, however, when he wanted to play with toys he would pick up a doll or play with teacups as easily as he would a car. At the centre of everyone's concern was the fear that he would become an adult sexual deviant. While all this occurred in 1974, Rekers (1995) still refers to Kraig as a foundational case in his *Handbook of Child and Adolescent Sexual Problems*. This handbook continues to be used in both clinical and research settings investigating GID.

Stanley

In 1986 three-year-old Stanley began treatment at the Psychoanalytic Institute in New York. Stanley was diagnosed with GID, and for him and his family this meant analysis five times a week for five years. Stanley was treated because, otherwise, "he would have developed into an adult homosexual" (Haber 1991, 107). "He liked kitchen toys, dolls and carriages. When he was two years old, he wanted to put on nail polish. He liked Cinderella, Wonder Woman and Princess Diana. He groomed and dressed dolls. He also had many childhood ailments, including sore throats, earaches, fevers and allergies. He received frequent allergy shots, and was on significant amounts of medication, which might explain why he 'avoided sports' and rough-and-tumble play" (Burke 1996, 100).

Stanley's greatest love was his grandfather, who lived with Stanley and his family and with whom he spent large amounts of time. After a short but serious illness Stanley's grandfather died without returning home from hospital. This devastated young Stanley. In his five-year analysis, Haber reported Stanley's behaviours in terms of his atypical gender behaviour and his future sexuality (Burke 1996, 103). In keeping with psychoanalytic theories, Stanley was thought to be harbouring castration anxiety, defending against damage caused by the loss of his mother as well as loneliness. Stanley's grandfather was also suspect in Stanley's psychopathology. The grandfather was married to a "vital working woman" and did light house cleaning while his wife worked.

Measuring for Gender Dysphoria

> Cross-dresser plans to switch to alternative school in Gresham,
> Oregon. A self-described "gay boy cross-dresser says he plans to
> transfer to an alternative school after being suspended for wearing
> women's clothes and a bra stuffed with socks."
>
> – *Columbian*, 5 May 2000

The development of measurement tools is an important area of research in GID. The Machover Figure-Drawing Test and IT Scale for Children are used to determine gender dysphoria and its severity. With the Machover Figure-Drawing Test the child is given a piece of paper and asked to draw a person. If a girl draws a boy or a boy draws a girl, then they are considered to have gender problems. The IT Scale for Children involves an exercise in which the child is shown a stick figure and, from various cards, is asked to pick appropriate toys, accessories, and clothing for it. If the child makes masculine choices, then s/he gets points; if the child makes feminine choices, then s/he does not get any points. Girls are expected to score very low on this test, while boys are expected to score high.

The Barlow Gender-Specific Motor Behaviour Form looks at body movements such as sitting, standing, and walking to determine normal masculine and feminine movements. Buttocks hold a special place in the Barlow Form: "if the distance between the buttocks and the back of the chair was four inches or more" points are given for masculinity (Burke 1996, 8). Close proximity of buttocks to the back of a chair is scored as feminine. This test is based on a seven-point scale.

GID maintains its status as science through these test instruments, which, in keeping with scientific principles, measure behaviours so as to provide consistent, reliable results. In their 1995 text Zucker and Bradley outline, in detail, the numerous assessment and test instruments available to GID specialists. According to them, "these assessment measures are the most readily accessible for clinical assessment ... all have shown at least some discriminant validity; that is they have distinguished gender-referred children from normal, sibling and/or clinical controls" (Zucker and Bradley 1995, 60-3). No doubt consistent, reliable results are obtained, but the foundational assumptions upon which these are made are solidified and naturalized based upon categories that are questionable. Assumptions about gender, sex, and sexuality, meanwhile, are left intact and unproblematized. The *scientia sexualis* of GID subjects children and youth to behaviour modification, drug therapy, shock therapy, and psychoanalysis (with "severe" cases being institutionalized), all in a concerted effort to shift non-conforming behaviours towards gender-appropriate performances (Burke 1996; Scholinski 1997).

The technologies of surveillance and intervention employed in producing correct gender seriously compromise notions of gender as naturally occurring, even while relying on these notions.

Displays of hyper-masculinity or hyper-femininity are considered a success even when, in most circumstances, these behaviours are socially inappropriate. For example, treatment is considered successful for feminine boys when "the boys become more verbally and physically aggressive toward their mothers" (Burke 1996, 54). For "gender-troubled" girls, therapists promote the use of makeup and a preoccupation with older males, who may be close family friends or part of the therapy team, as the pinnacle of successful treatment (Burke 1996). It goes without saying that, in other circumstances, it would be problematic to encourage girls to sexualize their behaviour with adult males, particularly those in a fiduciary relationship. For both girls and boys, disdain for the "opposite" gender is a hallmark of appropriate behaviour, even while the very best outcome is that children and youth diagnosed with GID become gender-appropriate heterosexual adults.

Theories and practices associated with GID were solidified during the same period that saw the emergence of second wave feminism. As feminist thinking worked towards opening possibilities for girls and women and towards the radical potential of liberating boys and men from their gender-rigid roles, GID worked to reify and rigidify gender. Both, however, depended upon essentializing notions of gender. While feminist thinking has moved beyond essentializing gender, GID discourse proliferates increasingly fossilized theory, therapy, and research.

Often parents – especially mothers, grandparents, and other loved ones – are blamed for gender inappropriate behaviours, even though it is most frequently relatives who, in the "best" interests of the child, turn children in for therapy. On other occasions, parents are not aware that their child is being treated for GID as this occurs within a school setting, with a teacher relying on outside assistance to "contend" with gender dysphoric problems present in the classroom (Burke 1996). The eradication of behaviours that might lead to later homosexuality is at the core of treatment for GID, even though experts are uncertain about the "causes" or outcomes of this "disorder." Zucker indicates, for example, that "we do not have any definitive studies that demonstrate one way or the other that treatment for GID in a child causes a heterosexual outcome or that cross-gender play in a child signals a homosexual childhood" (Zucker in Burke 1996, 100). Richard Green (1987), writing about the "sissy boy syndrome" and the development of homosexuality, supports psychological intervention with children not because these protect against homosexuality but because, he claims, parents have a legal right to seek treatment for gender dysphoric children and youth. Most chillingly, as we have seen, therapists Rekers and Lovass (1974) offer as their rationale for treatment the proposition that it is easier to change the child than the society in which s/he lives.

The discourse of GID is often confusing and contradictory, informed as it is by both biological and social constructionist arguments. What is not confusing about GID discourse, however, is the fear it perpetuates around the idea of children and youth growing up to be homosexual. This desire to eliminate homosexuality is not, of course, unique to experts of gender identity disorder. Even as parents claim to be amazed at the apparent ease with which their children conform to gender expectations, "something akin to gender terrorism aimed at children" operates to discipline children, youth, and all of us into gender conformity (Burke 1996, 125). When the influence of family, school, and friends fail, there are GID clinics to turn to; and, if therapeutic methods to "cure" gender identity disorder fail, there is the opportunity for sex reassignment surgeries.

Beyond GID: Sex Reassignment Surgery

> To "make" a man is to test him: to "make" a woman is to have intercourse with her. Like the dissymmetry of reference in Spanish between a "public man" (a statesman) and a "public woman" (a whore), "making a man" and "making a woman" mean two very different things, culturally speaking.
>
> – Marjorie Garber, "Spare Parts:
> The Surgical Construction of Gender"

In a technological twist on "making" gendered bodies, specialists in the surgical suite constitute another manifestation of the normalization of masculine male bodies and feminine female bodies. Through surgery and hormone therapies a man can be made from a female body and a woman from a male body. When GID therapy is unable to "make" sissy-boys and tomboy-girls into gender appropriate persons, sex assignment surgery can make sissy-boys into women and tomboy-girls into men, thus succeeding in matching bodies with behaviours. Kessler and McKenna, writing in 1978, indicated that "genitals have turned out to be easier to change than gender identity ... we have witnessed ... the triumph of the surgeons over the psychotherapists in the race to restore gender to an unambiguous reality" (120). According to Shapiro (1991, 252), transsexualism constitutes a fundamentalist approach to the relationship of sex and gender: "an inability to see an anatomical male as anything other than a man and an anatomical female as anything other than a woman."

In Canada the prerequisite for reassignment surgery is a diagnosis of GID. Without this diagnosis surgery is not insured through provincial health care and would be out of financial reach for most people. Sex reassignment surgery is not regarded as vanity surgery: "gender dysphoria" is regarded as life-threatening, requiring life-altering surgery. According to this logic, which is rooted in biological determinism, male brains are trapped in female bodies and female brains are trapped in male bodies. As Judith Shapiro (1991, 251) comments, "Whatever the reasons for it, even if we cannot ultimately specify what causes it, individuals can simply be recategorized, which has the considerable advantage of leaving the two-category system intact." Those with suicidal tendencies or who are gender non-conformists are the most suitable candidates. Being suicidal is further evidence of psychopathology, with the social realities of homophobia and heterosexism being somehow absent from the analysis. Once again, it is easier to fix the individual, this time through radical surgical procedures, than it is to fix the society.

Surgery to alter a body so that it lines up with the two-sex, two-gender, one sexual orientation system demonstrates the constructed nature of gender and sexuality. Or is this an instance of fixing up nature's little mistakes? Yet, if the demand for sex-reassignment surgery can be taken as an indicator, then "nature" seems to be erring at an ever-increasing rate. All too often transsexual surgery upholds the bipolar gender system by encouraging assimilation and erasing difference (MacKenzie 1994). And, of course, the body is not the only way, nor indeed an infallible way, for persons to become gendered. In fact, if we were naturally, essentially sexed, then "sex-change" surgery should not, would not, be necessary.

"Sex Assignments" and the Case of the Inter-Sexed

> In the face of apparently incontrovertible evidence – infants born with some combination of "female" and "male" reproductive and sexual features – physicians hold onto an incorrigible belief in and insistence upon female and male as the only "natural" options.
>
> – Bernice Hausman, *Changing Sex:*
> *Transsexualism, Technology, and the Idea of Gender*

Infants born with ambiguous genitalia, or inter-sexed babies, are subjected to surgical interventions to make them unambiguous girls or boys. Depending on what kind of external genitalia is present, a sex is assigned to the child and then surgical procedures are performed to match the infant's body to the assigned category (Hausman 1995; Kessler 1998).

The very label "inter-sexed" attests to the stubborn grip of a two-sex system. As Hausman (1995) shows in her analysis of medical, scientific, and narrative discourse on inter-sexed people and transsexuality, the range of hormonal, gonadal, and chromosomal variation among inter-sexed babies defies the idea of two sexes. The imperative of two sex/genders requires that inter-sexed babies become male or female. The idea of what constitutes the "best sex" for that baby is based on body morphology, most often on the size of the infant's penis (Kessler 1998), and on its perceived psychological makeup, which is derived from the work of Money (1968 [1994]; Money and Erhardt 1972). "After all, there can be no *true* sex if no single kind of sex (chromosomal, gonadal, hormonal, among others) can be invoked infalli-bly as the final indicator of sex identity" (Hausman 1995, 78-9, emphasis in original).

That "inter-sexed" babies might actually indicate that there are many sexes is not countenanced. Ambiguously sexed bodies are disappeared at birth or shortly thereafter. Gender discourse begins its work from these early and influential moments. Inter-sexed babies call into question the natural-ness of maleness-masculinity and femaleness-femininity, and so surgical procedures are required – *at birth* – to assign unambigous gender to ambigu-ous bodies. As Kessler (1998, 32) writes: "Accepting genital ambiguity as a natural option would require that physicians acknowledge that genital ambiguity is 'corrected' not because it is threatening to the infant's life but because it is threatening to the infant's culture." Ambiguous internal or external genitalia, chromosomes, or hormones are not life-threatening. The assignment of a sex category to the inter-sexed baby occurs prior to most socialization, and the surgical procedures are effects of rigid social constructs. These surgical procedures reveal the rigidity of gender rather than the natu-ralness of gender categories.

What is clear from sex-reassignment surgery, whether for infants or for adults, is the societal interest in altering bodies so that they match up to a two-sex, two-gender, one sexual orientation system. The implication is that, if one can achieve the correct body for one's brain, then one will have the appropriate desires for the opposite sex/gender mate and for gender appro-priate sexual performances. Discourses on wrong body/brain configurations assume that a brain that desires the same sex is displaying a behaviour, a desire, that belongs to the body of which the desiring brain is not a part. Unfortunately for the credibility of this discourse, some of those transitioning still desire the "wrong" sexual behaviours with the "wrong" kind of people. Queer icon Pat Califia, former leather dyke, is now Patrick Rice-Califia, a female-to-male who is in the beginning stages of transitioning and contem-plating marriage with a gay man. And queer theorist Eve Kosofsky Sedgwick (1993) confuses categories when she identifies as a gay man married to a straight male academic. What can this mean in the context of a two-sex, two-gender, one sexual orientation system?

Rather than reflecting the diverse and multiple ways in which people act and live in the social world, gender discourse misrepresents and distorts human life, producing bodies in such a way that some match rigid require-ments while others are categorized as defective, diseased, and mentally ill. However, the dangers to those who are pathologized are far greater than are the dangers to those who are misrepresented. For some gender non-conformists, the penalty for "deviance" is death.

When All Else Fails: Remembering Brandon Teena

Brandon Teena (formerly Teena Brandon) and two companions, a young single-parent woman and a young black man, were murdered on New Year's Eve 1993. On Christmas Eve 1993, exactly one week prior to his murder, Brandon Teena was brutally raped and assaulted by two former friends. The *Omaha Gazette*, in a sensational article entitled "Dressed to Kill," proposed that male clothing worn by a female body was central to Brandon Teena's murder. Brandon Teena's clothing did have something to do with why he was murdered, but this is not the whole story. Brandon Teena's murder is a sign of how deeply troubled our society is over gender ambiguity and homosexuality.

As the section on gender identity disorder conveys, many people will go to extreme lengths to eradicate both gender ambiguity and homosexuality. GID clinics attempt to erase unacceptable behaviours through psychothera-pies. Sex assignment of gender ambiguous infants eradicates "naturally" oc-curring ambiguous bodies. Sex reassignment of adults is designed to alter "mistakes" so that gender conformity is maintained. Taking the logic of gen-der rigidity to its conclusion, Brandon Teena's murderers erased gender am-biguity and the spectre of homosexuality by erasing Brandon Teena himself.

Teena Brandon was a sickly child who preferred to play with boys' toys and to dress in shorts, jeans, and shirts, unlike her ultra-feminine older sis-ter. As Brandon Teena in his teen years, he successfully dated young women, passing as male, offering further evidence (within the discourse of gender conformity) of psychopathology. Not only was he gender dysphoric, but his passing as a male was also evidence that he was a "pathological liar."

Brandon Teena's evasions or distortions about his body with most of his girlfriends varied after his early successes with girls. One of the young women Brandon Teena dated wrote, "he was a dream come true." At times he said that he was a hermaphrodite; at other times he claimed that he was transitioning from female to male (FTM). The truth was that Brandon Teena was genitally female and could not afford surgery. When two male friends of his last girlfriend discovered Brandon Teena's secret, they raped and as-saulted him in order to, in their words, "put her in her place." And they beat him severely to ensure that he did not press charges of rape and as-sault. The police officer who took Brandon Teena's "complaint" did not press charges and did nothing to protect him until it was too late. While

Brandon Teena was evasive and often lied about various things, his statement on public record expresses his clear and unambiguous wish to press charges and to go to court. After Brandon Teena tried to press charges the two young men murdered him and two other people.

Brandon Teena's story displays, in graphic detail, the deep and widespread intolerance and hostility towards, and individual and community inability to deal with, gender ambiguity and homosexuality. The community of Falls City, Nebraska, is a microcosm of larger societal anxieties and confusions regarding these issues. The confusion, intolerance, and ambiguity spawned by gender-rigid behaviours and attitudes are manifested at every stage of the authorities' interaction with Brandon. When the police uncovered his gender, they referred to him as "her" and used sexist language and assumptions while interrogating him during his complaint. Other examples demonstrate the very real structural problems that gender ambiguity creates: Brandon was "outed" when he was placed in the female side of a jail, and court records dishonoured his identification as male by using feminine gender pronouns.

As documentary filmmakers Susan Muska and Greta Olafsdottir discovered during their four-year investigation of *The Brandon Teena Story* (1998), the community in which the story unfolds is "more tolerant" of gender confusion but completely intolerant of the spectre and reality of homosexuality. The phrase "more tolerant" is dubious, given the way the narrative unfolds. The filmmakers find that many people accepted Brandon Teena on a personal level because they thought no one else knew. However, once "it" became public knowledge, complicity with Brandon Teena's secret was no longer possible.

Even as claims are made for a certain kind of tolerance towards gender ambiguity, the shallowness of that tolerance is unmasked once everyone knows and is forced to speculate about the link between gender ambiguity and their relation to Brandon Teena. The closet of silence that shrouds gender ambiguity and its queer cousin homosexuality, keeping them privatized and personalized, could not tolerate the gaze and scrutiny of public knowledge. This was especially acute for those who felt strongly about their own gender-conforming identities and sense of heterosexual selfhood. Brandon Teena posed a threat to all his girlfriends, who denied they were lesbian when they had to acknowledge that Brandon Teena was a biological female. For most of the community this constituted homosexuality.

Brandon Teena's last girlfriend, Lana Tisdale, and another friend are still ostracized as lesbian. Tisdale's friend, who is also Lotter's (one of the murderers) sister, never had any sexual contact with Brandon Teena but seemed to be guilty by association. In another twist, murderer Thomas Nissen was called a fag for raping Brandon. According to his girlfriend, the threat that this "pejorative" constituted to his sense of a masculine self was one of the reasons he decided to murder Brandon Teena. His sense of masculinity had already been seriously threatened through previous prison time, during which he was repeatedly raped and abused. Nissen's sense of his gender was threatened by the townspeople's questioning his "desire" during the rape of Teena as well as by his own rape in prison by other males. For the members of this Nebraskan community the threat posed by the spectre of homosexuality and ambiguously gendered females and males is so great that they are still in denial and refuse any responsibility.

For some, the threats to social norms and to one's intimate sense of identity are so dire that appropriate remedies take the form of radical and horrific actions. Being a man involves "making" a woman by taking her sexually, even if he takes her (as the murderers took Brandon Teena) against her will. Yet Brandon Teena is a "better" man than is either of his murderers because he pleases his female partners, while Lotter's and Nissen's relationships with women were weak and troubled, often consisting of forced sexual relations. Brandon Teena's murderers are fighting, hurting, drinking, male-bonded guys, and they are autocratic in their beliefs regarding gender and sexuality. So, too, was Brandon Teena as he successfully performed and outperformed them in many of the things related to masculinity. His murderers' sense of themselves was profoundly disturbed when they realized that the guy they let into their guy zone was, in their view, not really a guy. Everyone else, including Tisdale's mother, was fooled as well. The community of Little Falls was hoodwinked as effectively as were Brandon Teena's previous girlfriends. None of them was able to discern the "real" men. They were vulnerable to the enemy: those who successfully pose as men and therefore undermine "real" men. A normal man, vulnerable to an enemy, has to be brave enough to seek out and encounter that enemy in what might become a struggle for life or death. In Brandon Teena's case the struggle to maintain gender social norms was a death struggle.

The extreme homophobia of the murderers and the community towards Brandon Teena was acted out in the form of his execution. Eradicating Brandon had the immediate effect of removing the threat posed by his body. Killing him restored balance to the murderers' sense of their masculine selves and to an anxious and distressed community. Equilibrium was restored with the death of the gender/sexual deviant. Yet Falls City continues its struggle with the events that made up Brandon Teena's life and death.

The flimsiness of conventional gendered identity and sexual practice was exemplified by Hilary Swank's performance as Brandon Teena in the film *Boys Don't Cry* and her subsequent performance as a conventionally feminine woman when she received her Oscar award for best "actress." Swank's movie performance and her performance at the Academy Awards ceremony reveal the performativity of gender while also consolidating the common-sense notion that both Brandon Teena and Hilary Swank have a "real" gender behind the performance of masculinity.

Gender violators are variously punished, criminalized, psychopathologized, or, in the case of Brandon Teena, disappeared from public site/sight through murder. As Burke (1996) puts it, gender terrorism disciplines the majority of people into displaying conforming behaviour. Those who mostly get it "right" have an easier time forgetting the processes of gendering and come to believe they were born that way. Those who are different in childhood and adolescence may be subjected to a diagnosis of GID and concomitant therapies to eliminate gender inappropriate behaviours and, if these therapies are "successful," adult homosexuality.

Verbal and physical threats operate to discipline those unruly enough to "flaunt" their deviancy. For adult homosexuals "reparative therapy" purports to transform them into former, or recovering, homosexuals (Nicolosi 1991). If this treatment fails, then reassignment surgeries are available to ensure that bodies and gender appropriate behaviours match. Finally, in order to maintain the myth of heteronormative hegemony, the mutilation and execution of gender ambiguous/queer persons effectively disappears them from the body politic.

Even as heteronormativity appears to be a totalizing system, there are many interstitial spaces and cracks in the essentializing foundations of gender performances. Working, living, and breathing life into and in these spaces, queer bodies proliferate in spite of the relentless discourses of gender conformity. It is to some of these spaces that I now turn, with narratives framed by stories from queer youth in Alberta schools. These youth are subjected to the heaviness of the discourses of gender that insist on a coherency of bodies, behaviour, and sexual practice, yet they have found spaces in which to trouble the demands of conventional gendered identities.

Queer Youth in Alberta's Schools: Some Stories

The Case of the "Queer Young Dyke"

The early years of Jill's life were spent on a First Nations reserve close to a large city. Jill was the eldest of six children, and she often spent time taking care of her younger siblings, making sure they were cared for when her parents were not available. Often, Jill had to defend herself and her siblings, and by age six she was a highly skilled fighter who often became engaged in fist-fights with other kids, whom she described as bullies. Jill started school on the reserve and recalled liking it. However, she missed most of Grade 1 because she had to take care of her younger siblings. Sometimes her "uncle" would look after them as well. On one of these occasions, her uncle raped her. Jill's father died in hospital when she was seven years old, and her mother died about two years later. Jill and her siblings were separated and placed in foster care. Jill and one of her younger brothers went to the same foster home, which was located far away from their birth home and extended family.

Jill's foster family was a boisterous and engaging group, and both she and her brother quickly fit in. However, Jill was stigmatized in school as a "Native" in foster care. School professionals labelled her as incapable of learning and, throughout her school years, tried to place her in classes far below her achievement level. She was also labelled as difficult and disruptive. Her foster (and later adoptive) mother was a strong advocate for Jill and challenged the assessment of her learning abilities. However, she was unable to overcome her own and the school's assessment of Jill's "unfeminine" behaviour. Jill's love of rough-and-tumble play, which, "in psychological terminology, is the hallmark of the male child" (Burke 1996, 5), identified her as a gender non-conformist. Jill reported that teachers were all "weird about me ... they did not really like me and were afraid of my behaviours, especially when I did not act like a proper girl. I didn't even know how to act like a proper girl!"

I asked Jill how she knew the teachers were uneasy about her non-feminine behaviour, and she told me that they told her to act more like a girl. Meanwhile, Jill's adoptive mother admonished her to act like a girl, to keep herself clean and tidy, and to wear dresses more often. She also counselled Jill to talk "like a girl." As Jill demonstrated for me, this was to be accomplished by raising the pitch of her voice, something she still could not do easily. Jill reported to me that she had tried to reason with her foster/adoptive mother, explaining that she could not engage in the activities she loved if she was wearing dresses. These activities included "basketball, soccer, and climbing trees; and, oh yes, I loved fighting." Jill felt she had to fight as she and her brother were constantly teased because they were in foster care, because they were "Native," and because their last name was the name of an animal. Jill won all of her fights because she was not afraid, was highly skilled, and was bigger than those she fought. Not only were some of her teachers "weird" about her but, according to Jill, "some of them were afraid of me, I think because of my fighting but also because I was too big and they thought I was stupid. Some of the kids called me a stupid squaw, but I think some of the teachers felt the same way."

When she turned nine years old her foster parents adopted Jill and her last name changed: "I was thrilled because no one could make fun of my last name anymore, but I still had to fight all the time about other things." Still, life was secure and Jill loved her adoptive mother because she fought teachers and counsellors, even a principal, on behalf of her and the other children in the foster home. Through her adoptive mother's influence, Jill worked hard at school and, while never an outstanding student, progressed through grade school. Her adoptive mother provided her with love, care, security, and the protection that she needed. The only point of contention between Jill and her foster mother was over her tomboyism: "She was always on my case about being more like a girl and staying clean, wearing these dresses she bought, stop playing ball ... but she really liked me, she adopted me and loved me; that's all that mattered."

Jill's adoptive mother worried that Jill's behaviours would get her into trouble at school and later on in life because, as she tried to explain to her, she would not know her proper place. As for Jill's adoptive father, he did not figure in her narrative.

At one point two fourteen-year-old boys and a fifteen-year-old girl were placed as foster children in her home. Jill, age thirteen, was drawn into a mini-gang made up of these three and herself. For about six months they did everything together. One night, one of the boys went into Jill's room and raped her. Jill tried to tell her adoptive mother who told her "to please not tell her this thing, she could not bear hearing this stuff." However, the boy was quickly removed from the home and the gang fell apart, with everyone blaming Jill. Around this time, Jill's adoptive mother was becoming very religious and went to what Jill described as a "very Christian church, not one of your regular ones but one of those alliance ones or something." Increasingly, Jill's adoptive mother put pressure on all the kids in her care to attend church. She became more fervent in trying to get Jill to act like a girl and started telling her that she would never tolerate her if she was bad and wanted to be with other girls.

Around age twelve or so, over a two-year period, Jill became increasingly aware of her attraction to other girls. She still preferred to play and fight with the boys, but "I wanted to kiss and hug with the girls, especially the really cute ones." The cute girls, for Jill, were the ones who were physically active and smart. On many occasions she tried to tell her adoptive mother about this attraction but, as with the rape, she said she could not bear to hear what Jill wanted to tell her. Jill became increasingly agitated about this. "I love my mother," Jill said, "I wanted her to know about who I really am and I did not want to lie to her or mislead her because she saved me." Jill knew this was a highly contentious issue but she also knew that her attraction to other girls was a big part of "who I am." Jill was fourteen and a half when she came out to her adoptive mother. This woman packed Jill's bags when she went to school the next day and put them on the doorstep. Jill was not allowed in the house after that. She was forced into state care, where "I had to fend for myself, I was alone again ... I had lost my second mother." Not only was Jill not allowed to enter what had been her home, but her adoptive mother refused to see her and would not let her have any contact with her younger brother. According to Jill, "She said I was a bad influence."

Over the next few years Jill became increasingly alienated at school. She was constantly in fights and she flunked out. Her social workers and school counsellors did not know what to do with her. Teachers and students were either indifferent to her, afraid of her, or actively harassed her. Some teachers refused to have her in their classes, while students called her queer, a bull-dyke, or a lezzie. Others gave her a wide berth in the hallways and/or refused to sit close to her in class. Jill hated school and quit attending on a regular basis. She became defined as a problem student and was transferred from one school to another. An incident in one of her high schools stands out against the constant harassment and marginalization she felt at the others. Some kids ganged up on Jill after school and wanted to beat her up. She got away and reported the incident and perpetrators to a school counsellor. The school counsellor advocated on Jill's behalf and ensured that the perpetrators were disciplined. Jill could not remember any other positive incidents that occurred after she had been kicked out of her adoptive home.

She attempted suicide several times and landed in a psychiatric ward. The attending psychiatrist referred her to another psychiatrist, who was in charge of a program specializing in individuals whose troubles were perceived to arise from confusion about gender identity. During counselling, over a period of several months, the psychiatrist convinced Jill that she had "a male brain stuck in a female body" and that, through surgery and hormone treatments, this disjunction could be fixed. The psychiatrist told Jill "that all of [her] problems were because of this male brain thing." At first Jill went along with the psychiatrist, but in a feat of great bravery she was able to reject the starched white authority of *scientia sexualis* that, in addition to schools and family, has such a central place in the production of gender appropriate bodies. At the eleventh hour Jill refused to begin hormone treatments and instead insisted that she was not confused about her gender; rather, as she said, she was a "queer dyke." Jill was released from this program and went back into alternative state care.

From the time she was kicked out of home until the time of our interview, Jill's personal turmoil increased. State care was in the form of residential group homes, but with her suicide attempts and other misdemeanours (like fighting and theft), Jill was in and out of lock-up facilities. In one facility Jill was playing basketball with other girls in the gym and one girl accused her of feeling her up during a physically close moment. She yelled at Jill: "[You're] nothing but a stupid dyke! Keep your hands off me!" Jill punched the girl in the face, breaking her nose and knocking out one of her teeth. Although Jill was disciplined for fighting, the other girl did not receive any censuring; thus, Jill was also effectively disciplined for inappropriate gender and sexual behaviour, even though she denied that her actions bespoke any sexual intention: "I was just playing basketball and sometimes you touch the other players during intense play ... there was nothing sexual about it. As a matter of fact I hated her guts before that and loved pasting her in the face."

Jill did not complete high school. She reported that she has been raped at least once a year since her uncle raped her and that she has come to expect this. She was very matter of fact. Jill also reported that she is beaten up regularly because she is so "butch" looking. She fights back, she says, giving as good as she gets. She also confessed to attempting suicide on at least nine separate occasions. Several of these attempts occurred in the lock-up facility where she received counselling. After one such attempt she was referred to the psychiatrist who was knowledgeable about GID.

At the time of our interviews Jill worked security for a small local company. She was in a committed relationship with Ellen, another young woman her age who had also dropped out of school. Ellen was estranged from her birth family and did not work. She took care of Jill emotionally and both agreed, in a joint interview, that Jill was fragile. Ellen had pulled Jill out of several suicide attempts, which were not reported.

Jill missed her siblings and tried reconnecting with her extended birth family. She also visited her father's grave on the reserve. She was angry at her birth mother for dying but dreamed about her constantly. She missed her adoptive mother "dreadfully" and tried to reconcile with her repeatedly, with no success. The last time Jill phoned her adoptive mother did not recognize her voice. This devastated Jill. Her adoptive mother told her that she did not want to see her until she gave up her "lifestyle" and started acting like a girl. In Jill's words, "I still don't know how to act like a girl. I can't do it. Acting like a girl is not who I am. I can't wear a dress or talk differently. Yet, I am a girl."

The Case of Jack, The "Sissy-Fag Queer"

> He came home one day and asked me, "What is gay? Some boys said I am gay" ... they put him in a headlock, dragged him down a deserted concrete stairway, then sliced wildly at his leg, severing his femoral artery.
>
> – *Edmonton Journal*, 7 December 2000

> That BC teenager who killed himself over "fag" taunts had been called "geek" because he had good grades, "four eyes" because he wore glasses and "fag" because he had a high voice and liked the company of girls.
>
> – *Toronto Star*, 2 April 2000

Jack remembered his schooling and growing-up years as a continuous struggle to hide the fact that he was different. He passed as white although he is Métis from a two-parent, middle-class family. He had one older sister, whom he adored with all his heart. "She was so perfect, so beautiful, so much my very most favourite person ... next to my mother of course," Jack told me. He loved "my little ponies" and his younger girl cousins. He had a large stuffed animal collection with which his mother and aunt indulged him. Jack knew to hide his toy preferences during his first year of school. He was physically quite active at this time, thin and wiry. Although he preferred being with girls and playing with girls' toys, he also loved to play games outside and to ride his bike.

Jack's first year of school was traumatic. During the fall his beloved older sister was killed in a car accident on her sixteenth birthday. For Jack and his mother, the ensuing two years were extremely difficult as they tried to face life without their sister/daughter. Jack still mourns her loss and finds the fall, with its smell of decaying leaves, a very emotionally difficult time of year. Jack's father's work kept him away from home for long stretches of time, and Jack rarely mentioned him.

As a result of his sister's death Jack missed a significant amount of school during Grade 1. He and his mother would sleep in on school days, and his mother would not make him go to school late. She seemed tired and distant during this period and spent most of her time in his sister's bedroom. The result was that Jack's Grade 1 marks were poor, and he was held back while his cohort group moved on to Grade 2. Jack felt like he never fit in after that. He recalled that he was not invited to birthday parties or other after-school events. His former classmates made fun of him because he was "stupid." From Grade 2 to the end of Grade 5 Jack became a bully. He was given two- and three-day detentions for hitting other kids. One kid required five stitches after Jack hit him over the head with a bicycle chain. Jack also put on weight at this time. He did not want to go anywhere and withdrew into his house with his mother. He continued to gain weight and to beat on other kids. None of his teachers asked him why he hit other kids, but if they had, Jack would have said that it was because they teased him about his weight. He did not tell anyone that, from a very young age, he was called a "faggot" and would beat up other kids for this as well. The name-calling puzzled Jack because he worked hard to keep his love of what he called "girls' toys" a secret.

Over the years Jack and his mother kept his sister's room intact, a shrine to her. When Jack was stressed he went to her room and played with and looked at her belongings, wishing she were alive. He also took his stuffed animals and little ponies into her room and played with them there. Jack felt safe in her room. His mother, as Jack recalls, remained withdrawn and depressed throughout his time in grade school. She did defend him from neighbours and teachers when he was accused of being a bully. Towards the end of Grade 5, Jack ended his bully stage and decided that he was going to excel at school. He had gained even more weight and described himself as "a fatso, that was me ... I ate and ate and ate all the time, no one stopped me." Since his sister's death he spent increasing amounts of time alone, in a more and more sedentary manner, and spent long hours studying. Jack was able to excel because he had few friends, and once school was out, "I spent little time with any of my peers. Oh, I would walk part way home with some of them." His alienation from friends was related to being left behind in Grade 1, feeling older than his new cohort group, and being harassed and called names. He liked things that most of his male cohorts would not approve of, so he kept "that part of me silent, out of the picture," yet he was still harassed for being different. By the end of Grade 6 Jack was the top honour student in his class and had taken on all kinds of extracurricular activities: "I wanted all the awards, it was not enough to just be the honour student: I wanted to be the best in everything."

Jack knew that most of his teachers were uncomfortable with him. At first, he related this to the fact that he was a bully and that his sister had died. Then he thought that teacher discomfort was related to the fact that he was "a fat kid." Since he kept his like of playing with girls and girls' toys secret, he did not think the teachers knew about this aspect of his difference from other boys. It was not until Grade 6 that he became aware of another dimension to his difference, a "really serious" difference. At this point, Jack determined that teacher discomfort was because he was fat and because he was "showing." "Showing" for Jack meant that others could tell he was different because he liked boys "that way." "That way," for Jack, included kissing boys and living with them in the same house. Yet he played mostly, when he did play, with his girl cousins. "Showing" was also related to the way he walked and talked, which he thought were very feminine. By "feminine" he meant that he kept his arms tucked close to his sides; that he used his hands to emphasize what he was saying; and that he would "mince along" in smallish steps. He also felt that his voice was too feminine, too "girlie-like." Jack demonstrated a "girlie-like" voice for me, telling me that I knew what he meant.

During Grade 6 Jack fell in love with his music teacher, an attractive thirty-year-old man. Jack stared at this teacher whenever the opportunity arose but was increasingly afraid that this was making his difference show even more. He said he knew that he had to keep this difference a secret because no one would approve. Even so, he felt that, despite his academic achievements, his teachers did not approve of him because they knew his secret.

While he worked at not showing, other students must have known because they called him names.

One teacher stood out for Jack. In Grade 6 he discovered that he liked dancing, and the teacher, a woman, encouraged him and complimented him on his grace as a dancer. Jack was thrilled and worked hard at dancing. Unfortunately, other students made fun of him because boys were supposed to hate dancing. Nevertheless, the teacher's approval was a high point in Jack's school years and in his interactions with teachers. The following year, Grade 7, a group of boys pulled Jack's pants down to his ankles while he was getting his books from his locker and whispered "faggot" at him. Up until this time Jack wore jogging pants because they fit comfortably. He now made his mother go out with him and buy two pairs of jeans; he never wore jogging pants again. This incident was a horrific one for Jack and, as he told me about it, the shame and anger resurfaced: "I was so ashamed because I was so fat ... I felt myself turning bright red as I pulled my pants up and looked around to see if anyone else noticed. Afterwards, I was enraged at not being able to say or do anything back. I am still emotional about this incident five years later."

Jack worked harder at "not showing" and losing weight as he now knew what faggot meant and that people would make him miserable because, as he said, "I realized I was one." Jack was a top honours student until Grade 11, yet, for the most part, his teachers avoided him. A Grade 9 teacher physically moved back whenever Jack approached him, leaving Jack feeling "unwanted and repulsive." As Jack says, "he made it clear that he had to acknowledge that I was at the top of the class but that he didn't have to do anything beyond that, even though he made a big deal of inviting and including other students into his inner circle. Oh, he made it clear that he did not like me."

The lowest point in Jack's school years came in Grade 10. Jack had to take physical education and found himself in a class with most of the members of the high school football team. They all seemed to hang around together and gave him funny looks. He was "terrified of showing ... I did not want those guys to know about me." Also, although Jack was working hard at shedding pounds he was still overweight and out of shape. Being in the gym with the football team made Jack extremely nervous: "I broke into a sweat just thinking about phys ed and, in the class, I sweated buckets ... so much that I was constantly mopping my face and my armpits were soaked down to my waist ... it was embarrassing!"

One day, several weeks into the term, Jack found himself in the boys' washroom with the football captain, a particularly scary person. According to Jack, this guy "talked in a gruff voice and gave me looks that made me feel small and foolish and very afraid like he was going to smash me in the face if I said or did anything ... I was scared, I just kept thinking oh oh, oh oh ... I'm in trouble now." Jack hurried into a bathroom stall and slammed the door shut. When he came out he quickly ran his hands under the tap and smoothed his hair back so he could make a quick escape. As he was retreating, the football captain roared out, "What do you think you're doing?" Jack replied, "Me-ee? What do you mean?" The football captain roared again, "You haven't washed your hands properly!" Jack responded, "Oh, whatever" and raced out of the washroom.

The next gym class involved learning the rules for and playing basketball. When Jack passed the ball to his classmates, several of them could not seem to hold on to it. It was subtle at first, but over the course of several classes more and more of his classmates would not catch the ball and would begin whispering when play stopped. Jack heard them saying that they would not catch the ball because Jack's unwashed hands had "contaminated" it. With each class, Jack felt that everyone was focusing on him even more than they had previously, and he began sweating profusely. Some of the young men made a point of staring at Jack's armpits, and most of them began to avoid standing anywhere close to him. Whispered comments about his profuse sweating, the contaminated ball, and the fact that he was "one of those" circulated and were loud enough for Jack to hear.

Jack was devastated because he worked hard to ensure that no one knew his secret; he worked against his own "inclinations" in order to avoid "showing." For Jack, "inclinations" referred to the way he walked, gestured, talked, and sat. By this time, Jack was desperate to get out of the phys ed class and went to the school counsellor, who advised him to talk to his mother because, given his outstanding academic record, it was not a good idea to drop any course. He talked to his mother, who said that whatever he wanted was all right with her. Jack was not out to his mother or to anyone else. He went back to the counsellor, who wanted to know why Jack wished to drop the class. Jack was increasingly desperate and refused to answer that question with more than a "because." He quit attending classes.

Finally, the counsellor contacted the gym teacher who was also the coach for the football team. The gym teacher/coach went back to the class and chastised the students for discriminating against "someone like Jack." The gym teacher contacted Jack and told him what he had done. Jack was even more devastated – not only because he had been singled out in this way but also because the gym teacher had not asked him whether such an action were appropriate. Jack felt that he had been outed, with no input as to if, how, or when this would happen. To top everything off, the gym teacher's advice to him was: "Don't let them get you down and get back to class and face them like a man ... otherwise you will be a wimp for the rest of your life." Jack refused to go back to this class and, instead, negotiated a reduced mark. He spent the rest of his high school years avoiding members of the football team, his former classmates. His high school was large enough that he was able to accomplish this by ducking into rooms and turning his head whenever he saw anyone he wished to avoid.

Jack spent a huge amount of time and energy being vigilant because he never felt safe: "There were some ten of them in the class and chances of me coming across at least one of them every day were enormous. And besides, they were always together, so no matter what the counsellor or teacher said, I did not trust them and always felt afraid they would do something else to embarrass me or try to make me fight. I never felt safe."

In Grade 11 Jack found a friend, a young woman to whom he came out. She was respectful and encouraging. He came out to his mother next, and she told him that she already knew and was okay with this as she loved him, as he put it, "just the way I am." Because Jack had found a friend he did not put so much into his schoolwork; his time was spent elsewhere. "I was thrilled; this was my first real friend ever and I could tell her anything. I was afraid of losing her friendship, but now I have lots of friends, many of them girls because they seem to be more understanding." Jack began volunteering at the local HIV/AIDS centre and found a community that took him further away from schoolwork.

School just began to feel so irrelevant to my life. I was teased and harassed. I was afraid most of the time. Teachers did not like or respect me even when I had great marks. I never learned anything about myself that was useful. When I found my best friend, even getting good marks was not important. I contemplated dropping out of school.

Schooling was a constant struggle for Jack as he worked hard to avoid "showing" and to keep himself safe. Even though he had good marks and engaged in student activities, little at school alleviated his sense of alienation and isolation until he found a friend in Grade 11. He remembered observing how other boys were teased because they did not fit in, and he looked for reasons for his difference (i.e., the loss of his sister, his weight) because he was afraid to be like the boys who were teased. Yet he was one of those boys, a fact to which the constant teasing attested. Jack's knowledge of himself as a "sissy" became ever more apparent. And he knew that this was the "absolutely wrong thing to be in school if you were a boy ... I knew I was not a normal boy, but I could not help myself ... most of the time for being a sissy-fag, hey that's what I am ... that's what I was, even if school, teachers, other kids, whoever ... made sure I knew this was wrong, wrong, wrong."

Polymorphous Genders: Queer Identities in Formation

The relentless pursuit of a rigid two-sex, two-gender, one-sexual orientation system continues into the twenty-first century. Yet resistance to the dominant gender discourse surfaces with a frequency not possible thirty, twenty, or even ten years ago. The explosion of discourse around queer sexualities has greatly facilitated surfacing subjugated knowledges of sexual and gender orientations. Inter-sexed infants and queer transsexuals are evidence of the fact of polymorphous sexes; queer and transgendered youth are evidence of the fact of polymorphous genders. These categories show that Freud's notion of polymorphous sexuality referred not to a stage or phase we all pass through but, rather, to a range of sexual possibilities in which humans may engage. Even as polymorphous sexuality is alive and resisting, such resistance always occurs in relation to dominating and dominant discourses. The two cases of queer youth presented above show how each young person performed in relation to the rigid structuring of gender discourse. Each was hailed by gender discourse, yet each responded to this call differently than did gender conformists. They refused the dominant liberal demand to make themselves identical to those who are gender conforming. Each knew that their performances did not match up to what parents, teachers, and others expected of them. Yet both Jack and Jill refused to alter their behaviours. Jack hid his from public view until recently, while Jill tried but failed to perform femininity, even when faced with severe sanctions from her mother. Each first understood difference through knowledge of gender-appropriate toys, activities, and behaviours.

Even as gender discourse produced Jack and Jill as different from the gender normal, both were inflected with other differences as well. The effects of race, class, and gender are explicit in both narratives. The effects of poverty in Jill's early life were produced by the privileged indifference of a classist and racist society in which those who are poor are left without the resources to raise their children. Both poverty and racism were also manifest in Jill's narrative about her parents. Her father died from the effects of disease and malnutrition; her mother died from a drug overdose. These early traumas inform Jill's identity in multiple ways. Racist practices continued throughout Jill's life and were particularly active throughout her schooling. Today she is still read as Other because she is masculine and looks like she is Aboriginal. In order to understand her life, one must read the effects of gender alongside the effects of other cultural phenomena.

Even if school was a horrific place for Jack, he never knew the insecurities that Jill faced from a very young age. Jack was able to take for granted food, care, and shelter. In large measure, this security allowed him to become a high achiever academically. Jack was able to pass as white and thus never felt the effects of racism. Yet he knew the effects of a fat-phobic discourse. He knew that his body morphology did not match the dominant body configuration of a sleek and fit masculinity. The effects of his failure to conform were manifested in teasing and harassment.

As with Jill so with Jack: in order to understand his schooling years, one must read the effects of gender alongside the effects of other cultural productions. In school, the effects of gender produce Jack and Jill as unintelligible to those around them. According to Jack: "I never fit in anywhere until I found my friend." According to Jill: "This is not my world, no matter where I have been, I have not belonged ... I hated school because no one let me be myself." In their articulations with gender-rigid discourse Jack and Jill became, in effect, unknowable except as deviant Others. This is because inherent in gender-rigid discourse, or heterornormativity, is the spectre of homosexuality.

Through their production as deviant Other, Jack and Jill became the feared homosexual and, therefore, unintelligible. Unintelligible homosexual Others are discomfiting others. The net effect of gender discourse in schools is to relegate unintelligible, discomfiting homosexual Others to the margins, where they are either disappeared or rendered so peripheral that they can be ignored. This othering occurred in spite of the resistance Jill and Jack offered throughout their schooling and growing up years.

Heterosexuality: Gender Rigidity and Gender Melancholic Selves

> People picked on him and bullied him and called him a nerd, idiot, and faggot.
>
> > – *Edmonton Journal*, 30 April 1999

> Detailed investigations during the last few years have led me to the conviction that factors arising in sexual life represent the nearest and practically the most momentous causes of every single case of nervous illness.
>
> > – Sigmund Freud, "Mourning and Melancholia"

> Melancholic formation of gender sheds light on the predicament of living within a culture which can mourn the loss of homosexual attachment only with great difficulty.
>
> > – Judith Butler, *The Psychic Life of Power*

The preceding sections document the relentlessness of dominant gender discourse, which demands the cohesion of sexed bodies, gendered behaviour, and heterosexual desire and practice. There are, of course, other examples. The killings at Columbine High in Littleton, Colorado, and the high school in Taber, Alberta, are effects of the pathologies of gender-rigid masculine behaviours. In both cases the killers were perceived as threats to a normative masculinity. According to a dozen students at Columbine High, gunmen Harris and Klebold were taunted mercilessly by anti-gay jocks who called them "faggots" and "gay." The unnamed gunman in Taber was harassed daily at school by "male jocks" who also called him "faggot" and "gay."

What can one safely state about a culture that daily produces and reproduces acts of homophobia and heterosexism in relation to sexual life? Are homophobia and heterosexism deeply psychic disorders repressed and then displaced onto the bodies of the homosexual Other in daily occurrences of silence, exclusion, and violence? Rigid heterosexuality could be considered as a psychic disorder that is so widespread and pervasive that it infects all of us in the form of the daily production of gendered and sexualized bodies.

It makes sense to understand the heterosexism and homophobia emanating from rigid heterosexuality as a grave and pervasive psychopathology – one that requires strategies and therapies to alleviate its psychic distress and to relieve the daily indignities and violence that it displaces onto homosexuals/queers. Demands of heteronormativity in the production of a rigid heterosexuality involve a process of disordering a self that once was homosexual. As Butler (1997) points out, the lost object of mourning – homosexual attachment – is disappeared from the consciousness of the melancholic heterosexual, who mourns this lost object by acting out against actual homosexuals. Internalized by the ego, the lost object (i.e., homosexual attachment to the same-sex parent) becomes the self that cannot mourn its loss but, rather, that preserves it internally and that constantly plays it out by insisting on the disappearance of the homosexual.

Melancholia, according to Freud, is the unfinished process of grieving for what is lost to the self. Melancholia is thus central to the identity formations that produce the ego. For Freud, the identifications formed through loss (i.e., through grief and melancholia) are those that are internalized and that are preserved in and as the ego. Essential to understanding Freud's sense of ego development is the idea that the ego is "first and foremost a bodily ego" (Freud in Butler 1997, 132). Given the importance of masculinity and femininity for Freudian theory (as well as for social theory generally), we can assume that the bodily ego is a gendered ego.

The psychopathology of rigid heterosexuality results in there being very few cultural opportunities to mourn lost homosexual attachment. Cultural disavowals of homosexuality are so strong that the heterosexist or homophobe finds few opportunities (other than violent denial) to mourn this part of his/her self. The links between this psychopathology and discourses of gender (and their effects on conformists and non-conformists alike) is reason enough to advocate remedies that will enable disordered heterosexual selves to mourn their early homosexual identifications and, consequently, make it unnecessary for them to take out their unmourned loss on homosexuals.

The psychopathologizing of a dominant group identity is a viable, attractive, and politicized strategy. It is a counter-move – one that reverses the discursive order by casting rigid heterosexuality and its constitutive gendered bodies as not only troubled but also psychopathological.

2
Production and Consumption of Youth Identity

> Heterosexual ideology, in combination with a potent ideology about gender and identity *in maturation,* therefore bears down in the heaviest and often deadliest way on those with the least resources to combat it: queer children and teens. In a culture dominated by talk of "family values," the outlook is grim for any hope that child-rearing institutions of home and state can become less oppressive.
>
> – Michael Warner, *Fear of a Queer Planet:*
> *Queer Politics and Social Theory*

Youth studies has produced an immense body of social science research.[1] For the most part, this research naturalizes and solidifies what counts as knowledge about age-stage categories and who counts as normal within each age-stage. Youth studies research is almost entirely silent about sexual minority youth. In this chapter I look at how social science research has produced the category "youth" and how the queer youth discussed in this book negotiate how they are commonly understood in the dominant culture.

In some instances what these queer youth have to say directly contradicts the results of research that neither includes nor countenances them as subjects. In other instances, however, what these young people say is consistent with what mainstream youth studies tells us constitutes normality. This exposes the absurdity of assuming that young people are a monolithic group. Research and scholarship, some of it prominent (e.g., that of Margaret Mead and Sigmund Freud), and a large body of literature in queer youth studies and queer theory (some of which I present here) also disrupts the category "youth" produced by mainstream youth studies. Unfortunately, the former has had little impact on the latter.

Youth studies is comprised of what adults know about youth.[2] "Youth" and "adolescents" are reinforced as real, natural categories. Interestingly, those who are categorized as youth or adolescents do not themselves use these terms. In a 1990 survey in the United States, 64 percent of young people ages thirteen to seventeen polled on the question "What terms do you consider acceptable for describing people your own age?" chose "young adults" over the sociological term "youth" (29 percent) and the psychological term "adolescent" (19 percent) (Gallup, 1990).

Youth studies represents youth as irrational in relation to adults and as driven by hormones. It projects youth as a time of sexual innocence, sexual inactivity, and/or struggle over being sexually active, even while it posits it as a period of storm and stress. It claims that part of this storm and stress involves the struggle to remain sexually innocent. Contradictions occur in youth studies, in part, because it assumes a generic youth, ignoring the multiple axes of difference that comprise any given individual.

Production of the Category "Youth"

The idea that youth are distinctively different from humans of other ages and that they have special needs, wants, impulses, desires, and limited capabilities has occurred in Euro-Western thinking at least from the time of the ancient Greeks.[3] For Plato (429-347 BC) and Aristotle (384-322 BC), for example, youth was a third and distinct biological stage of life after infancy and childhood; it was thought to begin at age fourteen and to extend to age twenty-one. Both Plato and Aristotle viewed youth as the stage of life in which the capacity for reason first develops. Because of this, Plato (1956) argued in *The Republic*, serious education should begin at age fourteen. Education in science and mathematics was to be delayed until youth, when the mind is finally ready to learn to apply reason to the task of learning these subjects. Plato constructed a clear age hierarchy that placed youth above infants and children but behind adults, who were regarded as more reasoned. Aristotle thought children, like animals, were ruled by the impulsive pursuit of pleasure. For Aristotle the capacity for reasoning and making rational choices occurred only after childhood; for some, it did not occur at all. He argued that it takes the entire course of youth for reason to become fully established. At the beginning of youth the impulses remain in charge and even intensify because sexual desires develop during this time: "The young are in character prone to desire and ready to carry any desire they may have formed into action. Of bodily desires it is the sexual to which they are most disposed to give way, and in regard to sexual desire they exercise no self-restraint" (Aristotle 1954, 30). For Aristotle it is only at the end of youth, at age twenty-one, that reason is able to establish firm control over the impulses, including the sexual impulses.

Western discourses are informed by these ancient Greek writings, which depict youth as an impulsive (especially sexually impulsive) time of life. The idea that youth are generally irrational, impulsive, bored, alienated, sullen, or at odds with adults and the adult world is consistently marshalled in adult representations of youth in educational, psychological, sociological, psychiatric, medical, and popular cultural discourse. Note these examples from contemporary popular culture.

> Odd is not a useful definition when referring to adolescents. It's hard differentiating between a teenager with problems and one whose only problem is being a teenager ... [A] pie chart of the teenage brain reveals that 54 percent of the organ is devoted to tracking the state of their hormones, 21 percent does play-by-play analyses of their mercurial moods, and 10 percent is given over to calculations: what music they desperately need, what movies they'd die if they didn't see, and what items of clothing everybody else has but they don't. (Roberts 1999, 1)

> In preparation for meeting his children, Helma had read a book titled *Raising a Happy Teenager,* and attempted to watch music videos on television but surrendered after ten minutes ... the teenage years are confusing ... her mood will pass ... so where are those two adolescent nightmares? ... anybody over twenty-two is abysmally stupid and useless, and *such* an embarrassment. Don't you remember how you felt at that age? (Dereske 2001, 13, 24, 40, emphasis in original)

> You'll have plenty of time to hide your emotions when you're old. (Bonnie Bell advertisement for "Bottled Emotion" products, *Teen People*, November 2000)

Early Christian writings also represented the struggle between youthful reason and passion. In his autobiographical *Confessions* Saint Augustine (400, 354-430) described his life until his conversion to Christianity at age thirty-three. According to Augustine, as a teenager and in his early twenties he was a reckless young man who lived in an impulsive, pleasure-seeking way. Not only did he drink large quantities of alcohol and spend money extravagantly but he also had sex with many young women and fathered a child outside of marriage. As a newly converted Christian, Augustine repented his reckless youth, claiming that Christianity, not maturity, establishes the rule of reason over passion here on Earth. While Augustine favoured the position that youth are naturally, biologically impulsive and irrational in relation to adults, he nevertheless disrupted the alleged naturalness of youthful irrationality in contending that conversion to Christianity did not depend on maturity.

The idea of the innocence of youth was an effect of the increasing regulation of bodily habits, including sexual practices. Christianity, through the early Roman Catholic Church, consolidated the imperative that sex must be procreative within Christian marriage. Sexual pleasure, especially outside of marriage, was considered to be sinful pleasure of the flesh. Sexual innocence was thought to reside naturally in children and youth. Accounts of the innocence of youth can be traced at least to tales of the Children's Crusade, which took place in 1212 (Sommerville 1982). The Children's Crusade was a new attempt to conquer the Holy Land through peaceful means, inspired by the belief that Jesus had decreed that this would occur only through the efforts of innocent youth. While the Children's Crusade was unsuccessful, as an event it underlines a temporal distinction between youth and adulthood – a distinction marked by innocence, particularly sexual innocence. This youthful innocence was perceived as possessing a special value, as wielding a potent and persuasive power over adults that exceeds rational explanation. This notion of youth as a time of sexual innocence contrasts with Augustine's and others' accounts of youthful sexual activity, and it has little correspondence to the lives of the youth who appear in this book.

While notions of youth as constituting a period of life separate from adulthood existed prior to the nineteenth century, specific conditions in that century made possible a yet more rigid division between adults and youth. One such condition was the Industrial Revolution. There was a tremendous demand for youth and pre-adolescent children to staff mines, factories, and shops during this time. More physically resilient, younger people were better able to withstand the terrible working conditions of the time than were older people. The first stages of the Industrial Revolution occurred in Great Britain and distinguished younger people from adults by utilizing them as exploited labour while, at the same time, giving them many adult roles.

Urban reformers, youth workers, and early educators who were concerned about the physical and moral exploitation of young people were key to the enactment of laws to restrict child labour and to require children to attend secondary school (Kett 1977). Prior to the nineteenth century laws requiring children to attend school were restricted to primary school attendance (Tyack 1990). Between 1890 and 1920 increasing state legal changes required compulsory school attendance for "youth" (Arnett and Taber 1994). New technological demands required literate and more skilled workers. The idea of young people going to school for a prolonged period of time in order to train for an increasingly skilled workforce became entrenched during this time, with the result that, for long periods, youth became isolated from the world of adults and work. Discourses of youthful innocence still figured centrally, but this innocence was associated with notions of the need for prolonged dependence on adults in order to educate future workers. The need for a skilled work force in industrializing nations made possible an interface between youth as sexually innocent and youth as economically dependent.

The formation of human sciences during this time had a profound effect on the construction of youth as a category distinct from adults and children. Youth studies can be traced to this emerging "knowledge" about youth. In the sections that follow I present some of the most influential scholars of this new science and show how their work reinforced the notion of youth as a distinct social category with universal developmental attributes. This work variously understands youth as a period of storm and stress, as a period of maturation, as a time for proper sexual maturation influenced in particular by parents and family but also affected by friends and peers, as a time for prolonged dependency, and as a time in which internal problems (depression, anxiety, and suicide) and external problems (risky behaviours, aggression, and violence) are prevalent.

Youth as a Period of Storm and Stress

G. Stanley Hall (1844-1924) was a key figure in North America with regard to this emerging way of looking at youth. Hall obtained the first doctorate in psychology in the United States, was founder of the American Psychological Association, and was first president of Clark University. Significantly, Hall was the initiator of the child study movement and became a strong advocate of age-stage development theories about children and adolescents. He was, as well, an advocate for improved conditions for children and adolescents in the family, school, and workplace. In 1904 Hall published his landmark two-volume set of texts entitled *Adolescence*. This work reflected a culmination of many years of Hall's thinking about adolescence in addition to research by a range of adult experts on youth.

Adolescence became the intellectual proof of the distinctiveness of youth as a separate category of person and established the study of adolescents as a growth area of scholarly concern. Hall is particularly noted for his theory of recapitulation, in which he proposes that the development of each individual recapitulates the evolutionary development of the human species as a whole. Adolescence, Hall professed, reflects a stage in the human evolutionary past when there is a great deal of upheaval and disorder. Adolescents "recapitulate" this past, according to Hall, by experiencing "storm and stress" as a standard part of their development. The storm and stress period of youth is manifested in conflict with parents, mood disruptions, and risky behaviours.

Hall's views in *Adolescence* established what he believed were the natural, biological conditions of "youth," and these became the cornerstone of the science of youth. This science created a subject position consisting of brooding, irritable, petulant, impulsive, volatile young people who, while heterosexual, were considered to be sexually innocent. "Youth" was a time of sexual innocence even while young people were considered to be at risk for engaging in sexual behaviour that was considered normal for adults. Sexual activity engaged in by youth was regarded as out-of-control behaviour.

Throughout youth studies the link between out-of-control hormones and sexual behaviours is a cause for concern in relation to teenage pregnancy, sexually transmitted diseases, and single parenthood.

One of the effects of constructing the stage of youth as a time of storm and stress, even while a time of sexual innocence, is that those who are not stressed by the conditions of youth are characterized as unusual or abnormal. For example, Anna Freud (1895-1982) viewed the storm and stress of adolescence as both universal and inevitable. According to her, adolescents who do not experience storm and stress have serious psychological problems (Freud 1969). As she put it: "to be normal during the adolescent period is by itself abnormal" (Freud 1958, 267).

Like Anna Freud, the developmental-stage theory of Erik Erikson (1902-94) also postulated that an absence of storm and stress in youth is a sign of pathology. Erikson wrote that youth who seek security are psychologically impaired since a "total lack of conflict during adolescence is an ominous sign that the individual's psychological maturity may not be progressing" (Erikson 1963, 164). Suicide, the second most frequent cause of death for all youth, is implicitly linked with the storm and stress of youth. Moodiness, alienation, and depression are factors often listed in youth suicide research. All adolescents, according to this literature, require expert treatment in order to help them successfully navigate their way through this vexed phase of development.

Hall, Freud, and Erikson characterize youth as a universal stage in which youth subjectivity is naturally pathological. More recent scholars argue against a universal, biological experience of storm and stress during youth, pointing out that most adolescents like and respect their parents (Paikoff and Brooks-Gunn 1991); that for most, mood disruptions are not so extreme that they require psychological treatment (Arnett 2000); and that most youth do not engage in highly reckless behaviour on a regular basis (Arnett 1999). According to Arnett, conflict with parents marks early to mid-adolescence; mood disruptions peak at mid-adolescence; and risky behaviours, such as driving fast, substance use, and risky sexual activity, peak in late adolescent and emerging adulthood.

Arnett (2000) also reports that middle-class youth are more likely to experience storm and stress than are other young people. That working-class youth, even though highly constrained in other ways, may be less stressed because they are working and making decisions about their lives in relation to their more financially dependent middle-class peers is undertheorized in this literature. Middle-class youth are often more highly managed and controlled through the application of middle-class family values. This arguably produces storm and stress due to the young person's wanting to be in control of his/her own life. Because, for the most part, storm and stress has been taken up as a natural, biological stage, there has been little attention paid to other conditions of possible stress for young people, such as attitudes towards race, ethnicity, and/or religious background.

Despite the recognition on the part of some youth researchers that social conditions produce youth as relatively disempowered individuals in relation to the adults around them – a condition that many youth find "stressful" – social conditions are nevertheless downplayed in youth studies in favour of a biological/developmental explanation for storm and stress. The idea of an age-stage-segregated category linked to the biology of hormonal influence on moods and risky behaviours continues to underwrite even the most recent work in youth studies. In films, novels, magazines, and media headlines popular culture reinforces the notion of youth as a separate stage (Cote and Allahar 1994; Whatley 1991). Films such as *The Breakfast Club*, *Weird Science*, *American Pie*, *American Pie 2*, and *America's Sweethearts* reinforce the idea that youth are separate from adults and children, as do television shows such as *That 70s Show* and *Friends*. Special magazines such as *Teen People* and *Teen*, and media headlines such as "Teen Brains," "Are Tortured Youth our Future?" and "Smarten Up? Wild Teens Don't Have the Brains for It" have the effect of producing youth as distinct from other age categories.

Youth as a Period of Maturation
In addition to his contribution to the storm and stress literature, Erik Erikson (1968) advanced a developmental model for adolescence. Erikson's psychological model, replete with a specialized vocabulary based on years of study and practice, occupies a central place in most introductory texts in youth studies. For Erikson, and the many theorists and practitioners who follow him, the central developmental task of adolescence, generally viewed to begin with the first noticeable changes of puberty (Feldman and Elliott 1990), is the formation of a coherent self-identity. According to Erikson, the two variables that establish the attainment of a mature, or coherent, identity, are crisis and commitment experienced in relation to occupational choice, religion, and political ideology. Crisis refers to the adolescent's period of choosing among meaningful alternatives, while commitment refers to the degree of personal investment the adolescent exhibits in her/his choice. Erikson proposes that mature identity is only achievable when an individual youth experiences a crisis and becomes committed to an occupation and ideology.

> The most widespread expression of the discontented search of youth is the craving for locomotion, whether expressed in a general "being on the go," "tearing after something," or "running around"; or in locomotion proper, as in vigorous work, in absorbing sports, in rapt dancing, in shiftless

Wanderschaft, and in the employment and misuse of speedy animals and machines ... for ego identity is partially conscious and largely unconscious. It is a psychological process reflecting social processes; but with sociological means it can be seen as a social process reflecting psychological processes; it meets its crisis in the adolescence. (Erikson 1968, 9)

Crisis, not surprisingly, is yet another form of storm and stress.

Erikson's developmental model posits basic identity statuses during which youth work through crisis and commitment. Marcia (1966, 1980, 1989, 1993, 1994, 1999) constructed four measures based on Erikson's theory and used them extensively through the Identity Status Interview, which was used to classify youth in terms of their developmental progress. The four measures are: identity diffused, foreclosure, moratorium, and identity achieved. Identity diffused status occurs when a youth has not moved through a crisis, explored meaningful alternatives, or made a commitment to an acceptable identity. Foreclosure occurs when youth establish an identity without crisis or exploration, usually in keeping with parental expectations. Moratorium occurs when youth become embroiled in a continuous crisis and identity search because they have failed to make a commitment to ideology and occupation. Finally, identity achieved occurs when a youth goes through a crisis, explores the alternatives, and makes a commitment.

Many criticisms have been made of Erikson's theory, including the idea that youth do not necessarily move through these stages in exact sequence and may even enter adolescence from, for example, foreclosure (Marcia 1989). It is also assumed that all youth come from the same family background – nuclear, middle-class, white, and heterosexual. The possibility that different family configurations might have different crisis and commitment phases is rarely raised as an issue. Nonetheless, Erikson's work has been affirmed by other age-stage theorists (Adams, Gulottat, and Montemayor 1992; Grotevant 1987; Marcia 1989; Waterman 1992), thus solidifying the normative binary between youth and adults. Like other social science research in which the subject is assumed in advance, the research conducted by these theorists is bound to reinforce the categories with which they begin.

Youth as a Time for Proper Sexual Maturity: Influence of Parents and the Family

Capitalist democracies have relied on the heterosexual family (Kinsman 1996) and the unpaid labour of women in the home (Sayer 1991). Both the heterosexual family and the unpaid labour of women are premised on specific roles for those within the unit. Adult males and females act as role models for unemployed children and young people as the latter develop towards "normal" sexual and work-life maturity (Adams 1997; Parsons 1951; 1964). Psychosocial theories of development describe three distinct stages through which children and youth must move to reach maturity as auto-sociality, homo-sociality, and hetero-sociality (Miller 1990).

The traditional heterosexual nuclear family involves a system of power that is central to maintaining youth within a prolonged period of financial dependency within a highly specific form of subjectivity (Cote and Allahar 1994). In *The Trouble with Normal* Mary Louise Adams (1997) traces the ways in which youth and heterosexuality were produced in postwar Canada. One of the many ways this occurred was through notions of "family values" and what counted as the appropriate family structure. The idea that there is a "proper" family structure is assumed and familiar throughout social science research from Sigmund Freud (1964 [1940]) to Talcott Parsons (1964) to contemporary youth studies (Arnett 2000). In study after study, in theory after theory, the heterosexual nuclear family is described as the correct family – the one within which youth will succeed in maturing into "normal," contributing citizens. Any other family structure is suspect, thought likely to produce deviance in children and youth. For example, the infamous Moynihan Report (1965) in the United States "documented" the pathology of mother-headed black families and their role in the continuing pathology of black youth. A more recent example arises from research that found that children with homosexual parents were more likely to explore homosexual activity themselves. "Amy Desai, a policy analyst with the conservative group Focus on the Family, said the new report is 'alarming' in its suggestions children of homosexuals might be more open to homosexual activity. 'Kids do best when they have a married mother and a married father'" (Associated Press, *Edmonton Journal*, 2001, B7).

In order for children and youth to take on expectations and norms for gender and sexuality, families must be comprised of "opposite"-sex parents. Mothers and fathers are considered to be the initial and appropriate role models for proper gendering, and the nuclear, heterosexual family is the guiding prerequisite for ensuring this (Adams 1997; Arnett 2000; Erikson 1968; Parsons 1964; Rice 1999).[4] Appropriate toys and playmates are provided or approved by parents so that acceptable gendering occurs (Burke 1996). Female and male youth are to see their parents acting in appropriate gender and heterosexual roles (Smith 1999). According to this literature, two-parent, opposite-sex-parent families are more likely to produce "normally" maturing children than are other types of families (Adams 1997; Arnett 2000; Erikson 1950; Parsons 1964). That parents are heterosexual is assumed in this literature. The two-parent, opposite-sex-parent family is the taken-for-granted norm, and special chapters devoted to families who deviate from this configuration are included in many youth studies texts (Rice 1999). Even these families, however, are headed by heterosexual parents.

Appropriate maturation for youth within the traditional family establishes a moratorium on sexual behaviours,[5] even while youth are expected to identify as heterosexual (Adams 1997; Arnett 2000; Erikson 1950; Parsons 1964; Rice 1999). Traditional families are sites where sexuality is policed (Adams 1997; Burke 1996). The imperative that young people are heterosexual even while they are expected to be sexually inactive sets up absurd consequences. Take, for example, a recent controversy over the sexuality of fictional, yet iconic, Canadian literary figure Anne of Green Gables. At a scholarly meeting a professor read a paper in which she speculated about the possible sexual nature of some of Anne's friendships. This created considerable reaction by editorialists and letter writers in the mainstream press. The idea of a homo-social Anne was particularly vexing for a letter writer from St. Albert, who was awarded a Golden Pen Award by the *Edmonton Journal* for her letter about reading *Anne of Green Gables* to her children. The idea of reading Anne's desires as homoerotic was to her a repugnant and ridiculous idea. In response, I wrote the following letter to the editor:

Thank you to Barbara Stasuk and *The Journal*'s Cheryl Purdey. Both sure straightened me out! ("Anne Response Wins Prize for Top Letter," Golden Pen Award, *Journal*, 22 August). The very spectre of a Canadian cultural icon having same sex desire is just too beyond what could possibly be Canadian! Or is it the idea that children and youth may be sexual or have sexual desires that gets their goat? And yet, children and youth are sexualized all the time around heterosexual desire. If Jane and Dick play together too much, it is intimated they "love" each other and are encouraged to think of themselves as prospective mates in marriage ... As long as children and youth are heterosexualized, they can be homosexualized. Please, give the Anne of Green Gables thing a break and open your minds beyond your own immediate experience. (Letter to the editor, *Edmonton Journal*, 2000, A19)

While youth studies literature represents youth as (hetero)sexually innocent, youth are also represented as hormonally driven (Whatley 1991) or troubled (Arnett 2000; Rice 1999). Young males, in particular, are depicted this way, while young females are in danger of becoming pregnant, and both boys and girls are at the mercy of sexually transmitted diseases (Arnett 2000; Rice 1999). There is a substantive literature on appropriate youth behaviours with regard to heterosexual dating rituals (Kuttler, La Greca, and Prinstein 1999; Miller and Benson 1999; Paul and White 1990; Smith 1999). This literature provides guidelines for dating, research on dating, and descriptive information about dating (Arnett 2000; Rice 1999). Traditional families provide opportunities for youth to practice good dating methods as part of "normal" maturation. Like parents, schools are to help regulate dating practice, providing opportunities for non-sexual mating behaviour through dances and high school graduation ceremonies. This literature is replete with descriptions of non-sexual mating rituals with opposite-sex partners and is encouraged as constituting "normal" behaviour for maturing youth (Arnett 2000; Rice 1999; Smith 1999). The use of pictures and pronouns throughout these texts function to authorize and reinforce heteronormativity (Arnett 2000; Rice 1999).

Adults have long been concerned about youth sexual behaviours. The level of this concern has sometimes reached the level of moral panic. In the 1970s in Toronto one such panic surfaced over demands for better birth control information for young female teens (Sethna 2000). An articulate, fifteen-year-old spokesperson who requested better birth control information from the Toronto Board of Education was placed under RCMP surveillance. She was deemed a student activist and a risk to the state. Other adult panics surface periodically around teenage pregnancy and heterosexually transmitted diseases (Adams 1997) as well as the menace of homosexual predators (Kinsman 1996; Adams 1997).

Popular culture reflects this concern that young people might be sexual. In a recent newspaper article on Natalie Wood, the author lamented that "Wood had an affair with director Nicholas Ray when she was *ahem* age 15 [and that] afterward, you need a scorecard to tote the tumbles" (J. Smyntek, "Natalie Wood's Life a Study in Heartache," *Edmonton Journal*, 15 June 2001, E5). It is assumed that early sexual behaviours are harmful and that Wood is to be pitied for having engaged in them. According to the author, if Wood had had better parents and had not embarked upon an early path of sexual promiscuity, she would have had a better life and death. Of course, typecasting Wood's life in such a way works only if we accept discourses of youth that assume that happily matured sexual innocence and "good" parents produce happy, adult lives.

Adult moral panic over gay-straight alliances in high schools in various school districts also exemplifies concern over youth sexuality; however, more specifically, these concerns are about non-conforming sexuality and, in particular, homosexuality (GALE/BC 2001, 6). This adult behaviour is consistent with youth studies research that endorses a particular way of developing towards heterosexual maturity and activity. This involves authorizing a moratorium on sexual activity and encouraging youth to practise appropriate gender "roles" through dating practice.

The "deviant" behaviours of problem youth are traced back to family pathology. Suicide is linked to family dysfunction (Cole, Protinsky, and Cross 1992; Lester 1987), as are eating disorders (Lester 1991). Delinquency is linked to family conflict (Lester 1988), while depression is related to family pathology (Stack 1985). Youth at risk for these behaviours are thought to come from non-traditional families, still referred to as "broken" homes or single-parent families. When a youth identifies as homosexual, it is assumed that she or he is sexually active, whether s/he has had an actual sexual experience or is simply making an identity claim.

According to youth studies, parents have a significant but decreasing influence on youth as they mature. This reduced influence appears in relation to specific issues, such as education, work, risk behaviours, and dating (Arnett 2000; Rice 1999). As well, while time spent with parents and other family members decreases as youths get older, the amount of conflict with parents increases (Larson and Richards 1994; Youniss, McLellan, and Yates 1985). When youth have problems dealing with parents it is taken as evidence of storm and stress and their behaviours are regarded as irrational (Arnett 2000; Rice 1999). According to research reported in Arnett (2000) and Rice (1999) maturity for youth is measured by the degree of separation from parents. Moving away from home and living independently, if achieved at the appropriate time (i.e., after age eighteen) is considered to reflect both emotional and economic maturity (Cote and Allahar 1994). Leaving home prior to this is considered to be running away and is another indication of storm and stress or family dysfunction (Arnett 2000).

Youth whose parents expect them to do well often live up to those expectations, and consequently it is believed that parents influence independence and self-reliance, persistence, social skills, and responsibility (Baumrind 1991; Steinberg et al. 1992). Authoritative parents are reported as having the most favourable effects on the academic achievement of youth because they proffer high expectations to which youth respond (Steinberg, Brown, and Dornbusch 1996). Authoritarian parents, those who are demanding and punishing, often have a negative impact on youth (DeBaryshe, Patterson, and Capaldi 1993; Dornbusch et al. 1990; Melby and Conger 1996). Parents are rarely differentiated in these studies by gender, even though youth studies emphasizes the importance of children and youth modelling appropriate gender "roles" if they are to achieve proper maturation.

Not only does youth studies represent youth as undifferentiated, it represents good parents as those who are part of a traditional family; in this way it produces the majority of families as dysfunctional. The majority of youth are "normally" gendered and heterosexual regardless of their family configuration. Identifying a particular kind of youth as a "problem" and then tracing this problem back onto family configuration and parents does not account for the range of other discourses that affect youth. Youth studies has little to say, for example, about the effects of popular culture on youth.

Influence of Peers and Friends

Youth studies discusses peers and friends in relation to their influence on young people and their impact on socialization. According to youth studies, peers are those who are about the same age and who make up a large network of classmates, community members, and co-workers (Arnett 2000; Rice 1999). Friends are those from the same age group with whom youth develop a valued, mutual relationship (Arnett 2000). Implicitly, parents and other adults are not friends.

Arnett (2000) reports that the "progression to maturity" marks a change in quantity and quality of the time youth spend with parents as opposed to friends. Typically, the level of warmth and closeness between youth and parents is said to decline as youth move away from the social world of their families and become increasingly involved in that of their friends. One study of teenagers aged thirteen to sixteen indicates that the average time spent with parents is twenty-eight minutes daily, while the average time spent with friends is 103 minutes daily (Buhrmester and Carbery 1992). According to this study youth depend more on friends than on parents for companionship and intimacy. In industrialized societies this trend is related to the function of schooling as children and youth spend the better part of a typical day in school with peers (albeit supervised by adult educators). There is less adult supervision of youth outside of school than inside.

Whereas the literature reports that youth spend increasingly more time with opposite-sex friends in the final stages of normal psychosexual development (Miller 1990), earlier stages of childhood are measured as normal when children prefer to play and spend most of their time with same-sex friends (*DSM-IV*). Peer influence is reported as greater than parental influence in relation to school and schoolwork. For example, Midgely and Urdan (1995) indicate that, if their friends enjoy school and schoolwork, then this has an influence on how consistently teens attend class, how much time they spend on homework, how hard they try in school, and the grades they achieve. Youth studies pay considerable attention to the influence of peers and friends who have a negative attitude towards schooling (Arnett 2000). For example, low achievers who have high-achieving friends tend to have improved grades over time and are more likely to plan to attend post-secondary school than are those who do not have such friends. Another study found that teens who are concerned with what friends think about them perform more poorly in school than do teens who are not so concerned about this (Fuligni and Eccles 1992).

Socializing with friends and peers is the most common daily activity of youth in Euro-Western cultures (Arnett 2000). The amount of time spent socializing is related to grades: the more time spent socializing, the lower the grades. Having friends who denigrate school is reported to lower success even for teens with authoritative parents (Steinberg et al. 1992). A study conducted by Youniss, McLellan, and Yates (1986, 294) found that youth preferred to discuss more intimate matters – those involving sex, problems with sex, and feelings about the opposite sex– with friends than with parents. Youth have considerable influence on their peers with regard to the regulation of gender and sexuality, as does the popular culture produced for youth; yet youth studies has little to say about how youth use the imperative to conform to gender and sexual expectations in order to police conformity.

Arnett (2000) refers to "neglected adolescents lack[ing] the social skills necessary for making friends" (246) and "friends [as] the source not only of adolescents' most positive emotions but also of their most negative emotions – anger, frustration, sadness, and anxiety" (227); however, he does not explore the social conditions giving rise to these emotions. Given that youth studies emphasize the decreasing influence of parents and other adults on youth, the lack of attention to the social conditions within which youth influence each other is conspicuous by its absence.

Family, schools, peers, and friends police youth who do not conform to gender-rigid expectations (Bartky 1990; Burke 1996; Scholinski 1997). Young males are encouraged by male peers to act as heterosexual predators in the hunt for the next female virgin and to bully or denigrate homosexuality as further proof of their heterosexuality (Whatley 1991).

Popular culture – such as that found in teen magazines, movies, music, and music videos – plays a significant role in representing gender and sexuality to young people. Films directed at youth often depict male youth as hormone-driven creatures (Whatley 1991). Young males are cast as biologically driven and out of control, thereby reinforcing storm and stress and irrationality models of youth. Young females are depicted as morally superior unless they are heterosexually active, in which case they are viewed as promiscuous and, therefore, morally inferior. These films typically include male "nerds" who are sexually immature and innocent. Whatley claims that youth viewing these films long to assume these forms of subjectivity and come to expect these behaviours from their peers and friends. Youth studies considers female heterosexual activity to constitute problem behaviour because of how it manifests itself in teenage pregnancy and single parenting (Arnett 2000; Rice 1999).

Youth, like parents, are effective in enforcing and controlling each other's behaviour. Peers and friends do this through name-calling, teasing, bullying, and shunning. In extreme cases, youth police each other through the use of violence, even murder. The murder of Reena Virk, a British Columbia Asian-Canadian girl from a Jehovah's Witness background, is one such extreme example of the policing of difference. Reena Virk attempted to conform to the expectations of her peers but was unable to do so because of her size, colour, and comportment. While media attention has primarily focused on the violence of the killers, the role of other peers in disciplining Virk for her appearance and non-conforming behaviours has been given little print attention. The adult response to violence towards non-conforming peers is often dismay at what is perceived to be an increase in youth violence.[6] While Reena Virk's murder is an extreme example of policing non-conformity, violence remains a way for youth to influence others' behaviour.

According to Chakkalakal (2000), Reena Virk's death constitutes a Canadian lynching – an assertion that signals both the racism of this action and the refusal of the mainstream media to investigate it on this level. Despite her best efforts, Virk's bodily morphology, comportment, and colour did not match the expectations for a heterosexually conforming girl. Virk was alleged to have attempted to have sex with another young woman's boyfriend. This action was derided as ridiculous because of her appearance, but, at the same time, it was also taken seriously since it undermined another young woman's heterosexual relationship. When Virk refused to (could not) either conform or go away, her peers moved beyond the everyday regulatory mechanisms of gender and sexuality and murdered her.

The media represented Reena Virk as being complicit in her own death because she did not stay away from those who victimized her. Youth studies would identify her as someone who, having few peers and no friends, suffered from low self-esteem. It would see her attempts to find a way of belonging as evidence of her lack of social skills. It would regard her family as dysfunctional since Virk no longer lived with her parents. And it is likely that, given her gender deviant appearance, youth studies would blame her parents for providing inappropriate gender role modelling. Youth studies focuses on the idea that, for the most part, adolescents depend on peers and friends for companionship and intimacy, thus individualizing violent regulation by peers as instances of unchecked emotions such as anger, frustration, sadness, and anxiety (Arnett 2000, 227). It does not recognize youth violence as another way in which gender and sexual non-conformity is policed in this culture. Rather than individualize and psychopathologize Virk and others like her, we need to consider the regulatory role of peers.

Youth as a Period of Prolonged Dependency: Schooling and Transition from School to Work

A significant area of study within contemporary youth studies relates to schooling and the transition from school to work. This research examines the implications of schooling as a state-sanctioned institution concerned with the social control of youth.

The literature on the transition from school to work is concerned with the incidence and explanation of social inequalities (Griffin 1993). When school inequalities are considered, attention is given to lower- and working-class youth, youth from racialized groups other than whites (Hemmings 1998; Price 1999; Steinberg, Brown, and Dornbusch 1996), and gender, particularly girls (Sommers 1984; Bianchi and Spain 1996; Arnett 2000).

Premised on the assumption that youth experience a prolonged dependency within heteronormative families, schooling and transition from school to work research examines school drop-outs, exceptional students, underachievement, overachievement, effective achievement factors, peer influence, effective schools, effective class size, effective teachers, school transition from elementary to junior or senior schools, school climate, and transition to work (Arnett 2000; Rice 1999).

In his research Arnett found that the best teachers, like the best parents, are authoritative. Most of the literature on achievement is heavily influenced by psychologisms such as motivation, engagement, self-esteem, and resilience (Arnett 2000; Rice 1999). Social inequality issues are discussed in relation to socioeconomic, gender, and racial factors. Mainstream research rarely examines sexuality as an area of social inequality. The idea that an effective school would be a school in which sexual minority youth would be valued and safe within their learning environment receives little notice; instead, chilly climates are related to a perceived increase in youth violence. When other factors fail to explain the perceived increase in school violence, storm and stress theories and the related presumed irrationality of youth function as fallback positions.

Youth studies research on schooling is concerned with how prepared young people are for work when they leave school. Steinberg, Brown, and Dornbusch (1996) indicate, for example, that youth coming out of schools are ill-suited for the workforce. Concerns for the adequacy of Western education can be traced to the USSR's successful launch of Sputnik. Both the US education system and the youth prepared by this system were assessed to be lacking in the scientific and mathematical rigour needed to be competitive in the race to space (Arnett 2000; Rice 1999).

In the 1960s and 1970s education was criticized for being too far removed from real life. "Relevance" became the buzzword, and a focus on workplace skills, experience, and occupational training was emphasized (Arnett 2000). Throughout the last half of the twentieth century the lack of youth engagement in education was considered to be a serious obstacle to academic achievement. A major American study conducted by Steinberg, Brown, and Dornbusch (1996) stated that

> unfortunately, engagement is the exception rather than the norm in the school experience of American adolescents. Research indicates that a remarkably high proportion of adolescents not only fall short of an ideal of engagement, but are strikingly disengaged during their time in school, "physically present but psychologically absent." (67)

So serious is this disengagement that Steinberg felt compelled to provide the following summary:

> Today's students know less, and can do less, than their counterparts could twenty-five years ago. Our high school graduates are among the least intellectually competent in the industrialized world ... The achievement problem

we face in this country is due not to a drop in the intelligence of our children, but to a widespread decline in children's interest in education and their motivation to achieve in the classroom; it is a problem of attitude and effort, not ability. (183-4)

Nostalgia for one's own generation deflects attention away from the social conditions of schooling that many youth experience as intolerable obstacles to achievement. Schooling was, and still is, far removed from the lives of many youth who resist the social controls inherent within the school system as well as the social conditions found there. Mainstream youth studies pays little to no attention to the social conditions sexual minority youth encounter in schools.

Cote and Allahar (1994) write from an interdisciplinary focus (with an emphasis on political economy) about the prolonged dependency of youth in contemporary Canadian life. This period of dependence effectively keeps youth out of competition for jobs – something that, until recently (with globalization and the demand for cheap labour) was necessary for capitalist democracies. When youth are in the labour force, they generally work for low pay at low-skilled jobs in the service industry. Taking up Erikson's notion of moratorium, Cote and Allahar (1994) contend that youth are produced as citizens whose basic rights to work are placed in abeyance in order to satisfy legal and societal requirements. They recognize how gender affects schooling and the transition from school to work, but they fail to recognize that gaining independence after the latter event often confounds what is thought to be typical of youth.

Research in schooling and transition from school to work, like other mainstream youth studies research, neglects the experiences of sexual minority youth whose voices expose the inadequacy of the monolithic category "youth."

Externalizing and Internalizing Problems
Arnett (2000, 396) explains that "a variety of problems are more common in adolescence and emerging adulthood than at other periods of life." These are referred to as internalizing problems and externalizing problems, respectively. Internalizing problems occur when youth turn distress inward, toward themselves. These problems include suicide, depression, anxiety, and eating disorders. The literature tends to group these problems and indicates that they are more common among females than among males. In a study conducted by Petersen (1993), 35 percent of teens polled reported that they had been depressed at some point in the previous six-month period. This is significantly higher than rates of depressed mood for either children or adults. Arnett (2000) reports that depression is the leading internalizing problem of youth. Youth suffering from internalizing problems are said to

be overcontrolled by parents who maintain a tight psychological leash (Barber, Olsen, and Shagle 1994).

Externalizing problems involve those behaviours that are turned outward. They include delinquency, fighting, substance use, risky driving, and unprotected sex (Arnett 2000; Gottfredson and Hirschi 1990; Williams 1998). The literature associated externalizing problems with undercontrolled male youth whose parents are somewhat dilatory with regard to parental monitoring (Barber, Olsen, and Shagle 1994).

Unprotected sex is a special category of externalizing problem. The riskiness of this behaviour has effects ranging from sexually transmitted diseases to pregnancy and single parenthood. Debates about providing sex education for young people range from adult denial of the necessity of this information to highly biological how-to models of heterosex and reproduction (Adams 1997; Silin 1995; Moran 2000; Whatley 1991). Sex education for youth is not meant to encourage actual sexual practice. The concern is to help youth understand reproductive sex and marriage rather than safe sexual practices.

The political and moral anxieties of each era have found their way into sex education curricula (Adams 1997; Moran 2000). Not fully informing youth about safe sex because of the conviction that youth is a time for a moratorium on sex is a potentially deadly action. Patton (1995, 338) underscores the urgency of sex education:

By 1990, over 10,000 people under the age of twenty-five had been diagnosed with AIDS, with probably ten times that number infected with HIV (Boyer and Kegeles 1991, 2). Medical experts now believe that it takes an average of ten years from date of infection until serious symptoms occur; thus, most of these some 110,000 HIV-infected young people contracted HIV as teenagers. In the crucial first decade of the epidemic, some attention was devoted to instilling in young people a sense of tolerance toward people living with AIDS. Tragically, moralistic attitudes about sex combined with racism and homophobia ... delay identification of young people as significantly at *risk* and desperately in need of risk-reduction education.

Research indicates that youth suffering from both internal and external problems have especially difficult family backgrounds (Arnett 2000; Rice 1999). Sexual minority youth often have difficult family backgrounds; indeed, physical, psychological, or emotional migration from one's birth home due to family rejection, a form of diaspora,[7] is a common theme throughout sexual minority life narratives. Yet mainstream youth studies does not mention sexual minority youth as at risk of either internalizing or externalizing problems (Arnett 2000; Rice 1999).

Suicide, a behaviour related to depression, is the most disturbing problem behaviour reported in youth studies. One in three young people reports having suicidal thoughts (Arnett 2000); one in six report a suicide attempt (Rice 1999). Next to car accidents, suicide is the most common cause of death among people aged fifteen to nineteen. Koopmans (1995) refers to the significant body of empirical research that suggests that suicide is associated with family processes. Henry et al. (1993) indicate that suicidal youth come from disturbed family backgrounds; and according to Wade (1987) there may be a great deal of conflict between youth and parent(s) along with parental violence and/or negative attitudes towards youth. The absence or loss of one or both parents, or abandonment by the father, is reported as significant (Tishler 1992). Stivers (1988) found that those who attempt suicide have trouble communicating with significant adults and do not feel close to any adults. Emotional support from parents and other adults is reported as lacking for suicidal youth (Dukes and Lorch 1989). Three common characteristics of college youth who had thoughts of suicide were identified as: poor relationships with parents, poor relationships with peers, and a conviction of personal helplessness regarding the future (Lester 1991).

The best predictors of youth suicide attempts are said to be social isolation and loss of, or low, family support (Morano, Cisler, and Lemerond 1992). Multiple studies link suicide with some form of mental illness, including depression (Paluszny, Davenport, and Kim 1991). Symptoms include hallucinations, guilt deriving from voices directing them toward external aggression, and substance abuse (Rich, Sherman, and Fowler 1990). Suicide attempts are also linked to stress from low self-esteem and poor quality friendships (Peck 1987).

Psychological studies categorize suicidal youth as having immature personalities, poor impulse control, and little positive ego-identity development (Bar-Joseph and Tzuriel 1990). Positive ego-identity, according to the Erikson model, is necessary for feelings of self-worth, meaningfulness, and purposefulness. Other studies show that suicidal youth are highly suggestible and may readily follow the directions and examples of others (Hazell 1991).

Youth studies does not provide any information on queer youth and suicide. Tidy little boxes in textbooks list a variety of warning signs for youth at risk, but sexual identity is not one of them (Arnett 2000; Rice 1999). This absence is glaring, given the information available on gay youth suicide. One Alberta study found that gay youth are fourteen times more likely to commit suicide than are those from any other group (Bagley and Tremblay 1997).

A connection between suicide and homosexuality has long been recognized in the popular culture, reflected in music (e.g., *The Ode to Billie Joe*), movies (e.g., *The Boys in the Band*), theater (e.g., Hellman's *The Children's Hour*), and other art forms. Yet, few researchers have ventured to explore the link between sexual orientation and self-injury. Early evidence of an association appeared as incidental findings in studies of adult sexuality. They revealed that gay men were much more likely to have attempted suicide than heterosexual men and that their attempts often occurred during adolescence. Newer studies have provided consistent evidence of unusually high rates of attempted suicide among gay youth, in the range of 20 to 30 percent, regardless of geographic and ethnic variability. (Remafedi 1994, 1)

Given the myriad of risk factors listed for suicide in mainstream youth studies, it is truly astonishing that there is no mention of the impact of non-conforming sexuality. What perhaps is most poignant about this absence is that the biggest risk factor for suicide by queer youth may well be living within a heterosexist and homophobic family and culture. While some researchers decry suicide as an act of aggression expressed inwardly, they also suggest that successful suicide is actually directed at loved ones and society (Lester 1988). Queer youth simply get the message they should not exist, which is writ large everywhere. To blame the victim for acting on a message received over and over again is yet another instance of heterosexist aggression.

According to the US Department of Health and Human Services (1989) suicide is the leading cause of death for lesbian and gay youth.[8] Other studies (not from mainstream youth studies) affirm the deadliness of attempted suicide and suicide for queer youth (Gibson 1989; Herdt 1989; Herschberger, Pilkington, and D'augelli 1997; Kourany 1987; O'Connor 1993-94; Remafedi 1991, 1994; Rofes 1983; Rotheram-Borus and Koopman 1991; Schneider, Faberow, and Kruks 1989; Shafer and Fisher 1996). Young gay males have been studied more closely than have young lesbians, and it is reported that most attempts at suicide by the former occur before the age of twenty, when conflict at home and with one's self is most intense (Rofes 1983a).

In a survey of suicide studies, Remafedi (1994, 7) found "consistent evidence of unusually high rates of attempted suicide among gay youth, in the range of 20 to 30 percent, regardless of geographic and ethnic variability." Given that suicide is now recognized as the second leading killer of all youth in the United States and Canada (next to accidents), the astonishing fact about queer youth suicide is the overrepresentation of queer youth in suicide statistics and their absence from mainstream youth studies literature (Rice 1999). Mainstream researchers either completely ignore these studies, have special sections on lesbian and gay youth in which risk of suicide is mentioned in passing but not integrated into larger sections on youth suicide (Arnett 2000), try to foreclose discussion by charging queer researchers with having a political agenda, or quibble over numbers (Remafedi 1994).

The American federally commissioned *Report of the Secretary's Task Force on Youth Suicide* (US Department of Health and Human Services 1989) was almost rejected because of its controversial chapter on gay and lesbian youth (Remafedi 1994). When the report was finally accepted in its entirety, it was published in a limited printing of only 3,000 copies. As Remafedi (1994, 8) writes, "important but unfundable topics have a way of never becoming 'serious' science."

One of the major factors in the lives and suicides of queer youth is that they feel alienated from the social institutions to which most people turn in times of crisis. The family, church, and schools all fail to see homosexuality/ queerness as a viable human option (Rofes 1983b). Rather than providing support, these institutions are leaders in stigmatizing and regulating homo-sexuality. Many families react to queer youth by kicking them out of the home. Queer youth are overrepresented among the homeless (Brownworth 1992, 1996). While some empirical studies of homelessness ask questions about sexual orientation (Kruks 1991), much more research needs to be done. There is a dearth of shelter beds for all adolescents,[9] and there is virtu-ally nowhere for sexual minority youth to go except the street once they leave or are forced out of their homes. Homelessness often means that, be-cause of a lack of financial support from the family, education is rendered an unlikely option.

Financial vulnerability and the fact that there are few well-paying job options mean that street youth become involved in social networks com-posed of other homeless street people who support themselves by whatever means possible. Homeless female youth are exposed to prostitution as a way of earning a living (Perlman 1980). Prostitution is also a viable option for financially strapped, homeless sexual minority youth, both male and female. The numbers of sexual minority youth who earn a living as sex trade workers is underinvestigated (Coleman 1989). Even when youth do stay at home after coming out, they often face harassment, non-acceptance, or denial that queer sexuality is a valid choice. They are not safe within their own homes.

Disruptions of the Category "Youth"

The Influence of Margaret Mead

> Reading Margaret Mead's *Coming of Age in Samoa* was my introduction not only to the concept of culture but also to the critique of culture – ours. Before 1961, when I read *Coming of Age* in an introduction to anthropology course at the University of Michigan, Mead had already done a great deal to popularize the concept of cultural relativity. Her voice had reached into my teenage hell, where it whispered my comforting first mantra – "Everything

is relative, everything is relative" – meaning: there are other worlds, other possibilities, than those evident in 1950s suburban California. I was a scholarly minded half-Jew from New York (where I had spent my childhood) and a red diaper baby. I was athletic, hated dating boys, and resented pretending I was less than they were. Neither girls' clothes nor girlish attitudes felt "right" to me. And I was attracted – in some sweaty way that had no name – to girls and women (Newton 2000, 1).

In *Coming of Age in Samoa,* published in 1928, Margaret Mead contested the inevitability of age-stage developmental models for youth. This ethnographic work, like those of Ruth Benedict, Franz Boas, and Claude Lévi-Strauss, came out of anthropological paradigms that, from Freud to Erikson, contested the basic truths of age and stage theories of child and adolescent development. Mead's work was premised on the idea that the influence of a particular culture is crucial in determining the personality and behaviour of a developing individual. Because cultures vary with regard to social institutions, economic patterns, habits, mores, rituals, religious beliefs, and ways of life, culture, according to Mead, is relative. Anticipating work by post-structuralists Marcus and Fischer (1986), Mead used her ethnographic work in Samoa to form a cultural critique of modern cultural practices of child-rearing in the United States.

Mead's work did not deny the existence of an age period known as "youth." It did, however, deny that biological arguments adequately explain the experiences of youth. In Western, industrialized nations youth experiences are related to the cultural practices by which they are surrounded and are a response to conditions of dependency upon, and submissiveness to, adults. Sociocultural context is what determines the direction of adolescence and, therefore, strongly influences the degree to which youth are welcomed into the adult world. Given the strong and prolonged age separation of youth from adulthood, Mead argues that youth are *not* welcome in the adult world; rather, they are heavily discouraged from entering that world until they have developed "normally," as outlined in Erikson's (and other social psychological) work. Then, at a specific age – eighteen or twenty-one – youth are abruptly expected to become adults.

Samoan children and youth, in contrast to their American counterparts, engage in a relatively continuous growth pattern with no abrupt changes from one age to the other. Samoans are not expected to think or behave in one way as children, in another as youth, and in yet another as adults. The principle of continuity of cultural conditioning posits that there is no abrupt change from one pattern of behaviour to another. Three examples of this principle that Mead saw at work in Samoan culture are: the responsible roles of children in Samoan culture in contrast to the non-responsible roles of children in Western culture; the dominant role of children and youth in

Samoan culture in contrast to the submissive role of children and youth in Western culture; and, finally, the similarity of sex roles of children, youth, and adults in Samoan culture in contrast to the dissimilar sex roles of children, youth, and adults in Western culture.

Mead's observations of Samoan culture convinced her that sexual activity among youth was to be encouraged, while reproduction was to be discouraged until they were older. Multiple parenting and sexual freedom, radically different from the family and sexual role regulations of Western societies, opened up possibilities for human lives. In contrast, as youth mature within Western cultures, possibilities for sexual activity are limited. Minimizing the meaning of physical changes, as Samoan culture does, provides a different interpretation of those changes. Western cultures, with their preoccupation with physical changes in children and youth, produce particular subject positions for children and youth – positions that emphasize their distinctiveness from adults.

Mead's work of seventy years ago deconstructs the claim to universality of age-stage developmental models that are still so prevalent in the early part of the twenty-first century. Her work was and still is very controversial, not only because of its implications for social science research on youth and children but also because it implicates Western childrearing practices in the production of social problems – problems that youth studies represents as a natural and normal part of the maturation of youth. Based on her work in Samoa, Mead held that changes in Western childrearing practices would go a long way towards eliminating widespread social problems. While Mead did not use the language of poststructuralism, she made it possible to anticipate a range of youth subjectivities that, at that time, was severely limited by a culture that heavily circumscribed how it conceived of youth.

If we look at North American indigenous cultures, we can find other examples of the disruption of the assumption of universal age/stage categories. Given the egalitarianism of many Native American cultures, there was no place for arbitrary distinctions based on age or stage of development by which humans could be differentially valued. Kinsman (1996, 92) reminds us that, in Canada, central to the subjugation of indigenous peoples before Confederation, was "the marginalization and destruction of diverse forms of erotic, gender, and social life" and their subordination to "white, European derived social and sexual organizations." According to Wilson (1996, 305), "two-spirit Indigenous Americans" cultivate an identity that "affirms the interrelatedness of all aspects of identity, including sexuality, gender, culture, community, and spirituality." She goes on to say that "two-spirit connects us to our past by offering a link that had previously been severed by government policies and actions" (305). While most Euro-Western social science produces the "homosexual" as deviant, "traditionally, two-spirit people were simply a part of the entire community" (ibid.). Traditional Native American cultural values, like Samoan values, expose the arbitrariness of age-stage discursive hierarchies of youth as well as the heterosexism of mainstream youth studies. Moreover, because the subject positions produced by age-stage discourse were not subject positions for young people in these cultures, the "problems of youth" linked to them were not a part of these cultures.

Queer Youth Studies

> The history which bears and determines us has the form of *war* rather than that of a language: relations of power, not relations of meaning.
>
> > – Michel Foucault, *Power/Knowledge:*
> > *Selected Interviews and Other Writings*

> I think a lot about death. That's what comes of living in a war zone.
>
> > – V. Brownworth, *Too Queer:*
> > *Essays from a Radical Life*

Michael Warner (1994b, ix) writes that, when "social theory as a quasi-institution for the past century has returned continually to the question of sexuality," it has done so "with an endless capacity to marginalize queer sexuality in its descriptions of the social world." Prior to undertaking this research I did not, perhaps could not, begin to imagine the extent of this marginalization. It was only when faced with the juxtaposition of mainstream youth studies and queer youth studies that I realized that research about sexual minority youth is as inconsequential to research about youth as are sexual minority youth to a community's understanding of itself.

Sexual minority youth are produced through their absence or as a special area of interest, as the abject Other; that is, as a deviant outsider within the realm of youth studies. There is, however, a large body of research that takes the lives of queer youth seriously. Some of this research I have already referred to in the previous section on youth suicide. Queer youth studies pays attention to issues – such as coming out narratives – that are significant in the lives of queer youth. There is an acknowledgment that queer youth negotiate their sexuality in much different ways – with parents and other adults – than do non-queer youth. Strommen (1989) notes that many parents are often deeply dismayed to learn that their child is queer, and they require special support groups to come to terms with this.

I have come out to twenty-five or thirty people now and none of them knew or guessed. They were all surprised that I am queer. (Chastity, 1998)

He [best friend] finally told his parents and they were so awful he ended up moving out of home for a year. They wanted him to go to therapy and he was grounded indefinitely. They were so religious and it was against their religion. Once he left home, things were much better for him. He got to be so open about who he was and got his life back together again. (Chastity, 1998)

I lived on my own from the time I was fourteen. I signed off any right to my parents support so that I could get social assistance. I always felt more mature than my peers because I was paying my own bills and buying my own groceries and they were living at home and complaining about their parents. (Elton, 1998)

She [mother] went there for me. She wanted to give me and herself information to help us know what to do and what to expect. She knew there was lots of discrimination and wanted to know how to deal with this. She wanted to help me. (Chastity, 1998)

Organizations such as Parents and Friends of Lesbians and Gays (PFLAG) offer necessary family support for parents who are trying to come to terms with their queer daughter or son. Parents who cannot bear who their children have become meet with one another and talk and grieve their way towards accepting their offspring and themselves as the parents of a queer child. In a homophobic and heterosexist world other options are non-existent.

I think the information session was offered by PFLAG. I am sure that is where my mother got all the information for us. (Chastity, 1998)

While PFLAG is often helpful for those family of queer youth who have difficulty coping, hearing tortured lamentations of family members sorrowing over one's sexual orientation hardly qualifies as an act of love and acceptance, let alone of valuing. Small wonder that queer youth do not easily come out to parents and family.

My mother asked me if I was gay and we sort of talked about it but I did not come out. And she went to a session at the teacher's convention on gay and lesbian youth and brought home all this information. A big folder of information. And I was really uncomfortable but she had got all this information and she was fine with it. There was no problem with it whatsoever and she told my dad and my dad doesn't talk as much as my mum does. I've never had an important conversation with him, ever. But in his own little way, he came down into the TV room and sat on the couch with me ... so it was just kind of to say it was okay. (Chastity, 1998)

Yeah, well you see I was called sissy and everything by people at school and also my mother used to bug me about it. She would just say, "Why do you act like a girl?" Things like that: "I have never seen you play with a ball before. Why don't you act like a man?" (Rupaul, 1998)

Well, I think what happened is that my mom talked to my aunt, who talked to my grandma, who talked to my blah, blah, blah. Within a day everybody [in large extended family] knew. So that was pretty hard, but they all just figured "It's just a phase!" (Elton, 1998)

Queer youth are often caught up in protecting family members from homophobic or heteronormative harm. Fear that siblings will be targets of harassment or that their families will be viewed as dysfunctional figure in many queer youth narratives.

I had to be careful for my younger brothers. (Greg, 1998)

There was only one person who figured out that I was gay and I find that pretty shocking; but in school I was afraid to be out. Now I have to be careful because my sister might suffer if the kids at school know. (Svend, 1998)

They already thought my family was strange. I wasn't going to let them use my gayness against my sister and mother. (Virginia, 1998)

Mainstream youth studies has shown the effects of parental influence on youth. Queer youth in heteronormative families remains an unexamined dimension of family dysfunction and negative parental influence in the lives of young queers.

Well, I think everybody just thought I was just being rebellious. My father was really very physically abusive. And so, everybody thought that this was just a way to hurt him. A way to rebel against him for the way that he was treating me. (Elton, 1998)

I never knew my biological father. My stepfather is very abusive. My mum is real Catholic and I have a half sister. (Elton, 1998)

After my mother left my father, she fell apart and wouldn't get off the couch. So we had to fend for ourselves. There was never anything to eat and school was my safe haven. (Virginia, 1998)

My parents separated and divorced a few years ago. My father is Lebanese but he gave me nothing. All my artistic talent and everything came from my mother. (Greg, 1998)

My parents adopted me and my older brother. They got separated because my father was so brutal disciplining me and my brother. Then my mother was killed in a car accident when I was staying at the home. (Michel, 1998)

My family is very close and both my parents are very devoted to each other and us kids. I have a younger brother and sister. (Svend, 1998)

My mother and father are divorced. I live with my mother and sister and we are a paycheque away from poverty. We moved into this horrible place after my parents split up. My mum is Mormon and so am I. This makes life really, really hard for me. (Oscar, 1997)

I am very close to my mother, aunt, and grandmother. My grandmother is Aboriginal and tells me I am a good person. I had a half-sister, Mary, who I loved dearly, but she was killed in an accident on her sixteenth birthday. Me and my mother still mourn her. My father is not around much because of his job. When he is he doesn't say much and is very conservative. (Jack, 1998)

My family is so normal. I still live at home and get along well with both my parents. I think sometimes that we are too much alike. I don't have any brothers or sisters, but I like that. (Rock, 1998)

It is just such a relief to be out to my parents. This takes a big load off of me. But there still are so my things I can't talk to them about. At least they know this is who I am. (Chastity, 1998)

My mother always criticizes me for everything; she always tells me to stop acting like a girl, to be ashamed of myself. (Rupaul, 1998)

Schools reiterate the homophobic and heteronormative messages proliferating in silences and exclusions. As MacDougall (2000) argues, schools are a major site for teaching heterosexism and homophobia, including the internalized homophobia of queer youth.

I was very homophobic. I was very Catholic. And I played tuba with the provincial symphony on a six-weeks benefit tour around the province. There was a young man who was about sixteen years old who was a pianist. He was very flamboyant, very gay. And he was my roommate for the tour. I was very upset and went up to the band leader, the director, and I said, "No way,

*I am not rooming with that faggot." I was twelve at the time and very much
denying myself. (Elton, 1998)*

Schools regularly refuse queer youth access to facilities and school events
such as dances or gay/straight clubs. Given the importance that mainstream
youth studies attributes to socializing opportunities for friendships and dating purposes, queer youth are seriously disadvantaged by school policies.

*I went to my prom with my lover. I was not sure if it would really happen
even though everyone knew. (Elton, 1998)*

*It should be interesting at grad because I am going to take someone I want to
take [a girlfriend] and I sit at the head table because I am the president. I
wonder what Mrs. A [principal] will do or if someone will tell her ahead of
time. (Chastity, 1998)*

Dress codes in schools discourage cross-dressing. Transgendered young
people, in particular, are disciplined through school dress codes. Most school
professionals are reluctant to integrate queer issues into safe and caring
schools because they refuse to deal with controversial issues, deny that queer
youth are in their school, or contend that all youth in their school are treated
the same. Even so, teachers and other educational professionals are important to queer youth for many of the same reasons that they are important
for "normal" youth.

Peers and friends are important in the lives of queer youth, just as they
are in the lives of "normal" youth; however, patterns often differ as the
friends of the former may be of either sex.

*I didn't actually take a chance until the end of grade eleven to go out and
meet and talk to somebody. And then I did and I met this person and she is
my best friend now, since then. Like my life changed socially, a lot. I finally
had a friend. She was my very best friend and we would go shopping and talk
about fashion and makeup. (Rupaul, 1998)*

I have always been popular and had lots of friends. (Chastity, 1998)

My best friend is a girl. All the boys tease me. They always have. (Oscar, 1997)

I always preferred playing with the girls. We had more in common. (Jack, 1997)

*I was one of the boys for most of my childhood. I was a bigger and better
bully than any of them could be so I think it was survival instinct for them.
Me, I just liked the things they did better. (Jill, 1998)*

I was fairly involved in athletics and I was starting to become very popular. I mean with the girls. The girls all loved me. I guess because I wasn't a threat to them. I wasn't going to hit on them. I wasn't going to do anything to them. (Elton, 1998)

My best friend in high school was this guy named Alex. We talked about everything and he helped me come out. (Chastity, 1998)

I did have about three other friends in that group. Like, I don't know if they were the best people for me to hang out with because they were into drugs and stuff. But, basically, what group am I going to attract with my background, except these troubled kids, right? Like I am not going to attract the student president or her friends or anything. People who come from normal backgrounds. So basically I attracted these kids who were bad and did drugs. (Rupaul, 1998)

Within our school system queer youth rarely receive historical and cultural knowledge about themselves. Sex education speaks little about different forms of sexual practice, and even more rarely addresses these as valued and different ways of being in the world. When queer youth do encounter materials, they are negative.

When they used to put the gay stuff in [sex ed] ... it was a joke ... It was real quick, and like, why do we have to watch this? I didn't want to listen to it because I knew I was gay. I thought if I acted like I didn't care then no one would know. (Greg, 1998)

There was one book in the library ... you know the Coping With series? There was one called "Coping with Sexual Orientation"? I don't know. I looked in the back of the book and no one had checked it out. See, I think because they are scared to go to the library and check books like that out. (Rupaul, 1998)

In his research on schools in Toronto Smith (1993, 1998) writes about the ideology of the term "fag" and about schools as factories of violence. Other studies replicate Smith's findings regarding physical and psychological violence towards queer youth in schools (Frankfurt 1999; Hunter 1990; Khayatt 1994; Quinlivan 1996; Rivers 1997; Rostow 1999).

I thought, because I was so lonely and I felt I needed someone, something to help out with how I was feeling. I felt like I was going crazy. So I thought I am not going to approach anyone in school because I'm scared that they will call me faggot if they hear my voice or anything. (Rupaul, 1998)

If I touched the ball, they would back away and refuse to touch it after me.
They said the ball was contaminated. (Jack, 1997)

They would squeeze up against the wall in the hallway so they wouldn't
touch me. They were nowhere even near me. (Oscar, 1997)

The three years of junior high were the worst of my life. It was just terrible
because I tried to deny it to myself. And they called me gay and fag and stuff.
It seemed so hurtful. I guess because that is the age when kids are the most
vulnerable. You know the pre-teens and then going into teenager and what-
ever. And I had absolutely no friends for those years. I got picked on con-
stantly. (Rupaul, 1998)

Physical education classrooms, especially locker rooms, are horrific places
for many queer young males whose gender performance or identity is non-
conforming (Griffin 1993-94).

But the absolute worst was in the gym locker room because there was no
supervision or anything. So, I had to change with these guys from my class
and you are all in one class together. So, I ... it was hell. They taunted me.
Like, it was so severe. (Rupaul, 1998)

In the beginning, I wasn't athletic. I was a chubby kid. For me, phys ed wasn't
a great thing because, not because of the homosexual thing, but because of
my own vision of what my body was. So getting naked with all of these guys
who are in pretty good shape and here is chubby Elton, you know, getting
naked. Then when I was really out and everybody knew, there were some guys
who made comments. Like "change with your back to the locker." So phys ed,
in the beginning, was pretty awful. (Elton, 1998)

Other queer males, whose gender performance is more masculine, pass through
physical education relatively unscathed.

Well, before grade ten, I would just fight back. In grade eight, I didn't fight
back. I just let them beat me up. So they would still beat the crap out of me,
but they would leave with some bruises. And finally I said this is just stupid
and I started to become a jock. I became very athletic and very strong and I
started winning fights. In grade eleven was the last fight that I ever got into
about my sexuality. (Elton, 1998)

In its investigation of chilly climates in schools mainstream youth studies does not report the homophobia and heterosexism that queer youth
encounter in schools and in transit to schools.

Basically, I want to save up for a car, because I feel unsafe on transit. In my neighbourhood it is full of teenagers. Waiting for the bus and that, they call me fag and stuff. I just feel scared and I just feel scared riding the transit period. (Rupaul, 1998)

Underachievement, overachievement, and school dropout figure prominently in the lives of queer youth (Savin-Williams 1994). All three are linked to psychological isolation and alienation, a factor reported over and over in studies on the lives of queer youth (Hunter and Schaecher 1987; Jesuit Centre for Social Faith and Justice 1995; Khayatt 1994; Kielwasser and Wolf 1993-94; Martin and Hetrick 1988; Martin 1982; McCue 1991; Quinlivan 1996). For many queer youth, the notion of safe and caring schools is a farce.

Given the rejection queer youth experience, many are often in crisis. Unlike their "normal" counterparts, they cannot look to mainstream churches and counselling for help because these are often sites that mandate homophobia and heterosexism.

And I talked to my friend Alexander, whose parents are extremely religious ... they go to church every day ... [They are] Christian fundamentalist[s] ... He [friend] doesn't go to church. Every time he went to church they told him and everyone how homosexuality was bad and against the wishes of God and everything so ... he felt he had to tell his parents because he could not go on going to church knowing that he was who they were talking about. And it's been really, really hard for him. He can't talk to his parents about anything. His mum goes through his room and looks at posters and overreacts. I'm glad that this is not where I come from. I am glad my parents are not religious like that. (Chastity, 1998)

The failure of church and psychotherapy to offer support is a sad indictments of these so-called helping places.

I was raised in a very Catholic family. We went to church all the time. Sometimes, two or three times a week. I was an altar boy. By the time I was twelve years old I was teaching catechism, which is like Sunday school. My mom worked for the church. We were just a very involved family in the Catholic church. Which, to be a homosexual or to have an alternative lifestyle was very much against the Catholic beliefs. So when I came out it was pretty devastating to my mom. (Elton, 1998)

I come from a Mormon family and am very religious myself. One of my struggles is between my religion and my gayness. (Oscar, 1997)

Small wonder that sexual minority youth commit suicide and that substance abuse and risky sexual practices figure strongly in their lives. (Savin-Williams 1994). All too often mental health professionals and religious leaders psychopathologize sexual minority youth and continue their victimization instead of protesting this widespread social injustice.

They gave out lots of information on youth suicide [at the session] because it is such a big thing for gay and lesbian youth. But no one at school seems to know much about this. My mum was surprised at first but not after reading all the stuff she got at the convention. (Chastity, 1997)

Once a year, just like I get raped once a year. I try to kill myself once a year. Like clockwork for the last eight years. (Jill, 1998)

I just couldn't take it any more. I tried to kill myself. (Michel, 1997)

Sometimes I get so depressed. I am afraid of having what she [mother] has; she has bipolar stuff. I just want to die so I think about suicide. (Rupaul, 1998)

If my mom had a choice she would have been marching in that Christian Pride Parade, against me. My mom had a chip on her shoulder; we had no communication whatsoever. She had her Catholic faith and it said I was bad, I was a sinner. I was not going to take that shit. (Elton, 1998)

Mainstream youth studies assumes that youth are alike and, hence, has no room to countenance the difference that "difference" make to young people's lives.

Thank god I have a Canadian name. If they were to know I am East Indian they would be relentless. My brother has an Indian name and the other kids tease him about that. It's bad enough being called a sissy and fag, but if they knew my background things would be much worse. And I am still kind of embarrassed to tell them her [mother's] name because it is so East Indian. (Rupaul, 1998)

I was so glad when my foster mother adopted me and gave me her last name. So I didn't have to fight anymore. I always had to fight and beat up people because of my last name; it was the name of an animal and they [peers] would call me and my little brothers and sisters names because of it. (Jill, 1998)

I was brought up to learn English and to live in America and I have a white name. I am completely white. No one has ever guessed that I was East

Indian, because I wanted to be pure white. White people don't get any name-calling, barely. Kids like me get called Paki and stuff, and I just didn't want to be one of them; I just wanted to be pure white. (Rupaul, 1998)

The largest risk factor for sexual minority youth is not their queerness but, rather, living in a heteronormative world. Responsibility for suicides and risky behaviours needs to be firmly placed within the everyday dominant discourses of gender and sexuality that so relentlessly marginalize and condemn these young people. Research about queer youth is relatively plentiful, yet it is ignored in mainstream youth studies because sexual minority youth are not countenanced and because those who research this area are often queer themselves and, consequently, are dismissed as biased. The dilemma for queer scholars is that actively acknowledging our subjectivity places us in a double bind in which we risk not being heard because of our perceived deviance (Halperin 1995). The capacity to marginalize queerness is, indeed, limitless. The representations of mainstream youth studies reveal, yet again, where this bias rests. Remaining silent about these youth is not an option. As Audre Lorde (1984, 41) reminds us: "My silence had not protected me."

Polymorphous Sexuality: From Sigmund Freud to Eve Sedgwick

> All theories of adolescent development give sexuality a central place in negotiating the transition from child to adult. The nascent sexual urges that emerge at puberty must be blended with other aspects of teenagers' lives and channelled adaptively. It is especially important that the adolescent be able to integrate his or her sexual feelings, needs, and desires into a coherent and positive self-identity, which contains, as one aspect, a sexual self.
>
> – S. Moore and D. Rosenthal, *Sexuality in Adolescence*

The above epigraph accurately reflects theories of adolescent development after Freud. According to these theories adolescent identity must become coherent and positive, and adolescent sexuality stands as proof positive of the storm and stress phase of youth. This work ignores the radical potential of the early work of Sigmund Freud, which recognized that sexuality begins at the beginning of life, not at the time of puberty or adolescence. In his *Introductory Lectures on Psychoanalysis,* Freud (1972, 353) wrote that

> to suppose that children have no sexual life – sexual excitations and needs and a kind of satisfaction – but suddenly acquire it between the ages of twelve and fourteen, would (quite apart from any observations) be as im-

probable and indeed senseless biologically as to suppose that they brought no genitals with them into the world and only grew them at the time of puberty. What does *awaken* in them at this time is the reproductive function, which makes use for its purposes of physical and mental material already present.

Here, Freud effectively disrupts discursive notions of sex as reproductive and returns sex to the realm of pleasurable body experience, occurring in plural, or "polymorphously perverse," ways from the time of birth onward. His notion of polymorphously perverse forms of sexual pleasure recognizes that there are multiple sexual pleasures present in the early years of all human life and that these are tamed and restricted to culturally and socially acceptable heterosexual marriage, monogamy, and reproduction.

The notion of polymorphous perversion is captured in one of the axioms of queer scholar Eve Sedgwick; that is, that people are different from each other. Sedgwick (1990, 23) remarks that, despite the array of differences among people, "a tiny number of inconceivably coarse axes in categorization have been painstakingly inscribed in current critical and political thought: gender, race, class, nationality, sexual orientation are pretty much the available distinctions." She goes on to say that, in relation to sexual orientation, each of a long list of sexual differences (which I partially quote below) has the potential to "disrupt many forms of the available thinking about sexuality" (ibid.).

Even identical genital acts mean very different things to different people.

To some people, the nimbus of "the sexual" seems scarcely to extend beyond the boundaries of discrete genital acts; to others, it enfolds them loosely or floats virtually free of them.

Sexuality makes up a large share of the self-perceived identity of some people, a small share of others'.

Some people spend a lot of time thinking about sex, others little.

Some people like to have a lot of sex, others little or none.

Many people have their richest mental/emotional involvement with sexual acts that they don't do, or even don't *want* to do.

For some people, it is important that sex be embedded in contexts resonant with meaning, narrative, and connectedness with other aspects of their life; for other people, it is important that they not be; to others it doesn't occur that they might be.

For some people, the preference for a certain sexual object, act, role, zone, or scenario is so immemorial and durable that it can only be experienced as innate; for others, it appears to come late or to feel aleatory or discretionary.

For some people, the possibility of bad sex is aversive enough that their lives are strongly marked by its avoidance; for others, it isn't ...

Some people, homo-, hetero-, and bisexual, experience their sexuality as deeply embedded in a matrix of gender meanings and gender differentials. Others of each sexuality do not. (Sedgwick 1990, 25-6)

To draw attention to how youth studies reduces the differences of young people's lives to caricature, I close this chapter by introducing three queer youth and some of the differences of their lives. I follow each of these introductions with an account of their lives that could have been provided by mainstream youth studies. I do this to expose the fantastical adult discourse upon which the category "youth" is founded and to, once again, show how attention to the differences of queer youth reveals the limits of this type of categorization.

Chastity

Chastity lives in a two-parent, heterosexual, middle-class white family. Her parents are professionals and are non-religious. Chastity is close to her mother, and they talk extensively about everything. Her mother asked her about sexual orientation and sought out information for her before Chastity came out to her. Chastity's mother told her that she loves who she is. Chastity loves her father but spends much less time talking with him than she does with her mother. She engages in other activities with him, such as horseback riding and skiing. Chastity is a highly skilled snowboarder and currently teaches snowboarding. She is an active student in her high school and is class president, yearbook committee member, and organizer of her Grade 12 graduation. Her academic achievements have been outstanding, and she will be attending university. She has been awarded a provincial scholarship for her undergraduate education. Chastity has taken American sign-language courses and volunteers using these skills. She is popular within her school. During Grade 10 she met Alexander, a gay boy, and came to realize that she, herself, is a lesbian. She is now actively engaged in the queer community and bar scene. Chastity is the kind of person schools most desire in their student population. It is significant to note that her high school principal stated that no lesbian or gay youth attended his school. While Chastity has never experienced any overt homophobic harassment, she has definitely experienced the overwhelming silence about herself and her community at school.

"Assessment" of Chastity

While Chastity has a good disposition, she has some developing concerns. Her desire to please is extreme, and she will do anything to be accepted, including too much student committee work. This is evidenced as well in her excessive volunteerism, most recently with persons with hearing disabilities. She suffers from overachievement, competitiveness, and aggression, which is not acceptable for someone of her gender. She is too physically active, engaging in risky sports such as snowboarding. She is gender dysphoric and refuses to wear dresses. This may not have been so worrisome if she had not fallen in with a problematic group of peers in Grade 10. Under the influence of one particularly poor choice of friend, Chastity now believes she is a lesbian. This is a phase she is going through, and it will end when she reaches adult maturity. However, she seems to be proud of this psychopathology, as evidenced in her claim: "I'm here, I'm queer, I'm proud of it." This is likely evidence of the storm and stress period, typical to adolescence, in which she sees herself as alienated from the world of adult values.

While, at first glance, it seems that Chastity comes from a normal family environment, her parents are somewhat complicit in her present state of being. Chastity is an only child. As a result, her parents are too indulgent, have failed to check her deviant behaviours, and have left her at risk of developing into a full-blown homosexual. They show no interest in authorizing treatment to alter her gender-dysphoric behaviours. It is difficult to see a happy outcome for Chastity should she continue on her present path.

Elton

Elton comes from a two-parent family. His biological father is unknown to him. His stepfather was physically abusive. His mother is Catholic from a large, extended French-Canadian family. Elton was an altar boy and attended church regularly until his early teens. He was chubby and non-athletic during his younger years but began to get in shape and play sports when he realized this might help him deal with the constant teasing and bullying he experienced at the hands of other kids. He would fight back but was badly beaten for his efforts. Becoming more athletic helped him lose weight, which made him feel good. Elton is a talented tuba player and won the opportunity to play with the regional symphony, which was on tour for one summer. He met his first lover through this symphony tour. At first he was extremely homophobic but realized, over the course of the six weeks on tour, that he was physically attracted to the piano player with whom he shared his room. When he returned home and came out to his mother, he ended up leaving home and living with his first lover for about a year. He was fourteen years old. Elton beat up his stepfather, who baited his mother with the fact that her son was gay. In Grade 10 he also beat up a bully at school, and this checked much of the teasing and bullying he had endured. He wore his hair long, wore earrings, and described himself as swishing around school. Yet, because of his prowess on sports teams and his ability to beat up bullies, he became extremely popular with many peers and friends. He also dated girls and had sex with them but never relationships. Elton was extremely successful academically and maintained honour roll status throughout his school years. He worked hard to complete two years of high school in one year. Now he is mostly estranged from his family. He supports himself as a ward of the state and has signed off any parental obligations.

"Assessment" of Elton

Elton is an extremely aggressive young man with an inclination for physical violence. His pathology seems to lie in his deep-rooted hatred of his stepfather. This may be linked to his jealousy over sharing his mother as his stepfather moved in when Elton was five years old. While Elton is a high achiever, as demonstrated in his academic, music, and sports achievements, his intellect is overshadowed by extreme moodiness. His mother reports that he has a chip on his shoulder and that he likes to flaunt his gayness with her. She worries about his lifestyle and the people with whom he associates but feels that she lost control over him after he went on a six-week tour with the symphony the summer he turned twelve. Elton uses his extreme good looks in his quest for new male lovers. His early life without a father figure as a role model has left him prey to the homosexual lifestyle. He is at risk for depression, suicide, substance abuse, and HIV/AIDS.

Rupaul

Rupaul lives in a single-parent family with two younger siblings. He is from a mixed ethnic background: his mother is a non-practising Hindu from India and his father, now dead, was a white American citizen. His mother has bipolar disorder as do many of her family members, including her father. Rupaul's father was a substance abuser and was extremely abusive towards Rupaul and his mother. The family lives in poverty. Rupaul was always a very bright student. He cannot remember any time when he was not teased about being too effeminate. He did not have any friends until Grade 11, when he met a young dyke to whom he came out. She defends him when other people pick on him. His interest in school has fallen off because he is socially active with his friend, who is the first person to ever accept and like him unconditionally. He loves clothes and makeup and wants to be a model. His mother constantly ridicules him because he does not act like a boy or a man. He hates her and his father. He is depressed and has taken Prozac off and on for some time. He is afraid of having bipolar disorder like his mother and is afraid for his physical safety when at school or in more public places, including the transit system and the streets. He has been extensively harassed in all these places. He is thankful he has a white name because he is afraid people would torment him even more if they knew about his Indian background. At one point he documented the harassment he was experiencing at school and reported it to a counsellor, who was impressed with his documentation but who did little about the harassment. Rupaul may move to Texas, where he lived for a time when he was much younger. He has great hopes of finding a supportive community and returning to school with the help of an old family friend who has resurfaced after many years. This friend knows that Rupaul is gay and has offered to help him re-establish, and he will provide him with a place to stay. Rupaul hopes to shed the pain and sadness he experienced during his growing up years. He hopes to find a place in Texas where he will finally feel safe and accepted.

"Assessment" of Rupaul

Rupaul suffers from low self-esteem, motivation, and resiliency. He is depressed and at risk for the many internalizing problems of youth. Rupaul is gender dysphoric: he is extremely effeminate and lacks any masculine qualities. His effeminacy renders him preoccupied with the way he looks and what he wears. He is too thin and could be anorexic. He lacks appropriate peers and friends; he also lacks the appropriate adult role models. He comes from a dysfunctional family, one that is poor and racially mixed. His father has been absent most of Rupaul's life and was an alcohol and drug abuser who never worked for a living. Rupaul's father was emotionally and physically abusive towards Rupaul and his mother. His mother suffers from a mental disorder and, when she is in her manic phase, sleeps around with men who are strangers. She is emotionally abusive to Rupaul and constantly criticizes him. He has been the primary caretaker of his younger siblings since he was eight years old because his mother is often depressed and has been institutionalized twice. His younger siblings are at risk for deviant and non-conforming behaviours as well.

Rupaul is not interested in school, and it is likely that he is on a downward path leading towards under- or unemployment and a cycle of poverty. Increased drug use and casual sex with strangers in public washrooms make him a high-risk candidate for HIV/AIDS. Also, his ongoing problem with low self-esteem and depression make him a high-risk candidate for suicide attempts and even suicide. His mother is incapable of doing anything that would be helpful for Rupaul's psychological well-being. We do not predict a happy future for either Rupaul or his siblings.

Sexual Capital: The Contradictions of Exchange and Currency in Queer Youth Lives

> More centrally, one must also understand stories of desire
> and friendship that persist despite hostile conditions. Such an
> approach then, requires neither a discussion or refutation of
> attributes of causality or origin, nor a debate over whether
> children are sexual.
>
> – Deborah Britzman, "What Is This
> Thing Called Love"?

Drawing on the insights of Pierre Bourdieu's theory of cultural capital, Deborah Britzman, like Linda Singer (1993), takes up the idea of "sexual capital" in order to signal a political economy of sexualities, thereby flagging the need to create theories capable of incorporating the complexity inherent within research about sexuality. For Britzman (1995) sexual capital not only draws attention to processes of normalization that produce heterosexuality but also signals something "more transgressive." The notion of sexual capital marks "the lived experiences between and within those forms of sexuality that are valued and exchanged for social acceptance, social competence, pleasure, and power, and, those forms which have no currency *yet still promise pleasure even when they cost social discouragement and ostracism.* (Britzman 1995, 69, emphasis in original).

The stories of the queer youth related in this chapter and the remainder of the book are not the stories of victims, despite heterosexist desire for tales of the psychopathology of queer lives; rather, they are representative of lives of considerable pleasure, even if this comes at an extraordinarily high cost. The youth in *Queer Youth* experience pleasure and joy, and each of them has suffered many indignities. And it is crucial to understand that their lives, like the lives of most young people, simply cannot be captured by the reductionist vision of mainstream youth studies.

To be fully accepted for who I am as a queer person ... well that would be perfect. (Chastity, 1998)

3
Social/Legal Production
of Sexual Minorities in Canada

At the dawn of the twenty-first century sexual minorities have achieved a status in Canadian law that would have been unthinkable even ten years ago. Many Canadian provinces, for example, now include sexual orientation in their human rights codes. Quebec was the first, in 1977, to provide a legal mechanism for members of sexual minorities to seek redress for discrimination received from private actors such as landlords, employers, and businesses. In the late 1980s and throughout the 1990s sexual orientation was included as grounds for protection in human rights legislation in all other provinces. Only Alberta undertook this change reluctantly, having been forced to do so by the Supreme Court decision involving Delwin Vriend. The federal government incorporated sexual orientation into its Human Rights Act in 1996, but, more important, it has been challenged to change numerous pieces of federal legislation that discriminate against members of sexual minorities. This is because the Supreme Court has progressively read sexual orientation as grounds for protection under the equality guarantees of the Canadian Charter of Rights and Freedoms. In a partial response, the federal government introduced Bill C-23, which sought changes to the terms of more than sixty federal statutes that include same-sex and common-law couples in federal legislation, from income tax provisions and pension to immigration. The bill passed third reading in the House of Commons on 11 April 2000.

To many, Bill C-23 is a signal that sexual minorities have finally been recognized in law as full and legitimate participants in Canadian communities. In the first half of this chapter I explore this assumption, examining how legal discourses have produced sexual minority status in this country and how they function to maintain notions of "normal" and "abnormal" citizenship, even as possibilities have been opened up for sexual minorities.

The first section of this chapter was previously published with Debra Shogan (Filax and Shogan 2003).

In the second half of the chapter I turn to the impact of legal discourse on education in Canada. I look at three cases that focus on teachers but that hold broad significance for understanding how sexual minority youth are produced as outsiders in education practice. I also present three "stories" drawn from my interviews with queer Alberta youth. Each of these could constitute a charter challenge, but for a variety of reasons they did not receive the intensive attention necessary to push them into the legal system. In part, this is related to the storytellers' status as "youth" and to the contradictions between the discourses of youth and the discourses of homosexuality as these meet in educational settings.

It is important to emphasize yet again that I am interested in how discourse, in this case legal discourse, has affected sexual minority status. My concern is to identify features of what can be legitimately said about sexual minorities in the law rather than to produce an overview of all the legal cases pertaining to homosexuality. I am interested in the conditions that made it possible for sexual minorities to achieve legal status in Canada, and I am also interested in pointing out that this status has been established and maintained in relation to a heterosexual norm. The conditions I address include discourses about crime, sin, and illness; discourses about public and private sex; and discourses about equality and freedom. There are, of course, many other conditions that have produced sexual minority identity in Canada. The ones I discuss here, however, are a good place to start. In the sections that follow I demonstrate that the emergence of sexual minority identity in Canadian legal discourse is an effect of various conditions – some legal, some not.

Discourses of Sin, Crime, and Illness

In white settler societies such as Canada, Europeans, in the interest of the colonial state, took on an early and formative role as agents of successful nation building (McClintock 1995). Indigenous peoples were considered to be primitive, close to nature, and without culture, while Europeans were considered to be cultured, removed from nature, and enlightened (Bleys 1995). Entwined in this view of indigenous peoples is a belief that they engage in sexually sinful practices that have to be vanquished by Christian missionaries. Before Confederation indigenous peoples were subjugated to "the marginalization and destruction of their diverse forms of erotic, gender and social life and their subordination to white, European derived social and sexual organizations" (Kinsman 1996, 92).

Generally, the settler hierarchy considered non-reproductive sex practised by indigenous peoples to be not only sinful but also a "crime against nature," even though this claim contradicted other racial discourses, which linked Aboriginal peoples with nature. Within New France and Upper Canada being charged with a "crime against nature" could result in death (Kinsman 1996, 98). Non-Aboriginals who engaged in these activities were thought to have been contaminated by primitive practices after having been too long away from European culture. An effect of nation building in Canada was "to expel from reality the forms of sexuality that were not amenable to the strict economy of reproduction: to say no to unproductive activities, to banish casual pleasures, to reduce or exclude practices whose object was not procreation" (Foucault 1980b, 36).

European societies, as well as those of the New World, often punished homosexual activity; but it was not until the latter part of the nineteenth century and the early twentieth century that the "homosexual" was identified as a specific type of individual and as a member of a particular social group. The homosexual identity, most often thought of as male, emerged from a number of quarters: for example, from the social purity movement and from developing legal discourses. Most important, however, were the newly formed sexual sciences, including forensic psychiatry, sex psychology, and (later) sexology, which began to classify sexual behaviour (Kinsman 1996, 58). Not only did the sexual sciences produce a group identity where, before, there had been none, but those who were seen to belong to this group were considered to be mentally ill. A group identity was also established for heterosexuality. The "heterosexual" was part of the normal group against which the homosexual group was compared and, of course, evaluated as deviating from the normal.

Homosexuality, as a group identity, was strengthened by a shift in the nineteenth century in Europe and North America from agricultural, trading societies to urban, industrial societies. Capitalism became the dominant form of economic organization, and capitalist productive relations were premised on the reproductive relations of the heterosexual family (Sayer 1991). Consequently, capitalism reinforced the primacy of the reproductive family unit. It was supported by a universal prohibition against incest (Lévi-Strauss 1969) and a taboo against homosexuality (Butler 1990, 64).

The rise of urban industralized centres in Canada and elsewhere created public space (Kinsman 1996; Adam 1995). In other words, urban centres created the possibility for anonymity as well as places for those who wished to engage in non-reproductive sex to meet and socialize (Adam 1995). Once recognized only as isolated, individual acts, homosexuality became identified as being characteristic of certain persons and then of a specific group – those who engaged in same-sex sexual activity. Once named, homosexuals were seen in public in ever-larger numbers and were considered to pose a threat to community values.

The Canadian legal system responded predictably to these dangerous deviations from the normal. In 1869 "buggery was classified in criminal legislation as an unnatural offence, and from 1892 until the 1950s, it was classified as an offence against morality" (Kinsman 1996, 129). "Gross indecency" was introduced into Canadian statute law in 1890 and entered into the first

Criminal Code when it was adopted in 1892 (ibid.). Gross indecency referred to all sexual acts between males not considered to be "buggery." In the latter part of the nineteenth century and the early part of the twentieth century, social purity movements, in response to prostitution and to the utilization of public space on the part of men seeking sex with other men, advocated for the increased regulation of sexuality. Criminal Code classifications were used to direct the police against men engaged in this illicit activity (127). In effect, people were grouped and identified as criminals by virtue of sex acts such as buggery.

Canadian history is replete with examples, many quite recent, of arrest and incarceration as a result of being convicted of engaging in prohibited sexual acts. For example, in 1965, during the course of another investigation, a man confessed to the police that he was gay and engaged in sex with men. He was charged and convicted on four counts of gross indecency and sentenced to three years for each charge. A court later found that the man was a "dangerous sexual offender," and he was thus sentenced to indefinite detention in a federal penitentiary. It was also a regular practice, especially in the 1970s, for police to raid men's bathhouses and gay bars and to subject those arrested to publicity and humiliation.

The *Vriend* case provides a recent example of how an individual life can be caught up in the discourse of homosexuality as sin as well as in long and expensive litigation to secure what most others simply take for granted. Delwin Vriend, a laboratory coordinator employed at King's College, Edmonton, was fired from his job for the sole reason that he was gay, even though it was acknowledged by college officials that he was a competent instructor. Vriend turned for redress to the Alberta Human Rights Commission but was turned away because the province's Individual Rights Protection Act (IRPA) did not prohibit discrimination on the grounds of sexual orientation. Vriend thus challenged the constitutional validity of IRPA under Section 15 of the Charter of Rights and Freedoms. The Supreme Court eventually ruled in Vriend's favour in 1998, arguing that the Alberta legislation denied gays and lesbians the equal benefit and protection of the law.

The Supreme Court decision established that employer pronouncements of sin would not take precedence over fundamental human rights. The *Vriend* decision was thus an important advance for gays and lesbians in Canada. The reaction in Alberta, however, was less than celebratory. The editorial pages of the *Edmonton Journal* and the *Calgary Herald* soon filled with letters, some verging on hate-speech, accusing the Supreme Court of granting homosexuals "special rights" and of fomenting, among other things, sin, bestiality, pedophilia, and the destruction of the family. The Klein government, in turn, considered invoking the notwithstanding clause of the charter so as to avoid complying with the Supreme Court's decision. In the end, however, Premier Klein rejected this constitutional option. The episode, however, cast in stark relief the continuing political force of the discourse of homosexuality as sin in Canada.

Discourses of Public and Private Sex

For most of the past fifty years the legal identity of those who engage in homosexual acts was profoundly affected by British jurisprudence and public policy. Issued in 1957 the *Wolfenden Report* was a policy document that addressed homosexuality as a "large-scale deviation" that needed to be managed. The report made a distinction between public and private homosexual acts. This distinction created classifications that made it possible to officially police and regulate homosexuality (Kinsman 1996, 215). The public/private distinction also linked *crimes* with the public sphere and established the need to protect the public from homosexual acts. *Sins* were characterized as those homosexual acts that occurred in private. The public-private dichotomy produced by the *Wolfenden Report* officially created two subgroups of homosexuals – the appropriate/private homosexual and the inappropriate/public homosexual. The report created a safe yet sinful space for consensual acts between adults within the private sphere but criminalized consensual acts between adults if these acts should occur in what the law determined to be a public place.

The *Wolfenden Report* implied that heterosexuality was a "fragile and tenuous identity that is easily displaced by any positive image of homosexuality" (Stychin 1995, 41). The report promoted monogamous, heterosexual family relations as a way to prevent homosexuality, and it consolidated distinctions between adult and youth identities. Fears of homosexuals recruiting the young or engaging in sexual activity with children were extended into concerns about teachers and other adults who had contact with the young. Specifically, the report warned that homosexuals ought not to have contact with youth. Youth were characterized as easily seduced and, therefore, readily recruited into "sin" and "crime."

Canadian legislators relied on the *Wolfenden Report* in the preparation of the Criminal Law Amendment Act. This act included abortion and prostitution reforms as well as the removal from the Criminal Code of private same-sex activity between consenting adults. In supporting this amendment to the Criminal Code, then justice minister Pierre Trudeau made his now-famous statement: "The state has no place in the bedrooms of the nation." While the *Wolfenden Report* eased state regulation of homosexuality and while the Canadian amendment to the Criminal Code decriminalized it, the effect of both was an intensification of legal discourse about homosexuality. As a consequence of this increased legal interest in homosexuality there was a 160 percent increase in the conviction rate for homosexual offences in England and a similar increase in conviction rates in Canada (Kinsman 1996; Adam 1995). Increased prosecution of public homosexual acts, along with the production of the appropriate, private homosexual and the inappropriate, public homosexual, forced sexual minorities into the private realm or, worse, "into the closet." The overriding effect was to silence and to stigmatize all those identified, and identifying, as homosexuals.

The *Klippert* case provides a revealing example of the legal struggle over what is to count as public and private and what constitutes criminal or deviant activity. Everett George Klippert was convicted on four counts of gross indecency for having consensual homosexual sex in what was considered to be public space.[1] In 1965, based on the emerging psychiatric discourse that produced the notion of the "sick homosexual," Klippert was designated as a dangerous sexual offender (Kinsman 1996). Klippert's "crime" was having consensual sex in a car. This case underscores how legal distinctions, in this case the distinction between public and private spheres, were interpreted so as to criminalize homosexuality. Because heterosexuality was state-sanctioned and homosexuality was to remain hidden, heavy state regulations were imposed on the few places where many practising homosexuals were able to engage in sexual activity. In this case, a car was designated as a public place, even though cars were often sites of sex between consenting heterosexuals.

The *Wolfenden Report* and the Criminal Law Amendment Act further entrenched the notion of "the homosexual" as a group identity. Having a group identity was not necessarily an improvement over being labelled an individual criminal or sinner. Individuals still experienced silence, fear, and punishment; and now they were being considered part of a group that had been established by legal discourse. Although it did not help homosexuals, this homosexual group identity did help those who wished to control and regulate the lives of "sexual deviants." At the very least, a group identity produced legal mechanisms with which to force homosexuals into privacy.

Discourses of Equality and Freedom of Expression in the Canadian Charter of Rights and Freedoms

While Canadian law is based on a British parliamentary system, the 1982 adoption of the Charter of Rights and Freedoms, with its American-style, constitutionally entrenched bill of rights, made Canada into a more hybrid legal culture.[2] While sexual orientation is not listed as a protected category in the Charter of Rights and Freedoms, the charter has been very significant in designating sexual minority identity in Canada. Subject to certain limitations, the charter guarantees a series of individual and group rights. Of particular importance to the rights of lesbians and gay men are Section 2(b), which ensures freedom of expression, and Section 15(1), which ensures rights of equality before and under the law. Section 15(10) does not include sexual orientation in its list of protected categories; however, in some recent cases of discrimination against lesbians and/or gay men, judges have read it into the charter.

As a consequence of legal decisions based on the charter, lesbian and gay group identity and same-sex couples have been legally recognized. Other sexual minorities, such as bisexuals, transsexuals, and transgendered people, have not benefited from the charter in the same way. As well, sexual minority categories recognized in ethnic and Aboriginal cultures have not been legally recognized. Aboriginal two-spirited people, for example, can only be legally recognized if they abandon their own identification and take on the labels "gay" or "lesbian." It remains the case, however, that the term "sexual orientation" is used to refer to lesbians and gay men but not to heterosexuals. This erases the ways in which heterosexuality permeates Canadian law. By reading sexual orientation into Sections 2(b) and 15(1) of the charter, judges reinforce heterosexuality as the norm, with the result that lesbians and gay men have become "special" others who require legal intervention to prevent discriminatory behaviours. Legal discourse based on the charter constructs homosexuality and heterosexuality as dichotomous and as essentially different.

The Charter of Rights and Freedoms has improved the legal rights of lesbians and gay men in certain respects, but they continue to be denied things that heterosexuals take for granted – among them, benefits and freedom from harassment. The cases cited below demonstrate that Canadian law valorizes heterosexuality as the norm, to the exclusion of other sexual orientations. Moreover, these cases suggest that the full inclusion of gays and lesbians into the Canadian community will involve contesting the law on a variety of fronts.

The *Egan* Case

Egan and Nesbit v. Canada (1995) is an example of how, due to the assumption that people are heterosexual, the charter has not always worked to protect lesbians and gays. James Egan and John Nesbit had lived together for more than forty years, and, when Egan turned sixty-five in 1986, he applied twice for a spousal allowance for Nesbit under the Old Age Security Act, 1985. Nesbit was turned down both times because, in the Old Age Security Act, "spouse" was defined as a person of the opposite sex. Egan and Nesbit took the federal government to court and their application was dismissed, as was their appeal to the federal Court of Appeals (Greer, Barbaree, and Brown 1997, 174). They then appealed to the Supreme Court of Canada, where they argued that the definition of spouse in the Old Age Security Act discriminated against them on the basis of sexual orientation and thus denied them their equality rights under Section 15(1) of the charter. The majority decision of the Supreme Court ruled "that although there may have been discrimination in violation of section 15(1) of the Charter, because the Old Age Security Act defined 'spouse' to include only opposite-sex couples, such discrimination could be reasonably justified" (Yogis, Duplak, and Trainor 1996, 21-3).

Justice La Forest, in support of the majority decision, based his comments on the primacy of the "traditional family," in which procreating children is the primary function. According to La Forest, "marriage is by nature hetero-sexual." He continued, arguing that "it would be possible to legally define marriage to include homosexual couples, but this would not change the biological and social realities that underlie the traditional marriage" (*Egan and Nesbit v. Canada* 1995, 625). In effect, his point was that equality rights under the charter, which might have been expected to acknowledge same-sex relationships, could not be reconciled with the definition of spouse used in acts and laws covering families. In the words of Justice Cory, who dis-agreed with the majority decision, the distinction made between same-sex and opposite-sex couples reinforces "the stereotype that homosexuals can-not and do not form lasting, caring, mutually supportive relationships with economic interdependence in the same manner as heterosexual couples" (*Egan and Nesbit v. Canada* 1995, 677).

While the Supreme Court decided in the *Egan* case that sexual orienta-tion constituted grounds of discrimination with respect to Section 15 of the charter, it nevertheless decided that this discrimination was justified, thus denying benefits under the Old Age Security Act. This case shows how the charter made it possible for lesbians and gay men to assume some le-gitimacy in Canadian communities while, at the same time, they were ex-cluded from family law provisions that would have entitled them to spousal benefits.

The *Little Sister's* Case

Little Sister's Book and Art Emporium in Vancouver is a significant distribu-tion point for disseminating cultural materials into the gay and lesbian com-munities in western Canada. For many years, Canada Customs has consistently seized or detained publications that customs officers ruled to be obscene in content. While Little Sister's had often successfully contested the seizure and detention of materials through the appeal processes provided by the Customs Act, the detaining and seizing of materials did not stop. The sei-zures constituted a constant harassment of, and a financial hardship for, the store.

In order to remedy this situation, Little Sister's filed suit and charged that "the relevant customs regulations violated freedom of expression under Sec-tion 2(b) and equality rights under Section 15 of the Charter of Rights and Freedoms. The bookstore also sought a declaration that the customs regula-tions had been applied in a manner that violated Sections 2(b) and 15 of the Charter" (Greer, Barbaree, and Brown 1997, 171). While the Supreme Court found that custom officials frequently contravened the charter when they seized Little Sister's materials, it also found that the Customs Act did not itself violate the charter; rather, the Supreme Court ruled that the disadvantage to lesbians and gay men arose from Section 163(8) of the Criminal Code. The court ruled that "homosexual obscenity is proscribed because it is obscene (under s. 163(8) of the Criminal Code) not because it is homosexual" (Greer, Barbaree, and Brown 1997, 173).

This case is another example of the contradiction between charter rights and other laws, such as those governing freedom of expression and the Criminal Code, which limit homosexual erotica by labelling it obscene. Commentators have pointed out that this case reflects an inability to distinguish between homosexuality and pornography (Bull and Gallagher 1996, 163). Others suggest that gay pornography should be treated differently from heterosexual pornography because there are so few images of gay and lesbian sexuality available to gay and lesbian people (Stychin 1995, 56). Stychin argues that the freedom to create and have access to explicit sexual images is essential to the emergence of gay and lesbian identities that enable individuals to view homosexuality as a legitimate way in which to live one's life:

> The offensiveness of such attempts at discursive control through law is that they deny to some a right of citizenship; that is, a right to articulate a sexual identity within a shared communal space. Finally the material reality of these laws should not be ignored. Individuals have been lost unnecessarily, young people who are confused and miserable have been denied access to information that might instil a positive image, and prejudice and bigotry have been given an official outlet and *promoted*. (1995, 54, emphasis in original)

The Anglican Priest Case

On 22 June 1993 Daniel Webb was arrested by a police officer who had enticed him into the bushes by offering him sex. Shortly after Webb's arrest, the local newspaper printed a short piece stating that Webb had been charged with sexual assault while police were working to "clean up homosexual behaviour" in the park where the incident occurred. A day after the news item appeared Webb was asked to resign from his position as Anglican priest in Cambridge, Ontario. On 7 December 1999 Webb announced that he was "suing the Waterloo Region Police Service for close to $4 million and [was] seeking compensation for the turmoil that the 1993 arrest and media release caused him" (Humphreys 1999, A3).

It is clear from this example that police entrapment of men suspected of trying to have homosexual sex in public places contradicts Section 2(b) of the charter, which ensures freedom of expression, as well as Section 15(1), which ensures equality before and under the law. In the case of Webb, while sexual touching occurred between two consenting adults, nothing more occurred in this public place. This case underlines that, despite the charter, homosexual consensual contact is not treated in the same way under the law as is heterosexual sexual consensual contact. Except in the case of prostitution, looking for heterosexual sex is seen as a common, public activity that interests neither the police nor the courts. Nor do people lose their livelihoods for engaging in this kind of behaviour. To the contrary, the image of young heterosexual lovers embracing in the park is idealized both in advertising and in films.

Emergence of Queer Sexuality as Post-Group Identity

In legal terms, in the early part of the twenty-first century the status of sexual minorities is largely defined by the provisions of Bill C-23. The legislative changes that this bill enacted have provided some new-found legitimation for lesbians and gay men. Same-sex domestic partners, common-law partners, and, of course, married couples can have similar legal relationships within the federal state, especially with respect to taxation. However, there has been considerable resistance to legal recognition of same-sex partner status. Some argue that this limited recognition isolates those who are not in long-term same-sex relationships as abnormal in relation both to legally recognized same-sex partners and to "normal" heterosexual couples. Others point out that the federal government's willingness to expand the definition of family has come precisely at the moment when governments everywhere are downloading the costs of care and security onto the family unit.

There are sexual identities that remain unrecognized by Canadian law. These "outlaw" identities have been created in popular culture, including in films, on the Internet, in music videos, in alternative presses, in bookstores, in theatres, in clubs, and in activist discourse. Among these are the television shows *Ellen, Will and Grace,* and *Queer as Us;* movies such as *All about My Mother* and *Ma Vie en Rose;* publications such as *The Advocate, Out,* and *Curve;* gay pride marches and the Gay Games; and queer figures such as Rupaul, Dennis Rodman, and Patrick Rice Califia. Identities are also produced from resistance to such things as police raids, court decisions, and AIDS policy. Popular cultural representations and performances of a range of sexualities disrupt the notion that the only sexual minorities in this country are adult same-sex couples who work and have the resources to take advantage of benefit packages along with tax and immigration provisions.

Central to the emergence of queer sexuality in the 1990s and the early part of the twenty-first century is resistance to attempts to make everyone the same. To identify as queer is a strategy that opposes group sexual identity and that resists regimes of normalcy (Warner 1994a). Queer strategy exposes and resists the way in which "the heterosexual" is constructed as the norm, but it also exposes and resists attempts to make sexual minorities more like this norm. The very idea of "queer" challenges how legal discourse has managed and minimized sexual difference by only recognizing gay men and lesbians. Queer strategy also opposes the control of difference within sexual minority communities, which judge and punish those who, while not heterosexual, are also not gay or lesbian. Queer identity is hybrid, partial, not fixed, and it stresses "the fractious, the disruptive, the irritable, the impatient, the unapologetic, the bitchy, the camp" (Dinshaw and Halperin 1993, iii-iv).

When reading "sexual orientation" into the Charter of Rights and Freedoms, judges and legislators have understood it to refer to same-sex sexual activity. Sexual orientation, as it has been read into the charter and subsequent legal decisions and legislation, refers to the gender of a person's sexual object choice; that is, to whether the person is male or female. In queer terms, fixing sexual orientation in this way is rigid and significantly reduces the opportunity to recognize differences in sexual practice.

By questioning how sexual minority status has been produced by legal discourse, queer politics and theory also reveal how heterosexuality is limited by it. Not only does legal discourse confine sexual minority status to same-sex activity, but heterosexual status is constrained to include only those practices that can be understood when they occur in long-term relationships. It is, however, no more possible for the law to fully contain or describe the various forms of heterosexuality than it is possible for it to contain or describe "queer."

Canadian Legal Discourse and Education

> The most important factor in the perpetuation of homophobia and marginalisation of homosexuals, including self-hatred in homosexuals, is the intense indoctrination in heterosexism that children experience, a great deal of it in educational institutions. Society loses much of its rationality when it comes to homosexuality and children. Children are "sheltered" from contact with homosexuality and homosexuals, who are presumed to prey on them.
>
> – Bruce MacDougall, *Queer Judgments:*
> *Homosexuality, Expression, and the Courts in Canada*

The dangers of homosexual access to children and youth permeated debates over the 1969 Criminal Act Amendment. In the 1950s and 1960s across Canada there was a series of moral panics related to children, youth, and homosexuality (Kinsman 1996, 313, 336, 338, 341; Adams 1997). Far from preventing children from being affected by homosexuality, the proliferation of legal and civic discourses about homosexuality and children ensured that children and youth were profoundly affected by fears of homosexuality. At the heart of these public discourses about homosexuality, masquerading as age-of-consent issues, were the assumptions that children are either asexual because of their age or that children/youth are heterosexual. I turn now to legal cases in which "the homosexual" had to be eradicated in order to protect innocent youth in educational institutions.

Strange Judgments 1: The *Saskatchewan Human Rights Commission* Case, 1976

In 1976 Douglas Wilson complained to the Saskatchewan Human Rights Commission that, through his employer, the University of Saskatchewan, he had suffered employment discrimination because of his sex and, in particular, because he was homosexual.[3] Wilson's complaint arose because he was dismissed as a supervisor of practicum student teachers in the College of Education. He was dismissed when it was brought to the attention of the dean of education that Wilson had advertised in the local student newspaper, seeking parties who might be interested in joining an "academic gay association." While the exact focus of Wilson's proposed group is not apparent from the advertisement, it was not about having public homo-sex on campus. His call was similar to many others of the late 1960s and 1970s, a time when large numbers of student groups organized on campuses.

Wilson's call for a gay group on campus did not materialize in any visible way. Gays on campus remained invisible for fear of being dismissed or suffering other punitive measures. In fact, many gays on and off campus were angry with Wilson for "causing" a problem where none had existed. The message was clear: whereas other social justice issues were enjoying public attention on university campuses, gay and lesbian issues were to remain closeted, outside the norm of public spaces. Through the Douglas Wilson case both the gay community and the dominant community reinforced the spectacle of the public and, therefore, "bad gay" of politico-legal discourse.

Wilson argued that his sexual orientation was an immutable, not chosen, sex characteristic and that, therefore, it was not a legitimate basis for discrimination. The Saskatchewan Human Rights Commission, before proceeding with the application, ruled that, in their code, "sex" included "sexual orientation." The University of Saskatchewan applied for a judicial review of the commission's ruling *(Board of Governors of the University of Saskatchewan, Kirkpatrick and Stinson v. Saskatchewan Human Rights Commission).* The higher court found that the category "sex" had nothing to do with sexual proclivity; that is, sexual orientation (Herman 1994, 21). The substance of the case was never reviewed because the higher court ruling disallowed the Saskatchewan Human Rights Commission from investigating complaints related to sexual orientation on the grounds that no category – and certainly not the category of "sex" in the Saskatchewan Human Rights Code – covered complaints of discrimination related to homosexuality. Further, in a move that reaffirmed long-standing discrimination against homosexual employment rights, the high court "stated that if the legislature had intended to cover homosexuality in the legislation, it would have said so clearly and unmistakably" (Yogis, Duplak, and Trainor 1996, 3).

Many things may be said about the case of Doug Wilson. His work as a teacher in Saskatchewan schools prior to his graduate work had been exemplary. His work as a supervisor of practicum teachers had also been exemplary. The call for colleagues to join an "academic association" was a call to establish an association for the purpose of engaging intellectually with other homosexual/lesbian academics at a time when student organizing around social justice issues was particularly strong. It was not a call to have sex on campus or in public. Yet publicly using the words "gay" or "homosexual" was (and still is) taken as a sign for sexual activity. Few, if any, of his mentors and professors at the university were aware of Wilson's sexual identity until someone brought his ad to the attention of the dean. Wilson's low profile was the exact opposite to, for example, that of the dean of education – a known married heterosexual man often seen socializing on and off campus with his straight wife in attendance. In fact, the entire campus knew that the dean was married. In contrast, Wilson's orientation was never on public display. In 1976, if a member of a sexual minority displayed the same privileges that heterosexuals took for granted, then s/he quickly lost the privacy and security of the closet.

Most students, then and now, take for granted the right to post notices, especially in student newspapers, in order to advertise to form new groups and to tackle a range of issues. The 1960s saw widespread campus agitation regarding student rights, which, in the 1970s, produced welcome changes (for example, the right to be voting members on departmental, faculty, and university committees). Yet, in Wilson's case, the violation of student rights was submerged within a larger homophobic impulse. What this case highlights is the cultural currency of the myth of homosexual predation and recruitment of youth. Through Wilson the myth that young pre-service teachers, children, and youth are vulnerable to homosexuality was solidified in a highly public way that had at least five immediate effects.

The first effect was that children and youth were portrayed as weak-willed, sexually innocent, sexually vulnerable, and therefore substantively different from adults. Children and youth were considered to be so completely vulnerable that having a homosexual in close proximity to them, even if they did not know her/his identity, placed them at great risk of harm. The second effect was the production of adults as a distinct category in relation to those under the age of eighteen. Those who are close to eighteen – the student-teachers Wilson was supervising – were cast as vulnerable and recruitable. Meanwhile, some adults were represented as both weak-willed and as powerful homosexual predators; while most adults, such as the dean of education, were represented as strong-willed, invincible older people who dedicate themselves to protecting the young from the homosexual menace.

The third effect of this case was the identification of Douglas Wilson, formerly an exemplary teacher and supervisor of pre-service teachers, as a hypersexualized adult and as a sexual predator whose work history and academic record were incidental. Wilson was produced as immoral and, therefore, as not suitable for a job that would bring him into contact with young teachers. He was fired. His exemplary work record was wiped out because of the "offence" of homosexuality. He was further humiliated when a higher court ruled that the law was not "intended to cover homosexuality"; if it had been so intended then it would have said so clearly and unmistakably. Douglas Wilson did not teach again and did not finish his graduate studies. Ironically, the negative publicity directed towards sexual minorities throughout this ordeal resulted in Wilson being the target not only of the University of Saskatchewan and the Canadian court system but also of the gay and lesbian community, whose anger at being spot-lighted was intense.

The fourth effect of the case was the continued silencing and marginalization of sexual minorities, and the fifth effect was that, by definition, children and youth were to be understood to be heterosexual. Any notion that a child or youth could be homosexual was simply not possible within the constraints of the legal and social discourse set up around this case. Not surprisingly, this myth has had a continuing impact on the status of sexual minority children and youth in schools.

Wilson's case had other important effects as well. The high court ruling exposed a confusion around categories of sex and sexual orientation. In part, this confusion relates to the inability of heteronormative discourse to countenance the fact that persons categorized as male or female may engage in sexual practices that are not heterosexual. Indeed, within heteronormative discourse, to be male or female is to be heterosexual. In order to be able to hear what it clearly thought was a case of employment discrimination, the Saskatchewan Human Rights Commission chose to include sexual orientation under "sex," thereby exposing the limitations of such categories within heteronormative discourse. This attempt by the Human Rights Commission to move towards inclusion by using categories that disallowed inclusion anticipated contemporary deconstructive understandings of sex and gender discourse – understandings in which the homosexual exceeds the limits of such categories and exposes the falseness of the assumed coherence of sex, gender, sexual desire, and sexual practice.

Strange Judgments 2: The *Vriend* Case, 1991

The *Vriend* case is remarkable for exposing the arbitrariness of categories such as public/private sex. As in the Wilson case, an issue of employment was hijacked and transformed into an issue of immorality. Fear that Vriend's homosexuality, even though he was not out in the classroom, might interfere with his teaching and influence students was so strong that religious leaders at King's College sought to have him fired. With regard to Vriend, these people, through their fear of homosexuality, transformed what should have been an issue of employment equity into an issue of morality. By making Vriend's homosexuality a work issue, they created a crisis of public space where none had existed.

The contradictions between Canadian charter law and provincial human rights legislation are exposed when heteronormative moralizing and religious freedom are pitted against individual and group protections. What also becomes apparent is the confusion around identity, imagined sexual activities, and actual sexual practice. Admitting to a homosexual identity does not mean that one is sexually active. Vriend was not sexually active during his employment hours at King's College (O'Byrne and McGinnis 1996). His dismissal was directly related to imagined activities that may or may not have occurred outside his employment hours. As MacDougall writes (2000, 107), it was the imaginings of his superiors that could not be countenanced, not Vriend's real-life actions (about which little or nothing is known).

The consequences of the heteronormative, homophobic, and religious fundamentalist discourses associated with the *Vriend* case are far-reaching, and they include reproducing representations of youth and children as sexually innocent, as heterosexual, and as easily recruited and/or victimized by homosexuals. Even though Vriend won at the Supreme Court level, the fervour with which his case was taken up in Alberta reinscribed old fears: fears about the effects of homosexuality on youth and children, fears about the transmission of HIV/AIDS, and fears about the "origins" of homosexuality. As with *Wilson* and the *Surrey School Board* case (which I describe next), *Vriend* is one of the rare cases in which the confluence of homosexuality and education is directly taken up through the courts.

Strange Judgments 3: The *Surrey School Board* Case, 1998

In the spring of 1997 the Surrey School Board voted four to two against approval of the use of three books in kindergarten and Grade 1 because these works featured same-sex parents.[4] Board chair Robert Pickering saw the books as both a way of promoting a lifestyle and as a mechanism for recruiting for it. It is worth noting that Pickering was a director of the Citizens' Research Institute, a right-wing Christian organization that promotes and recruits potential followers of "family values." In another action, the school board supported a principal's decision to remove a child from the classroom of a gay teacher, James Chamberlain. At the same time, the Citizens' Research Institute conducted a "family rights campaign" in which parents were asked to sign a declaration stating that their children were not allowed to be involved in any school program that portrayed the "lifestyles of gays, lesbians, and/or transgendered individuals as one which is normal, acceptable or must be tolerated" (GALE/FORCE, February 1999, 2). In keeping with these other actions, the board voted overwhelmingly to poll Surrey parents on "the gay issue."

Education Minister Paul Ramsey called the board's actions intolerant and noted Pickering's anti-gay activities and affiliations. James Chamberlain filed a grievance. Gay rights advocates took the Surrey School Board's book banning to the British Columbia Supreme Court. Meanwhile, Surrey trustees planned to spend whatever it would take (over $500,000) to keep the three books out of their school system. In December 1998 BC Supreme Court Justice Mary Saunders ruled that the board's actions were influenced by the trustees' religious views and, further, that these contravened the BC School Act. An independent arbitrator, Stephen Kelleher, ruled in September 1999 that the board discriminated against Chamberlain when it supported the principal's decision to remove a student from his class. Meanwhile, the new board chair, Heather Stillwell, said the board did the right thing by supporting the principal in removing the student from Chamberlain's class. The board vice-chair, Gary Tymoschuk, stated that the board would think up new ways to ban the three books, that Kelleher's ruling was "ludicrous," and that the board would continue to remove children from classrooms if it was in their best interest (GALE/FORCE, November 1999, 4).

When the BC Teachers' Federation heard about Tymoschuk's comments, it paid, along with the Surrey Teachers' Association, to have Kelleher's ruling registered by the BC Supreme Court so that, if the Surrey School Board broke the ruling, then it would be in contempt of court and face fines and jail time. Countering this action, the Surrey School Board forced the Surrey Teachers' Association's lawyer to appear before the BC Supreme Court, arguing against the filing of Kelleher's ruling. This was dropped when Surrey School Board chairperson Heather Stillwell and vice-chair Gary Tymoschuk both filed affidavits with the court stating that they would abide by Kelleher's ruling.

Clearly there have been a number of changes in how sexual minorities are treated in education since Douglas Wilson's dismissal in 1976. Then, Wilson's fate as an outed homosexual working with young and aspiring teachers was coldly predetermined. There simply could not have been any other decision based on the public/private split enshrined in the 1969 Criminal Act amendments and the statements regarding teachers and children that arose out of *Wolfenden* and the Canadian derivatives thereof. What *Surrey* points to, in particular, is just how uneven these changes have been. It is worth noting that both the *Surrey* and the *Wilson* cases occurred within the context of publicly funded institutions, while the *Vriend* case occurred at a "private" religious college. *Vriend* is most clearly about religious intolerance. And yet, in *Surrey*, religious values came into play as well. In both public institutional settings public values of inclusion collided with religiously inspired fears about homosexuality and children.

Surrey again reveals the contradictions between the Canadian charter and religious discourse. While school boards are to represent the mandates of public school education (of which inclusivity is one) religious and other private schools have no such requirements. This leaves human rights issues affecting sexual minorities vulnerable to contestation by those with anti-gay religious beliefs not only within private schools but also whenever such people assume control of public school boards. According to provincial and federal law, religious beliefs are to be kept separate from public education and schooling. Fortunately, Justice Mary Saunders found that the religious attitudes of the board members interfered with the public school mandate of inclusion and, therefore, contravened the BC School Act.

As with the *Wilson* and *Vriend* cases, the *Surrey* case shows that, even in the late 1990s, children and youth coming into contact with a gay teacher or reading materials with gay-positive content can fuel a moral panic. An amazing amount of energy was expended on preventing "recruitment" or "contamination," including petitions, meetings, and conferences in which Kari Simpson (an anti-gay crusader) gave keynote addresses across the province. The Surrey School Board spent over $500,000 to keep three gay-positive books out of the classroom. The cost, as various levels of the judiciary heard this case, implicated tax-payers beyond Surrey. Although this should not happen within a publicly funded educational system, the religious beliefs of a relatively small group of adults was imposed on the majority, including children, parents, teachers, and the surrounding community. What this reveals is just how vulnerable public education is to moral panic about sexual minorities. This vulnerability occurs even though inclusion of all is the primary mandate of school acts across Canada, not to mention the cornerstone of Canadian charter values.

Emerging: One Step Forward, Two Steps Back?
What distinguishes the *Surrey* case from *Wilson* is that the challenges to gay rights in the former were unsuccessful. James Chamberlain is visible and,

significantly, visibly supported. Various levels of educational professional associations provided much needed support, as did the queer community. More critical, when *Surrey* was heard important human rights legislation relating to gays and lesbians was in place in British Columbia. Legislators and the judiciary were prepared to back gay human rights and inclusive education. Book banning brought out public fears around censorship, so that concern was widespread, also affecting those who did not have children in schools.

Yet *Surrey* constituted a costly battle in both time and dollars. For several years the Surrey School Board was able to spread its anti-gay message and to act on this within a school district and province that, as part of a larger framework, was openly bringing about educational change supporting gay rights and content. For example, in 1997 the British Columbia Teachers' Federation (BCTF) had passed recommendations to strike a committee to study homophobia and heterosexism and social justice issues. In many ways the Surrey School Board's actions were a reaction to these broader, inclusive educational changes as well as to the BCTF's specific recommendations. What the struggle in Surrey reveals is the deep-seated response on the part of some Canadians to the idea of including sexual minorities as full Canadian citizens. It also reveals that, unlike in the *Wilson* case, sexual minority people are willing to resist and to be visible. A crucial effect of this visibility is the solidification of group identity.

One of the issues that underpins all three cases is that, for some people, any hint of homosexuality in schools constitutes recruitment and endorsement of a "lifestyle." Breaking the silence about sexuality constitutes an assault on the traditional family. Having their children exposed to homosexuality is to risk having them recruited into a life of pathology and sin. For these people, the threat of homosexuality is equal to child theft. And yet, historically, marginalized groups of people are the ones whose children are at risk of being taken, whether physically, spiritually, or emotionally. Gays and lesbians either have their children taken from them or leave them behind because of the threat of custody disputes. First Nations peoples in Canada have had their children taken and placed in residential schools.

The Surrey School Board's actions presume that one "becomes" a sexual minority by being introduced to this "lifestyle" through reading or other ways of interacting in the world. Those concerned with where sexual minorities come from simply miss seeing that they are most often produced in "normal" heterosexual families. Sexual minority offspring are most often produced within heteronormative family and community structures.

Douglas Wilson is dead and, after 1976, never practised as a teacher. Delwin Vriend was given leave by the Supreme Court of Canada to complain to the Alberta Human Rights Commission, but given the time lag between the actual event, his dismissal from King's College, and the high court decision, Vriend had moved on. It remains for another case to test homosexual rights in the Province of Alberta. Both Wilson and Vriend paid high emotional and financial costs – costs that we can only begin to imagine. Vriend had the good fortune of receiving widespread community support from queer and straight people and organizations, while Wilson was vilified by most and is only recently being positively remembered through a series of conferences at the University of Saskatchewan entitled "Breaking the Silence."

Each of these cases has had the effect of erasing the sexual minority child or youth. Again, the production of children and youth as either heterosexual or asexual is assumed. The very existence and, therefore, the rights of sexual minority youth and children are not countenanced. Yet, as the following accounts reveal, sexual minority youth do indeed exist.

Sexual Minority Youth: Three Proposed Cases for Charter Challenges

What follows are accounts drawn from interviews with sexual minority youth in Alberta schools. Significantly, none of these has become a charter case. The contradictions between discourses of homosexuality and the construction of youth (through these discourses) are exposed when we confront the reality of queer youth. Since Canadian law continues to construct sexual minority status outside the norm and to effectively mandate heterosexuality as the centre from which all other sexual practices deviate, schools (like most other institutions within the Canadian cultural context) are unable to deal with sexual minority youth in any other way than to "socially derange" them (Corrigan 1987).

Charter Non-Case 1: Ellen

Ellen was an outstanding student.[5] She was a high-achiever in both sports and academics. She was in the top five percentile of her school district, and she was active as a student on the school council, the yearbook committee, and in other extracurricular activities, including athletics. Her teachers knew her well and found that she was rarely disruptive, asked great questions, and finished her homework on time and in an exemplary fashion. They told Ellen that she was a wonderful student, "a pleasure to have in the classroom." Ellen was popular with her schoolmates, both female and male. She was cooperative, confident, and fun to be around. Ellen had always loved school and found it a haven from her neglectful home life, spending long hours there from the time she was in elementary school.

Ellen knew about her sexual identity since her late junior high school years. It was increasingly important for her to be "true to herself," to be an out "baby-dyke lesbian." In Grade 11, so there would be no confusion, Ellen deliberately wore clothing that she thought announced her orientation.

This clothing consisted of jeans, work boots, and a leather jacket. Ellen's hair was short and spiky. She did not want anyone to mistake her for someone she was not.

In Grade 11 she was best friends with another young woman, Anne, who was also the girlfriend of the captain of the school football team. Anne had difficulties in her relationship with the football captain and thought he took her for granted. In an effort to shake his assumptions, Anne flirted openly with Ellen in front of the football team and Ellen flirted back. The captain became increasingly angry and finally threatened Ellen.

One Friday, while Ellen was walking down the school hall during what, for most students, was scheduled class time, she saw the football captain coming from the other direction. Ellen felt unsure and unsafe, and decided that the best course of action was to keep her head down and not to make eye contact. As they drew closer together, out of the corner of her eye she saw the football captain veering sharply towards her. Wham! Ellen was slammed into a set of lockers with a body check that knocked the breath out of her. Some of those who witnessed the assault came forward to assist her. Ellen was taken to a hospital emergency room, where she was treated for two broken ribs and severe bruising.

Ellen complained to school counsellors and the principal on the following Monday. All of these people knew her well because of her high profile as an outstanding student. The principal told her that there was not much he could do because a major interschool football competition was under way over the next few days and the school could not be without one of its star players. He suspended the football captain for two days but only after the competition was over and only in response to pressure from Ellen and a teacher.

Both the principal and counsellors suggested that Ellen not be so visible. They asked her why she flirted with Anne anyway. They agreed that the assault was not the best way to handle things but believed that the football captain was threatened by Ellen's sexuality. They indicated that they thought it was okay for Ellen to be gay but that she had crossed a line by flirting with a heterosexual girl. Ellen was shaken by their accusations. School, once her haven, was no longer safe. If school authorities felt she was "asking for it" because she was "too out," then how could she feel safe, especially given what had happened? Ellen felt publicly shamed and humiliated because very little had happened to the football captain while her life had altered completely.

According to the law, Ellen had been physically assaulted. At the time of the assault, the perpetrator was over sixteen years of age and could have been charged. Yet school authorities either failed to recognize this or refused to take action. School professionals failed to provide the kind of learning environment for Ellen – a safe and caring environment – promised under

Alberta's vision for education. Further, her high school, which operates under provincial imperatives concerning inclusivity, had failed in its mandate to provide her with fair and equal treatment. Rather than seeing the assault on Ellen as an issue of freedom of expression, the right to equal treatment, or the right to safety and inclusion, school professionals chose to take a moralizing approach to the issue, whereby Ellen became the perpetrator and the football captain became the victim.

Ellen's outsider status was guaranteed through a heteronormative discourse that produces all sexual minorities as outside the norm of heterosexuality – a norm that functions just as harshly in schools as it does within the larger Canadian context. Ellen was seen as flaunting her sexual orientation and deserving of punishment. Ellen's flirting in response to Anne's flirting was misconstrued as a deliberate attempt to seduce a regular heterosexual girl into a lesbian "lifestyle" and away from a normal relationship with a high-profile heterosexual male. Anne was regarded as "normal," and, therefore, her actions were seen to be in fun. Ellen, however, was regarded as deviant, and, therefore, her actions were seen to be threatening. The football captain was justified in his anger because Ellen had no right to violate heterosexual norms. Following this line of thought, because Ellen had flirted openly with Anne, she had humiliated the football captain and had called his masculinity and his heterosexual prowess into question.

Ellen's transgressive actions were violations of school and cultural norms and, therefore, were punishable actions. The football captain disciplined Ellen for these violations. Ellen was put back in her place – the place of all sexual minorities who dare to act as though they have the right to inclusion, freedom of expression, and equality before the law. The discipline that was foisted on Ellen was a sharp reminder that tolerance in Alberta schools is thin at best and that you'd better know your place; otherwise, retribution will be swift.

This case represents "school as usual." Social control and discipline, active indifference, and unwillingness to counter a homophobic assault all work to ensure the continued functioning of heteronormativity. The abuse of one sexual minority student is considered to be incidental, even if this person is an exemplary student. Yet, according to the Canadian charter, Ellen's fundamental right to freedom of expression and association are guaranteed and protected. Ellen has a right to express herself as an "out baby-dyke lesbian" in a public institution without fear of punishment. Like the football captain and Anne, Ellen has the right to flirt with whomever she wishes. Ellen has the right to equality of treatment before the law and before school authorities. However, over one minor interruption of heteronormativity, the football captain and school authorities *both* violated Ellen's rights and got away with it.

Prior to this incident, Ellen thought she would be protected from physical assaults, especially those that occurred on school grounds. She believed that those responsible for such actions would be punished accordingly. Ellen thought that she enjoyed the rights and protections guaranteed by her status as a Canadian citizen. The school act in her province as well as Canadian charter law guarantee this.

Ellen thought she lived in a different world than did, say, Douglas Wilson and Delwin Vriend. Ellen did not know about Wilson, but she certainly knew about Vriend. And she had expected that her life in school would be better because of his high-profile struggle as well as because of her discussions of this struggle, over a two-year period, with teachers and counsellors. The latter had made her believe, falsely as it turned out, that the educational professionals in her school were different and that the times were different. In the aftermath of her assault, Ellen's sense of violation and alienation, combined with her strong sense of lack of safety, were such that she completed the few remaining weeks of school and decided to do her final year by correspondence. Ellen, an "out" student, was effectively disappeared from school.

Charter Non-Case 2: Michel

Michel was not an exemplary student.[6] He did all right at school but it was not a priority in his life. He hated sports and would not dream of being involved in school committees or student counsel. Primarily, school was a social occasion for Michel – a time for him to gossip and a place to wear fashionable clothes and to see what everyone else was wearing. Michel planned to be a lawyer but, in the meantime, he wanted to take full advantage of his youth.

Like many other youth Michel had some close friends in his high school; however, he was especially close to a young straight woman, Barbie. She was the only person at school to whom Michel was out. His other main source of social support came from the local queer youth group, which had a drop-in night as well as an information night, both of which Michel attended regularly. Through this youth group Michel was invited to talk on a local radio show about his experiences as a sexual minority youth. He was assured that his voice would be disguised so that he could not be identified. Michel saw himself as a closeted community activist, so anonymity was very important to him.

The day after the radio show aired was a school day. Michel was not expecting anything unusual, and at first nothing out of the ordinary occurred. His first class of the afternoon was career and life management (CALM). Michel went in and seated himself in his usual place, waiting with the rest of the class for the teacher. As he read over some work from another class, bits of balled paper started landing on him, his desk, and the floor around him. Michel looked up as bits of paper continued to be peppered at him, and those throwing them started chanting, "fag-got, fag-got, fag-got." Not everyone in the class was engaged in these actions, but no one did anything to stop what was happening. Michel described the time prior to the teacher's walking in as endless. Once the teacher arrived, the volley of paper bits and chanting continued but in a more restrained way. At this point, Michel, who was already frustrated and frightened, slammed his books together and started to storm out of class. The teacher, appearing oblivious to what had happened, stopped Michel with her hand and asked him where he was going. Michel threw her hand off, shoved her out of the way, and shouted that he had had enough of this "shit." He stormed out of the class and left the school.

The teacher filed a complaint with the vice-principal concerning Michel's "violent" behaviour. Michel went to a school counsellor and complained about the actions and inactions of the students and teacher in his CALM class. He was furious that he had been identified as having been on the radio talk show as this was the only way he could make sense of the harassment. He had been "outed" without his permission. He was also angry that the teacher was indifferent to what he thought were obvious actions against him. Michel was quite certain she had heard the word "faggot" being chanted at him and had simply chosen to ignore it.

The counsellor, vice-principal, and teacher then involved the principal. In a meeting between them and Michel, it became clear that the school authorities were incapable of handling, or were unwilling to handle, what had taken place. Michel knew that his school district had recently passed a public "safety action plan for lesbian, gay and transgender youth" and that there was someone working for the school board who could assist him. He was aware of this through his youth group rather than through any information provided by the school. He contacted the board person, Eve, and asked her if she would intercede on his behalf. There was a meeting between Eve, the school counsellors, the CALM teacher, the principal, the vice-principal, a social worker, and Michel. Once again it became evident that the school had difficulty coming up with any clear action with which to address what had happened. Eve's suggestions were rejected either as not practical enough or as too controversial. The fear on the part of the principal, teachers, and counsellors was that parents would become upset or even enraged at having gay rights "shoved down their throats." The principal asked why Michel talked on the radio show, thus exposing himself as a "homosexual." He further suggested that Michel should have known better than to talk so openly. In the principal's view Michel was deliberately holding out a red flag and antagonizing those who do not like homosexuals.

Between the actual event, the first meetings with school professionals, and the final involvement of the school board a period of over two months had transpired. Michel had been encouraged by all school professionals to continue attending school during this time; however, when he did so, harassment accelerated both in and out of classes. Name-calling, bumping, and avoidance (some gasped and inched along the walls when they saw him coming) were just some of the actions engaged in by a small group of students intent on making Michel's sexuality an issue. Michel named these students but none of them was disciplined. It was his word against theirs, and other witnesses, even those who were his friends, did not materialize on his behalf. Michel felt his safety was completely compromised and he dropped out of school. He volunteered at his local HIV/AIDS network and took a correspondence course. The following year, Michel attended a different high school across the city.

As with Ellen, so with Michel: discourses of homosexuality as adult and discourses of youth as innocent and/or heterosexual produced him as both deviant and as impossible for schools and professionals to deal with. He is a category violator by virtue of being a youth who is queer. According to these discourses, Michel should not exist. Yet, according to Alberta Education, Michel, like all other students in the province, is promised "excellence." It is difficult to see how this promise materialized for Michel. His learning environment became unsafe due to the "outing" actions of someone else, and dropping out became the only way for him to escape an increasingly hostile environment. Further, although the Alberta School Act promises inclusion, due to the lack of action on the part of school professionals and the punitive action on the part of some of his schoolmates, Michel was excluded from the schooling and benefits offered to most other students. Under Section 15(1) of the Canadian Charter of Rights and Freedoms – the equality rights provision, which guarantees equality before and under the law – Michel was treated in a manner that compromised his right to equal treatment, inclusion, and accommodation in his school; therefore, his fundamental charter rights were violated. In direct opposition to charter guarantees, he was treated like a social inferior.

Michel's identity and experience were "socially deranged" in such a way that his experience of harassment could not be addressed by school authorities. As Corrigan writes:

> It is not, I insist, the *self*-concept that is damaged, but the *social* identity which is deranged. More specifically in validating a particular value and its ways, civilization in short – people who *cannot* come to that value with an experience which connects, find themselves *not there*, or and these are twin practices – find themselves there only as negative examples: *their* family

form, *their* sense of *their* value and ways is acknowledged (i.e., found in a discourse valuated as knowledge) only to be named (thus claimed) as partial, traditional, faulty, on the way to ... (1987, 21)

Michel's experiences of homophobia, like Ellen's, were turned into occasions where his judgment was questioned and then rendered as a lack of judgment. Michel's valuing of his difference, his very right to be different – both of which he revealed on the radio show – were rendered questionable. Talking about his negative school experiences was recast as waving a red flag for those who found him objectionable. Being sexually different was turned into a moral issue, too controversial for normal students, their parents, and the immediate community. This was possible because Michel's social experiences were outside the parameters of what is normal; thus, he could be marginalized.

Michel argued that the series of meetings at which he was on display and where he was grilled about his intentions and actions were a continuation of the discriminatory behaviours of his classmates and students in the hallways. He was on trial for thinking he had the same rights as his student-colleagues, while the perpetrators of homophobic harassment were never interviewed and never reprimanded for their actions. Rather than guarantee Michel's right to equal access to schooling and all this implies, school professionals became part of and extended Michel's harassment. The net effect was that Michel and what he experienced were kept outside the parameters of what could be successfully dealt with by school professionals. Rather than inspiring excellence or equality, Michel's experiences were effectively disappeared from the high school and a heteronormative cloak of silence again closed over the school. Discourses that maintain the illusions – that sexual minorities are deviant Others and that all youth are heterosexual – worked effectively to restore this social order. Other sexual minority youth in the school stayed silent, and those who knew of this episode with Michel learned a basic lesson in exclusion, harassment, and hatred.

Charter Non-Case 3: Oscar

Oscar was an intense student.[7] He loved English literature and had read far more than had most of his friends and fellow students. He was witty and loved discussions and intellectual arguments. Oscar's written work was excellent and intense, much like himself. He also wrote poetry. He was not afraid to address issues of his sexual identity either in his written work or in conversations. He was openly gay, and even though this was something he struggled with because of his religious upbringing, his sexual identity was also something he was proud of and actively exploring.

Oscar realized he was "different" in elementary school, and, in junior high, he recognized this difference as having to do with his sexuality. Prior to junior high, Oscar thought his feelings of not fitting in were related to his religious practices and to the break up of his parents' marriage. When he was nine years old, he was curious and asked his father about homosexuality. His father told him that it involved two people of the same sex loving each other sexually. Oscar asked if this was okay, and his father said yes. He came out to his mother first, and he found her supportive of his sexual identity. When he came out to his father, his father said that he already knew and that it was fine with him. Having supportive parents gave Oscar confidence.

Oscar did not, at first, come out at school. He was very aware that school taught him little of positive value about himself or about homosexuality and that it was only through outside cultural sources that he could learn to value himself and to know about others who were like him. Gradually, through his own reading of novels and queer publications, through watching television shows such as *Roseanne* and *Oprah* (with their affirmation of homosexuality), and through his involvement with the local youth group, Oscar decided that he had a right to live his life as openly as did everyone else. For him, this meant being out at school. Throughout Grade 10, Oscar became increasingly visible as a young gay. He talked about homosexuality in classes where this was appropriate, and he identified himself as gay when this seemed right. At first, teacher and student reaction was minimal. Sometimes Oscar felt that others found him tiresome and boring, but mostly he experienced indifference from teachers and students alike. Some claimed that they already knew he was gay and were curious about what being gay meant for him and other gay people. Oscar was happy to have an opportunity to talk about his experiences and what he knew about being gay.

In Grade 11 things shifted. Oscar was never able to pin down what caused this shift. He knew the atmosphere was more antagonistic towards him but no particular reason for this stood out. When the school year began he had feelings of unease. Some students began to hiss at him and call him names in the hallways, but, when he turned to confront them, it was not clear who they were. On other occasions students in the halls called him "faggot," and he responded by saying, "No, we prefer 'gay' most of the time." On other occasions when he was called a faggot, Oscar responded with, "Redneck!" and the name-caller scowled at him. Oscar replied, "Look, if you want to use derogatory labels towards me, I will respond in kind!"

Because he felt that school should provide him with information about "his people," Oscar requested that his school library carry gay-positive magazines like *Out* and the *Advocate*. He was especially strong-minded about this since the library carried "homophobic magazines like *Alberta Report*." His requests were never successful. Given the increasing harassment in the halls, at one point Oscar decided to conduct his own survey of homophobic actions in his school, and, over a five-day period, he observed sixty-four separate instances of name-calling, shoving, or negative joking. He shared this information with a school counsellor with whom he had talked before, when he had felt depressed and suicidal. The counsellor said there was nothing the school could do about these incidents because no one else had complained, because the incidents had not been witnessed, and because, in any case, homosexuality was taboo within the school system.

Several days later, in English class, Oscar went to the washroom; when he returned to class, his daily planner had disappeared from the top of his desk. He knew it was there when he left because he had been doodling on the pages. After class, he searched all the desks but his daily planner did not show up. He checked in the lost and found the next day, and there he found it.

On opening his daily planner, Oscar found the following words scrawled across the current day-timer pages: "faggots burn in hell." He was upset but decided not to report the incident since his earlier complaints to the school counsellor went unheeded.

Several days later, Oscar found the words "all fagots burn in hell" printed in ink across his locker. He did not want to take this incident seriously because he rationalized whoever wrote the graffiti could not spell. When he related this incident to me,[8] he also speculated on whom he could tell. But he clearly felt that his complaint would not be taken seriously anyway. When he told his story to his youth group, they expressed concern, telling him that homosexuality as an identity is not banned in school and that what was happening to him should not be happening. The following Monday Oscar complained to the counsellor, who advised the principal and vice-principal. The graffiti was removed from his locker, but several days later the same message was scratched into the paint on his locker. Meanwhile, hallway hostilities towards Oscar continued unchecked.

When Oscar and his mother approached the school for solutions, they were advised that he might have to go to another school. The counsellor suggested that if Oscar were not so openly gay then these things would not happen. In a meeting with Oscar's mother, both the counsellor and the principal noted that Oscar had escalated his openness about being gay, with the result that everyone in the school knew. Meanwhile, the locker was scraped and repainted. Oscar and his mother decided he should stay in the school and "tough" it out for the balance of the term. However, once term ended, he changed schools because the atmosphere had simply become too hostile. Those who expressed concern for his well-being at school included his mother, his youth support group, and me. School professionals, on the other hand, blamed Oscar and his homosexuality for creating the situation.

The confluence of discourses about homosexuality and youth effectively prohibited any successful solution to the violence directed at Oscar and, in fact, produced him as a social deviant. School professionals failed to provide Oscar with the "excellence" in education mandated by Alberta Education. As with Ellen, so with Oscar: because he was too openly gay he was blamed for the violence that was perpetrated against him. In the parlance of the school professionals, Oscar created the situation by being out. Yet, according to the Canadian charter, fundamental freedoms such as freedom of religion, expression, and association are protected, guaranteed rights. Section 15(1), in particular, guarantees equality before and under the law and equal protection and benefit of the law without discrimination. Oscar could charge his school, school professionals, school board, the Alberta Teachers' Association, and Alberta Education, as all were involved in violating his fundamental charter rights.

As with Ellen and Michel, so with Oscar: instead of ensuring that he had the same access to excellence and safety in his learning environment as did other students, school professionals became a part of the continuing violence perpetrated against him. Oscar's school exacerbated this epistemic violence by insisting that the threats and harassment perpetrated against him were his fault. Oscar was produced as outside the normal, as unworthy of protection, as outside the purview of what can be countenanced within normalizing school discursive practices. Like Ellen and Michel, Oscar disappeared from his school. Heteronormativity was restored to the school and the idea that sexual minority youth do not exist was reaffirmed.

The Canadian Charter of Rights and Freedoms, the Human Rights Act, the Alberta School Act, and mission statements written by Alberta Education state, unequivocally, that all persons have the right to be treated equally. As Canadian legal theorist Bruce MacDougall (2000, 104) writes, "Actions by schools or school boards are state actions subject to Charter scrutiny." One must ponder, along with MacDougall, why so little legal attention has been paid to what are clearly charter violations. Yet, rather than see discriminatory acts perpetrated against Michel, Ellen, and Oscar as what they so evidently are, school professionals were quick to turn issues of equal access and freedom of expression into issues of blaming, shaming, and moralizing.

The 1969 Criminal Code Amendment shapes the experiences of sexual minority youth by positing a dichotomy between public and private. The very naming of the existence of sexual minority youth in schools constitutes a public spectacle. The conflation of persons with sexual actions – that is, the overdetermination or hypersexualization of sexual minority people in public space – creates a moral panic over imagined sexual acts. Within the heteronormative imagination, out or outed sexual minority youth, like sexual minority adults, are equated with the immorality of public sex. For sexual minority people to be safe, they must be private; that is, they must be in the closet.

School authorities are able to abandon any moral responsibility for sexual minority youth, to whom they are supposed to have an ethical and professional commitment. Sexual minority youth are produced as outsiders to the discourse of equitable and fair treatment in education. As well, school authorities constitute yet another source of repressive disciplining in the production of sexual minority identity in Alberta schools. While individual counsellors, teachers, or administrators may feel badly about the outcomes, none of them is able to disrupt the course of heteronormative, homophobic education.

In the late 1990s, for Michel, Ellen, and Oscar, the protection of Canadian legislation and generic promises of provincial educational mandates and/or school acts offer little improvement over the violence levelled at Doug Wilson at the University of Saskatchewan in 1976. In the late 1990s, as in the 1970s, this violence has the effect of increasing victimization by forcing those victimized out of the school.

Conclusion

In this chapter I identify some of the conditions that made it possible, at the beginning of the twenty-first century, for Canadian legal discourse to produce a particular type of sexual minority status. The Criminal Law Amendment Act, the Charter of Rights and Freedoms, and Bill C-23 each assume a heterosexual norm. Opening legal discourse to include sexual minorities has not diminished the force of heteronormativity in legal discourse. The Criminal Law Amendment Act privatized homosexual affection and sex, while heterosexual affection and some sexual activity retained its status as public sex. Court interpretations of the Charter of Rights and Freedoms established sexual orientation as something that pertains to lesbians and gay men, while heterosexuals retained their status as the unnamed norm. Bill C-23 made it possible for same-sex couples to take up many of the benefits previously afforded only to heterosexual couples, but it also protected marriage as the preserve of those who are "normal." In other words, it recognized same-sex relations only when they mirrored heterosexual partnerships. Those who identify with other sexual arrangements remain outside legal discourse.

In Canada "the homosexual" was produced as an identity category through social conditions that made it possible for people to congregate in urban centres and to engage in sexual behaviours outside the purview of marriage and the heterosexual family. Social purity movements, sexology, and legal discourse that cast homosexuals as sinners, as mentally ill, or as criminals reinforced this category. The category "homosexual" also created positions from which individuals could resist these ascriptions and from which counter-movements could be built. Without the creation of a group identity for same-sex sexual activity the decriminalization of these acts, the reading of sexual orientation into the Charter of Rights and Freedoms, and Bill C-23 could not have happened. The latter, in particular, has created opportunities for inclusion for people who, for more than half of the twentieth century, were subject to punishment for same-sex sexual activity. It is worth emphasizing, however, that since legal discourse in Canada assumes that people are heterosexual, it is not possible for sexual minorities to be fully protected or acknowledged by the law. The pattern of recognizing sexual minorities in legal discourse only when they appear to act in the same way as do legally recognized heterosexuals continues to deny full inclusion to those with sexual practices that refuse to be fixed by dominant norms and discourses. As the cases of Michel, Ellen, and Oscar underline, notwithstanding the Charter of Rights and Freedoms, harassment of queer youth will continue until principals, teachers, and superintendents are willing to take their rights seriously.

4
Queer Identities and Strange Representations in the Province of the Severely Normal

In October 1997 a group of students from Scona Composite High School in Edmonton approached local businesses, including Orlando Books (a lesbian owned and operated bookstore), to place ads in their student newspaper. Scona High was close to home for me, less than two blocks from my residence and the school my son attended for one year. Jacqueline Dumas, owner of Orlando Books, obliged the students with an ad that included the phrase "books for lesbian and gay youth and their friends." A few days later the student editor of the paper phoned to say that there was a problem using the preceding phrase and offered to run the ad for free if that line could be deleted. Dumas declined this offer. Shortly after, the faculty adviser called Orlando Books and advised Dumas that the newspaper went out to all students and their parents. The ad, he said, was not inclusive because it did not include heterosexual students; thus, refusing the ad was in keeping with school policy. Dumas countered that the ad *was* inclusive since heterosexual students were included as "friends," and she asked for a copy of the school policy. That the newspaper had such wide circulation seemed to be a red herring – until it became evident (through subsequent dialogue) that school professionals were afraid that inclusion of "controversial issues" would be evidence of the school's approval of the gay "lifestyle" and that this would become known to parents and the community beyond the school.

The next day the principal, Rick Anderson, called Dumas and reiterated that the ad would be refused unless the words "gay" and "lesbian" were removed. The ad would be free if Dumas agreed to the deletion. Dumas again refused the offer, and the ad did not appear. According to Dumas (1998, 26), "He [school principal Anderson] must have thought that the stories about gays in the school library's copies of *Alberta Report* provided sufficient information for his students."

Representations of queer people are significantly absent throughout school curricula, and it is still uncommon for there to be a policy to enhance the safety and well-being of queer youth in Alberta schools. As I complete this book, a twelve-page booklet about safety issues for lesbian and gay youth is still circulating among an ever-widening audience of school professionals before the Alberta Teachers' Association will finally release it for publication. Ostensibly, this unusual review process will strengthen the booklet by ensuring that all contentiousness is removed prior to publication. Meanwhile, neither education professionals nor anyone else reviewed *Alberta Report* (hereafter *AR*) before permitting its inclusion in school libraries and as a supplement to curriculum materials. Whether this was deliberate or an oversight has led to the same consequence. Given that *AR* was heavily involved in constituting and maintaining the challenge to sexual minority rights in Alberta, and that it was welcomed in the province's schools, it comes as no surprise that there has been a significant imbalance in how sexual minority people have been represented in Alberta schools.

When I first began to investigate the conditions in which queer youth negotiate their identities in Alberta I was met with the following sorts of reactions from what was then Alberta Education: "no one does *that* kind of work here," and "we do not have any materials about *this* topic on hand." Consistent with the sensationalized production of queer Albertans in *AR*, Alberta Education was able to provide me with one document that specifically mentioned "gays," and this had to do with sex education and HIV/AIDS. Alberta Education mirrored the representations of homosexuality that appeared in *AR*, which equated homosexuality with gay maleness, disease, and pathology.

As the 1990s unfolded the signatory case regarding homosexuality in the province was the one that turned Delwin Vriend, Alberta citizen, into the *Vriend* case. Prior to *Vriend*, on several occasions the Alberta Human Rights Commission had tried unsuccessfully to have sexual orientation written into the Individual Rights and Protection Act. The refusal of Alberta's elected politicians to provide human rights protection, together with the *Vriend* case, made Alberta unique among Canada's provinces for its state-produced and state-sanctioned homophobia. In order to comprehend how queer youth understood their place in this province, it is vital to recognize the role the Alberta government played in the production of "the sexual minority deviant" as well as *AR*'s relentless obsession with "homosexuality." These queer youth lived their identities in the cultural vacuum of school and family, where the only homosexual content was negative, where heterosexism was widespread, and where homophobic harassment was common.

> *Yeah, it's Alberta. And they sort of hide under that pretence of "it's equality for all." Because I really believe that there are people out there who really believe that if everyone is equal then we don't need that special sort of clause in there. But really they are just deluding themselves ... because ... Alberta is*

so conservative ... and then we have the Reform [party], and it's very right wing. We do not have equality in this province. (Virginia, 1998)

Because Alberta – the people here, you know, aren't that bad. They're mostly pretty decent. It is kind of sad when you see them lagging behind like this. My friends are really great and really support me and who I am. They prove that not everyone in Alberta is homophobic. And all my friends are straight but care about me and who I am as gay. (Svend, 1998)

In this final chapter I show how the discourses of gender, youth, sexuality, and legal status that I identified in previous chapters are taken up by *AR* for the purpose of promoting a particular version of who counts as a legitimate member of the Alberta community. I utilize a number of strategies to present the material in this chapter. The text is marked off by significant dates in the *Vriend* case, and this is often followed by a barrage of headlines and, in some cases, magazine covers or inserts from *AR*, all of which intensify in number and sensationalism as the case gets closer to a Supreme Court decision. I also quote extensively from some of *AR*'s editorials and "news" pieces in order to illustrate the ferocity of that magazine's agitation around "homosexuality." The voices of queer youth are meant to disrupt these representations of the "disgusting homosexual" by contrasting the complexity of their lives with *AR*'s reductive hate-mongering. A range of life exigencies were important to these young people – often more important than was their sexuality.

The following presentation of headlines, magazine covers, excerpts, interview material, and analysis is not meant to provide an easy read. The fragmentary nature of what follows is deliberate: its purpose being not only to underscore the absurdity of the coherent narrative of the deviant homosexual portrayed by *AR* but also to insist on the humanness of queer youth. I refuse to confine the richness and diversity of these young people's lives in a tidy box of statements and stories. In other words, I intend this text to be exhausting – as exhausting as was living life as a queer youth in Alberta during the 1990s.

The theme of moral panic is evident throughout the text. Moral panic may be said to occur when a

> condition, episode, person or group of persons emerges to become defined as a threat to societal values and interests; its nature is presented in a stylized and stereotyped fashion by the mass media; the moral barricades are manned by editors, bishops, and politicians and other right-thinking people; socially accredited experts pronounce their diagnoses and solutions; ways of coping are evolved, or (more often) resorted to; the condition then disappears, submerges or deteriorates. Sometimes the panic is passed over and

forgotten, but at other times it has more serious and long-term repercussions and it might produce changes in legal and social policy or even in the way in which societies conceive themselves. (Kinsman 1996, 45)

In *AR* the hysteria over homosexuality was never submerged, passed over, or forgotten. Sensationalized accounts of homosexuality pulsed through this magazine. Every week it produced at least three editorials, articles, or letters that presented homosexuals as a group of persons posing a clear threat to societal values and interests. For many Albertans, queer and otherwise, it seemed that the only available information about homosexuality came from *AR*.

> *I am really discouraged by living in the prairies because it's as if we [gays]*
> *don't exist or we are openly disliked, even hated ... on one side we have a very*
> *gay friendly atmosphere and on the other side we have the Stockwell Days*
> *and the Rutherfords and the* Alberta Reports *of the world and the Ted*
> *Byfields. (Oscar, 1998)*

As is apparent from the previous chapters, moralizing discourses about homosexuality are highly potent for queer youth because they are economically dependent on adults (usually family members), who demand from them a moratorium on sexuality and employment (Cote and Allahar 1994). The notion of family is premised on rigid ideas regarding gender roles. Youth are expected to be sexually innocent – that is, inactive yet heterosexual; therefore, homosexuality among youth is rarely accepted by parents or other adults.

Alberta Report: **Marshalling the Struggle**
In celebration of their first twenty-five years of publication, editor-operators of *AR* produced a special edition on 11 January 1999, in which they summarized their history. The following quote tells some of this story.

> We learned one other lesson in the latter 1980s, as we started branching out
> with other editions, first *Western* and then *BC Report.* Instead of reverting to
> clear conservatism on the social issues of the day, we began to drift, subtly,
> into what could be called "lifestyle" coverage. That is, we gradually lost our
> interest in the deeper and more difficult questions posed by *sex, family,*
> *school, and faith.* There was a reason for this drift. *Back in the 1970s, weirdo*
> *things like radical feminism and gay rights could be dismissed, at least in Alberta,*
> *as an amusing madness.* But by the late-1980s they couldn't. They had become rooted in public policy everywhere, underlying social programs, court
> rulings, and school curriculum ... well, values-neutral is not just gutless, it is
> dull, *and circulation was slipping anyway.* (L. Byfield, "Our Next 25 Years: The

Battles to Be Fought Will Be Harder – but Like Some Earlier Ones, They Can Be Won," *AR*, 11 January 1999, 19, emphasis added)

Keeping their eye on a formula for fiscal success, those in charge of *AR* determined that their 1980s approach did not sell magazines and that the 1990s approach would reverse this trend. The following is a summary of the issues *AR* took on in the 1990s:

> In 1990 we got back on course. We challenged the feminist sacred cow on campus ("Women's Studies: Academics or Propaganda?" Jan. 7, 1991), nut-case environmentalism ("Father Earth," May 11, 1992), the global thrust for what are deceptively promoted as "children's rights" ("The Pied Piper of Ottawa," Aug. 8 1994), poisonous but powerful liberal currents in the churches ("See No Evil," July 8, 1996), and Ottawa's continuing abdication of responsibility for Indian justice ("Canada's Mythical Holocaust," Jan. 26, 1998). We once again, adopted causes: gun owners' rights, removal of abortion from medicare, direct democracy and taxpayer activism. *We attacked as provocatively as we could the fatuous and sinister new acceptance of the gay lifestyle; it reached its apogee with our Aug. 16, 1993, cover "Can gays be cured?"* ... but the theme which re-emerged in our pages in the '90s which dwarfs all others in significance is that of *the family*. (L. Byfield, "Our Next 25 Years," *AR*, 11 January 1999, 19, emphasis added)

Issues such as feminism, environmentalism, Aboriginal rights, and homosexuality are interrelated because, according to *AR*, they all pose threats to its concept of the family. According to *AR*, "the good" is exemplified by white, Euro-Western descendants who are progressive yet traditional, natural yet highly cultured, and who are ordained by God to live within a traditional family, with "man" as dominant over the planet and all its life forms. The *AR* family is heterosexual and nuclear; that is, it is a father-led family consisting of two parents of "opposite" sexes. This is a family that, "left to itself ... very naturally resumes its ageless pattern: father-led, mother-inspired and child-centred" (L. Byfield, "Our Next 25 Years," *AR*, 11 January 1999, 20). This form of the family, according to *AR*, has existed throughout the history of "mankind" but is now increasingly under threat as it has been "invaded, plundered and demoralized over the last generation" (ibid.). Queer people, which *AR* reduces to "homosexuals," pose a particularly nasty threat to the viability of this family structure.

When I was first finding out about it, my parents didn't know but they got hold of a number that I had gotten hold of when I was in Grade 9. My parents sat me down and told me that if I was, because they were Christians and believed it was wrong, then I would have to leave. They would pack my

things and I had to go because they did not want me in the house. That being
gay was evil, blah, blah, whatever. (Jill, 1998)

AR drew the battle lines in what it would eventually come to describe as a
"war." Sexual minorities were to go back into their closets, along with envi-
ronmentalists, feminists, human rights activists, Aboriginal peoples, and
pretty much everyone else who was not a conservative fundamentalist Christian like those in the Byfield family. That this magazine could effectively
launch an all-out attack that, throughout the 1990s, contributed to moral
mini-panics about homosexuality, reflects the fact that its representations
of homosexuality resonated with those of a significant number of Albertans.

Kissing n' Telling in Banff, Alberta, November 1992

In November 1992 the Walter Phillips Gallery, part of the Banff Centre for
the Arts, hosted a ninety-minute performance, *True Inversions*, as part of its
three-month-long celebration entitled, "Much Sense: Erotics and Life." This
work, by Vancouver's Kiss and Tell, consisted of a film and live talk performance that included a visual and oral exploration of lesbian sexual practices. While lesbian sex is often either conflated with gay male sex or erased
by "what-do-lesbians-do-in-bed?" rhetoric, neither evasion or effacement
of lesbian sex was possible with *True Inversions*. Lesbian sex was made public
through graphic black-and-white photographs of the Kiss and Tell collective members, stories, vignettes, and mini-plays.

Taking note of this public display of lesbian sex and dedicated to boosting flagging readership with "gutsy and lively reporting," *AR* sent reporter
Rick Bell to cover the performance and to investigate funding for "the latest
in subsidized 'alienation' and lesbian porn" ("Kissing and Telling in Balmy
Banff," *AR*, 7 December 1992, 33). Bell revealed that the Banff Centre was
provincially funded, with $14.5 million coming from Alberta's Department
of Advanced Education, while the Walter Phillips Gallery was granted $15,000
from the Department of Culture and Multiculturalism, headed by Doug
Main. Canada Council, a federal agency involved in funding the arts, funded
Kiss and Tell.

Doug Main, minister of culture and multiculturalism, responded to Bell's
article with a letter to the editor of *AR*, in which he admonished the magazine for its "slavish devotion to point-making at the expense of good journalism" (*AR*, 21 December 1992, 4). He was especially offended that the
story and cartoon made the suggestion that he was personally responsible
for, supportive of, and even proud to be involved with *True Inversions*. Main
accused *AR* of being ignorant of facts, especially the fact that "the minister
of culture is not the arbiter of taste in Alberta" but, rather, is responsible for
the provision of infrastructural support that allows for artistic expression
within the province. Departmental support for the arts, according to Main,

ought not to be confused with his personal support for a specific work, in this case the work of Kiss and Tell. Main finished his long letter with the following statement: "By the way, I think the event and its line-up of performances was disgusting. I wasn't asked to provide any special specific funding for this event. If I had been asked I would have said 'No!'" (*AR*, 21 December 1992, 4)

AR's Link Byfield responded to Main's letter with an editorial in which he stated that, if "Mr. Main wasn't responsible for subsidizing those Banff lesbians, then who was?" (*AR*, 21 December 1992, 2). Byfield's editorial referred to *True Inversions* as a performance by a "troupe of foul-mouthed, sex-obsessed Vancouver lesbian activists." Further, he admonished Main as follows: "If Mr. Main says he isn't responsible for making us pay women to masturbate in public, then who does he think is?" (ibid.). Speculating as to what Main might say if he properly shouldered the responsibility of his portfolio, Byfield wrote: "Please be advised that as minister responsible for cultural subsidies I am accountable to the voters and taxpayers of Alberta for what you do. When we take their money we owe them the courtesy of respecting common norms of decency and religious tolerance" (4).

The panic engendered by the *AR* coverage of Kiss and Tell continued elsewhere in the province and went on into the New Year. In the words of Kiss and Tell member Susan Stewart (Kiss and Tell 1994, 72), the "offshoot of the *Alberta Report* article was a syndicated story that appeared in at least twenty little community papers sprinkled throughout Alberta, Manitoba, and environs."

AR's Kevin Avram focused on taxpayer dollars. Three examples of headlines that make use of the original *AR* story are: (1) from the *Hanna Herald* of Hanna, Alberta, "Government Coffers Are Never Empty for 'Art'"(6 January 1993, 1); (2) from the *Watson Witness* of Canora, Saskatchewan, "Even Lesbianism Is Government Funded" (6 January 1993, 1); and (3) from the *West-Central Crossroads* of Kindersley, Saskatchewan, "Tax Dollars Funding Smut" (6 January 1993, 1).

Ken Kowalski, deputy premier of Alberta, pronounced in *AR* that he thought the performance was "god-awful" (*AR*, 15 January 1993, 24). Even though he did not actually see the performance, he asked Advanced Education Minister Jack Ady to speak to institutions such as the Banff Centre and "tell them such shows are not acceptable if the public is footing the bill" (*Edmonton Sun*, 1 February 1993, 43). What this implies is that only some Albertans – those who work and who are heterosexual – pay taxes. This is "assiduously damaging" and "effective in furthering a deeply homophobic right-wing agenda" (Kiss and Tell 1994, 72) because it also implies that sexual minority cultural events, unlike other cultural events, are completely unworthy of any kind of government sponsorship. Politicians and other concerned citizens do not actually have to read or view a thing: they simply have to read or hear about it from *AR*. If whatever was reported was related to homosexuality, then they pronounced a judgment, demanded censorship, and threatened the withdrawal of funding.

> *I think it is way worse to be a dyke in Alberta than anywhere else in Canada. But if I had to choose, it is better in Edmonton than it is in Calgary. (Virginia, 1998)*

Pejoratives such as "unacceptable," "disgusting," "spectacle," "lesbian porn," "foul-mouthed," "sex-obsessed," "sacrilegious obscenities," "women masturbating in public," "perversion," and so on were juxtaposed with notions such as respecting common norms of decency and religious tolerance. As well, a new twist was introduced to this proliferation with Main's reference to "special specific funding" in relation to homosexuality. This phrase worked its way into one of Ady's statements and then became part of the cant of Community Development Minister Dianne Mirosh, who railed against "special rights for homosexuals."

Along with *AR* the negative comments from Alberta politicians such as Kowalski as well as from other media resulted in a potent mix of homophobic discourse informing public knowledge about the sexual identities of queer Albertans. Unfortunately, this was often the only available public discourse. Those most vulnerable to the effects of adult phobias were sexual minority youth who were both financially and emotionally dependent on parents, teachers, and other adults. One unintended effect of *AR*'s venom was that its publicity for the work of Kiss and Tell did function to break the silence surrounding lesbianism and lesbian sexuality.

Rights Talk: Specifying, Specific, and Special

While then federal justice minister Kim Campbell undertook to recognize legal rights for sexual minorities, *AR* stated that "Alberta courts and legislators have for the most part resisted pressure from the gay lobby to accede to demands for similar legislative action" (R. Frey, "A Self-Legislated Mandate: AHRC Boss Sayeed Forges Ahead with Gay Rights," *AR*, 21 December 1992, 9). This comment was made in an article written in response to Alberta Human Rights Commission (hereafter AHRC) chief commissioner Sayeed's decision to investigate complaints of discrimination based on sexual orientation in the wake of federal changes to the Canadian Human Rights Act. Sayeed's decision was in keeping with other AHRC requests, on three prior occasions, to change the Individual Rights Protection Act (hereafter IRPA). Provincial Labour Minister Elaine McCoy supported Sayeed, stating that he had not overstepped his mandate or exceeded his authority, both of which were suggested by *AR*. In support of *AR*'s position, MLA Jack Ady indicated that it would be a mistake to single out small minorities in legislation. He added that "the act should protect people as Albertans, not as a member of this or that group. The question is, where does it end when you start specifying specific groups?" (ibid.).

We have to start somewhere, right? And starting somewhere is gonna be having that little phrase that says sexual orientation. (Virginia, 1998)

AR contended in Frey's "A Self-Legislated Mandate" that there was little evidence to suppose that homosexuals were discriminated against and that they were not in need of human rights protections. As evidence, *AR* relied on an unnamed 1988 survey of 25,000 consumers, in which most gay men had some postsecondary education and reported an average annual income of $62,000 – a figure achieved by only 20 percent of the general population. Nevertheless, *AR* argued that a lesbian who, because of her sexuality, had been fired from her job with a deaf boy from a Christian family had not been discriminated against and, therefore, should not receive human rights protection. Further, when homosexuality came up against Christian values, according to *AR,* common sense favoured Christian values.

I was totally lost in the medication and was actually set up for an operation [to begin transitioning]. When I first agreed to it, the only reason I agreed to the operation was that maybe this was a way to get my parents back. Well maybe, if I become a guy and I am straight, then, well hey, they are going to love me, right? (Jill, 1998)

Federal Justice Minister Kim Campbell introduced a bill to amend the Canadian Human Rights Act (CHRA), the most contentious change, according to *AR*, being the inclusion of sexual orientation as a "human characteristic worthy of special protection" (J. Woodard, "Ms. Campbell's Sly Compromise: Critics Say Her New Legislation Will Give Gays Family Status Soon Enough," *AR*, 28 December 1992, 26). Calgary North federal MP Al Johnson, member of a group of Tory MPs dubbed the "Family Caucus," declared, "I don't think 'sexual orientation' needs to be named as something we protect. If we start naming all the things government should protect, where will it end? Will we include protection of obesity next?" (ibid.). Johnson implicitly acknowledged the need for protection of sexual minorities but preferred not to be explicit since naming sexual orientation would make the realities of discrimination public.

From Special Specific to Special Rights: Dianne Mirosh

According to the cover of *AR*, on 18 January 1993 Alberta found a new champion for the growing cultural war over gay rights. Entitled "'Homophobe' or Heroine?" a six-page report asked the question, "Can

Mirosh stop the gays?" (J. Woodard, "Can Mirosh Stop The Gays? Alberta's New Rights Minister Checks the HRC and Enters a Social War Zone," *AR*, 18 January 1993, 6-11). With this headline, *AR* signalled that it and others expected government resistance to rights for homosexuals. The cover featured a rather boxy and dykey looking Mirosh, with her right hand up in a gesture that evoked a pledge of allegiance to *AR* and their agenda and that also suggested an official "stop" to the homosexual rights movement. In her other hand Mirosh held a book which may have been a Bible.

Alberta Report cover, 18 January 1993

Dianne Mirosh, rookie provincial community development minister, became an instant heroine for *AR* when she stated "gays and lesbians are having more rights than anybody else" and then made clear her intention to investigate the matter. Mirosh also declared: "A lot of heterosexuals feel uncomfortable about this" (J. Woodard, "Can Mirosh Stop the Gays?" *AR*, 18 January 1993, 6). Both the *Edmonton Journal* and the *Calgary Herald* decried her as a homophobe, while *AR* touted her as a proud but quaking heroine. Link Byfield prefaced the "special" report on Mirosh and gay rights by stating that "the rise of the homosexual rights agenda" had the Klein cabinet tied in knots and Mirosh hiding under her desk (2). Further, claimed Byfield, when it came to sodomy (his favoured word for describing homosexual practices), most people have the sensible attitude that "what those people do with themselves is their business, not mine ... yet somehow those people keep making it our business, whether we want it or not" (ibid.).

In this editorial, Byfield wondered why gays couldn't just go away and do whatever it was they did without laying guilt trips on others. According to him, rather than staying private, homosexuality had become a public and odious form of "hyper-political" activity, in which a significantly noisy element of sexual minorities terrorized "poor Mrs. Mirosh" while seeking the right to feel good about themselves in public. Byfield concluded his editorial with the following admonishment: "If they want their personal habits to remain private, they should stop making them so public" (*AR*, 18 January 1993, 2).

Sure I want everybody to have the same jobs and same opportunities and I also want integration into the community at large, but I think that what happens is the ghetto is a safe place. The ghetto is – well, I think of the ghetto as the place where a person is out to the gay community, absolutely uncloseted in the gay community, and the moment he is out of the gay community, he's back in the closet. I think that is dangerous. I think we have to stay out of the ghetto, get out of the closet. (Oscar, 1998)

It is really hard to come out. The kids are sort of coming out silently, in their own little groups. But there is no sort of acceptance. In Vancouver, it's no big deal. (Virginia, 1998)

But I always knew I was different. Early on I realized these differences would make me unpopular so I hid them until ... well, I'm still hiding them around most people. (Rudolf, 1998)

When told by an *Edmonton Journal* reporter that sexual orientation was not yet protected by the IRPA, Mirosh's surprise exposed her ignorance. Continuing pressure from Sayeed and former AHRC chair Fil Fraser, along with mainstream press coverage and organized gay community activity, had the effect of turning the story national. Mirosh made more statements about the discomfort of the "majority of Albertans." Sayeed stated she was over-reacting, and another former head of the commission, Marlene Antonio, called for Mirosh's resignation. Other Alberta politicians stepped into the fray.

Provincial Tory cabinet minister Ernie Isley declared: "If the human rights commission does not stop acting on homosexual claims, they will have to be stopped" (J. Woodard, "Can Mirosh Stop the Gays?" *AR*, 18 January 1993, 7). As a result of continuing pressure, Human Rights Commissioner Sayeed admitted in an interview shortly after Isley's statment that the AHRC was not proceeding with any investigations. Inadvertently invoking lesbian Kiss and Tell's *Drawing the Line* art show (mounted in Edmonton's Latitude 53 Gallery the previous year) among other battle-line analogies, *AR* reported that "in one small theatre of the continuing culture war between the traditional family and 'progress,' by a narrow margin, and only temporarily, the line has once again been held. If Alberta democracy does hold the line, then it may avoid having to undertake serious repairs later on" (7).

According to *AR*, the battle continued and democracy itself was under threat in Alberta. Homosexual rights were pitted against the traditional family. Homosexual rights were "special rights"; that is, rights that no one else seemed to have. Homosexual rights were "'elite' rights of a well educated and wealthy minority thus the homosexual movement was already very powerful" (J. Woodard, "Can Mirosh Stop the Gays?" *AR*, 18 January 1993, 7). According to *AR*'s Woodard, homosexual lobbying had become so powerful that American commentators referred to it as the new McCarthyism. Figures about money raised in support of AIDS research were used as evidence of the strength of this powerful homosexual agenda. "Why," asked Woodard, "are gays so militantly asserting their status as victims?" Quoting from author William Donohue, Woodard answered this question for readers: "Tell a militant homosexual that he already has toleration. He'll explode with indignation. Toleration's not enough; he wants social affirmation ... why should affirmation be so important ... their lifestyle constantly brings them in contact with death. But they can't cheat death the way the rest of us do, by having children who carry on after us. If they're going to reproduce, they have to do it politically, basically by taking over other people's children" (8).

Fears of homosexual predators taking over other people's children existed alongside assumptions that other people's children are not homosexual, that homosexuals themselves do not have children, and that all humans who defy death through reproduction are cheaters. Implicitly, heterosexuals were positioned as morally weak, requiring "special" protections. The vulnerability of fragile, traditional families to gay threats was also implicit. These families were likely to simply collapse under the weight of the "gay agenda."

The centrality of reproductive sex within the sanctity of heterosexual marriage was a cornerstone of *AR*'s beliefs, as was the sexual innocence of children and youth. The representation of homosexuals as threats to children, youth, adults, and traditional families was not enough for *AR*: it was also concerned with the "progressive compulsions" of homosexual behaviours. These behaviours were reported to exclude productive work and behaviours related to family and kin. Homosexuality was considered to exist outside of youth, work, citizenship, and family. *AR* was unable to understand queer people as human beings whose lives and experiences consist of far more than sexual practices; rather, it relied on "information" culled from a right-wing research foundation network supported by fundamentalist Christians in the United States.

> From a quarter to two-fifths of gays engage in some form of torture-sex, anywhere from a sixth to two-thirds (depending on the survey) report having sex in public washrooms and two-thirds sex in gay bathhouses ... 90% of homosexuals use illegal drugs ... yet most disturbing is the high incidence of sex with minors ... according to sociologists A. Bell and M. Weinberg in their book *Homosexualities,* 25% of adult white gays admit to sex with boys 16 or younger ... between one-quarter and one-third of homosexual men and women are alcoholics ... homosexuals are at least six times more likely to commit suicide than heterosexuals ... with so much indiscriminate contact, homosexuals would probably spread infection even if they only kissed ... 90% of practicing homosexuals engage in anal sex, and over two-thirds in mouth-to-anus contact ... the vast majority of homosexuals ingest medically significant amounts of human feces, with 5% to 10% eating or "wallowing" in them ... and despite propaganda to the contrary, AIDS is still overwhelmingly a homosexual disease ... homosexual medical problems begin with compulsive promiscuity ... even sky divers live longer than homosexuals ... even homosexuals dying from other causes survive, on average, to only 41. (J. Woodard, "Can Mirosh Stop the Gays?" *AR,* 18 January 1993, 9).

> *And I think, I used to think it was fear. But now I just think that it is blatant ignorance, because they don't know what they are afraid of. They can't even identify something to be afraid of. It's not even coming out of hatred or "I know what I am hating." It's that they have no clue. There's no – it is total ignorance. (Virginia, 1998)*

There was very little information regarding homosexuality circulating in the province to counter the *AR* discourse. Key to this discourse were notions of special rights, sexual practices linked to pathologies, diseased and dying bodies, death at a young age, sex with vulnerable heterosexual minors, and choice of this horrific lifestyle when wholesome alternatives were available (J. Woodard, "Can Mirosh Stop the Gays?" *AR*, 18 January 1993, 10).

As if this litany was not enough to frighten off the "average Albertan," *AR* included another article in the same edition, entitled "The Next Step: Lessons on Same-Sex Love – Alberta Considers Introducing a Homosexuality-Friendly Sex-Ed Course" (J. Woodard, *AR*, 25 January 1993, 11). Given the purported link between homosexuality and immoral and criminal activities, parents and educators alike were advised to be vigilant.

"Special rights for gays" was the slippery slope down which everyone in Alberta would slide towards depravity. Meanwhile, as the new elite coalition of "homosexuals, feminists, and other civil rights advocates" (J. Woodard, "Can Mirosh Stop the Gays?" *AR*, 18 January 1993, 10) marched towards queer anarchy, heroic government minister Mirosh "bends but does not break," reiterating her intent to recommend against the inclusion of "special rights" based on sexual orientation (L. Gunter, *AR*, 25 January 1993, 10).

Special Treatment for Winning Albertans: k.d. lang
It should be clear by now that *AR* was not writing in a cultural or political vacuum but, rather, had widespread support from within the elected provincial government. As noted throughout the previous sections, statements and actions on the part of provincially elected politicians functioned side by side with *AR* in the production of homophobic and heterosexist discourse. Even if individual Albertans did not subscribe to or read the numerous free copies of *AR* that were in circulation, it would have been difficult for them to ignore the homophobic statements and actions of politicians as these were reported in mainstream radio, television, and print media.

One such occasion occurred in the midst of the "gay-rights-as-special-rights" skirmish. In January 1993 national attention was focused on k.d. lang, an Albertan from the town of Consort, who had previously won numerous music awards and had again received a Canadian music award. When Albertans gain widespread recognition for outstanding achievements or performances, the Alberta government honours them by citing their name in the legislature and sending them a message of congratulations on behalf of all Albertans. lang, however, was not to be lauded in this manner. She was given different treatment – some might argue "special treatment" (even though the Alberta government was openly anti-special treatment for homosexuals). The government refused to honour lang. The reasons for this refusal varied, depending on which politician one addressed. One reason given was that lang, who is a vegetarian, had made a "meat stinks" advertisement several years earlier that had riled the cattle ranchers of Alberta. Premier Ralph Klein stated that his refusal to honour lang was related to her anti-beef campaign (A. Panzeri, "Province Honours lang for Third Grammy Win," *Edmonton Journal* [hereafter *EJ*], 26 February 1993, A1). Other members were more forthcoming. Tory MLA Ernie Isley stated that he would not support sending lang a message of congratulations because she had openly declared she was a lesbian (ibid.).

Opposition member New Democrat William Roberts tried to introduce a motion to send lang congratulations, but unanimous consent was required and significant support was not forthcoming from many members of the Klein government. In March 1993 lang won a third Grammy Award for her music, and finally the Klein government sent her a letter of congratulations: "Klein said he hoped the gesture would make up for the bad press the province received when the legislature refused to honour lang in January" (A. Panzeri, "Province Honours lang for Third Grammy Win," *EJ*, 26 February 1993, A1).

> *Well, Albertans are made up of many different communities, and there is no one type of Albertan. And when you look at the population as a whole you can see that it is not likely going to have a huge backlash against rights except from a very small – small and vocal, yes – but still a small group of people that don't represent what the people in the province want. (Svend, 1998)*

The unwillingness of elected politicians to acknowledge openly queer Albertans for outstanding achievement made it clear that such Albertans and their achievements were not worthy. The message was that queer Albertans were not real Albertans and that it would be better if they lived somewhere else – perhaps, according to *AR*, the Sodom of the west, Vancouver, British Columbia. Central to homophobic discourse is the belief that queer people are defined solely by their sexuality. Any other characteristic must be ignored, even when queer people stand out in ways recognized by mainstream Canadian culture.

Earlier, *AR* praised Mirosh for saying that gays and lesbians did not deserve special anything: yet special treatment is exactly what the Klein government meted out to lang. Maintaining homophobic policies that cater to the special interests of minority religious groups required politicians to flip flop on what they understood by special treatment.

Significantly, *AR* reported lang's awards ("Those Bigoted Backbenchers Again," 8 February 1993, 29) as well as commenting on her "virtuoso singing voice" (26 July 1993, 32). In a later edition, however, *AR* commented: "You could not help but feel that the singer was using her prodigious talent and fame to mess with youth, impressionable minds" (P. Bunner, Editor's Notes, *AR*, 26 August 1993, 4). Again, *AR* represented queer people as contaminating and predatory homosexuals and reinforced the assumption that youth are heterosexual and easily recruitable.

Of Chemicals and Sex: Can Pollutants Cause Promiscuity and Homosexuality? (R. Owen, *AR*, 1 February 1993, 16)

Away We Go Down the Next Slippery Slope: Guard Your Children (L. Byfield, 15 February 1993, 2)

The Radical Agenda Gains Acceptance: Sex with 12-Year-Olds Isn't Necessarily Harmful, Says the Grey Nuns Head Psychiatrist (J. Demers, *AR*, 15 February 1993, 28-29)

"Rage against the Dying Light": Western Evangelicals Mobilize against Gay Rights (R. White, *AR*, 19 February 1993, 37)

The Gay Sore Erupts Again: As the UC Agonizes, a Cleric Appears in Full Frontal Glory (R. White, *AR*, 15 March 1993, 36-7)

Gays Are the Worst Victims of Their Own Propaganda (J. Nicolosi, *AR*, 15 March 1993, 40-1)

Helping Kids Become Gay: A Medical Conference in Edmonton Promotes Teen Homosexuality (J. Demers, *AR*, 10 May 1993, 40)

Repudiating the Special Rights Lobbyists (J. Woodard, *AR*, 21 June 1993, 3)

Of Course There Can Be a "Gay Theology," also a Pedophile or a Con Man's Theology (T. and V. Byfield, *AR*, 5 July 1993, 40)

Special Rights for Sodomites!

In 1993, 1994, and 1995 *AR* produced an onslaught of articles dealing with the issue of human rights for lesbians and gays. The federal Tories had fallen from power, along with their proposed changes for inclusion of sexual orientation as a protected category in the CHRA, and new federal leader Jean Chretien's Liberals were in charge of the Canadian state. Within this frame *AR* marshalled a different argument in its battle on homosexuality and flagging readership. In a story entitled "Special Rights for Sodomites," reporter C. Champion wrote: "Canada's human rights czar makes a last plea to legitimize the homosexual lifestyle" (*AR*, 8 April 1996, 25). Before his retirement, federal human rights chief commissioner Max Yalden wrote in his final report that by failing to add sexual orientation to the CHRA, Ottawa was complicit in widespread intolerance towards lesbians and gays. Further, Yalden roundly condemned critics for stating that inclusion of sexual orientation amounted to special rights.

The response of Alberta's community development minister, Gary Mar, to the Yalden report provoked a new and immediate skirmish with *AR*. Mar stated: "it's interesting that when blacks were marching in Alabama in the 1950s, people would hold up signs saying 'no special rights for blacks'" (C.

Champion, "Special Rights for Sodomites," *AR*, 8 April 1996, 25). The *AR* charged Mar with confusing discrimination against blacks, which occurred within a different historical context, to the contemporary Canadian refusal to endorse legislative protection for homosexual practices. Again, *AR* saw human rights protection as an endorsement of homosexual practices rather than as being about job security and apartments (MacDougall 2000, 106).

AR also argued that black rights are not analogous to homosexual rights because blacks do not have a choice regarding skin colour, while gays and lesbians do have a choice about taking up the "homosexual lifestyle." To shore up its argument, *AR* interviewed Dean William Allen, a black man attending James Madison College in Lansing, Michigan, who also disagreed with Mar's analogy between blacks and homosexuals. "For all important social purposes ... homosexuals are a 'trans-social category' – belonging to all classes and walks of life, and not readily identifiable unless they choose to advertise their proclivities ... and they [blacks and homosexuals] are in no way comparable, and there is no justification for using such as [sic] analogy to advance the homosexual cause" (C. Champion, "Special Rights for Sodomites," *AR*, 8 April 1996, 25).

According to the *AR* special features of 8 April 1996, choice operates in two ways in relation to homosexuality. First, relying on evidence and arguments made as early as 1993, *AR* presented "research" and included special stories on reparative therapy in which gays and lesbians chose to be treated and restored to a happy heterosexual existence complete with a traditional family of their own (J. Woodard, "Out of the Closet – and Then Some: A Reformed Calgary Homosexual Goes Public to Help Other Gays Change," *AR*, 19 April 1993, 30-1). Unlike blacks, who have no choice regarding skin colour, homosexuals choose to make themselves public by announcing their "proclivities." Homosexuals choose to be out; if they did not, then they would not be noticed. Heterosexuality, of course, does not need to announce itself publicly as heterosexuality is the default position – the "normal," "natural" position. Meanwhile, *AR* reported federal Liberal backbencher MP Tom Wappell warning that "it is not an end, but the beginning of a quest to have homosexual behaviour treated as the absolute equivalent of normal heterosexual relations" (C. Champion, "Special Rights for Sodomites," *AR*, 8 April 1996, 25).

Prepare for Ramming: Chretien Will Push Gay Marriage Rights through in One Week (T. McFeely, *AR*, 6 May 1996, 8)

The Skater-Boy Who Wasn't: A Lesbian in Drag Seduces Young Girls (D. Sheremeta, *AR*, 6 May 1996, 25)

Homos at Twelve O'clock! An Alderman Wants to Buzz Trysting Gays with a Police Chopper (L. Sillars, *AR*, 6 May 1996, 40)

Rock's Gay Bill: What Thou Doest, Do Quickly (L. Jenkinson, *AR*, 13 May 1996, 8)

The Beating Reform Was Doomed to Suffer: Manning Learns There Is No Such Thing as a Populist Position on Human Rights (M. Jenkinson, *EJ*, 20 May 1996, 6-8)

A Forced March toward Chaos: Critics Assail Manning's Refusal to Accept that Many Forms of Discrimination Are Essential and Good (T. McFeely, *AR*, 20 May 1996, 9-11)

What Exactly Was It That Gained for Sodomy Such a Fine Reputation? (T. Byfield, *AR*, 20 May 1996, 44)

Mr. Manning's Evasive Ideas about "Rights" Are Worse than Mr. Rock's (L. Byfield, *AR*, 27 May 1996, 2)

The Mask Comes Off: With Gay Rights in the Bag, Homosexuals Plot Their Next Move (P. Verburg, *AR*, 27 May 1996, 8)

Queering Gropes for the Moral High Ground (C. McGovern, *AR*, 27 May 1996, 34-5)

The Dirty Politics of Homosexual Health (P. Verburg, *AR*, 3 June 1996, 36)

While advocating the extermination of all gophers in the province ("So Why Not Gophers?" cover, 6 May 1996), the *AR* staff sensed that another of their special exposés of homosexuality was in order. Several years had passed since the last report, and the cause was taking a further battering from one of their own – federal Reform leader Preston Manning. Manning's position on human rights involved removing all protected categories and, instead, legislating that all discrimination was illegal. The administration of the law would be left to existing human rights commissions and commissioners, another group of people *AR* found reprehensible.

Drawing on the "expertise" of twenty-four-year veteran medical doctor Grant Hill, who was also a Reform MP, the special report on homosexuals hit the stands in June 1996. The article introduced Hill's credentials: married, father of seven, a former graduate of the University of Alberta Faculty of Medicine with first-hand experience "treating hundreds of people for sexually transmitted diseases, including many homosexual men" (P. Verburg, "The Dirty Politics of Homosexual Health," *AR*, 3 June 1996, 36). Hill advised *AR* that, during his tenure as a medical doctor, "he formed a 'vivid impression' that the homosexual lifestyle is unhealthy" (ibid.).

The evidence Hill provided to *AR*, along with his personal experiences, relied on *one* medical study about the increase of hepatitis A in homosexual populations. *AR* drew further on studies from 1992, 1993, and 1994 concerned with HIV/AIDS infections, and these were used to "prove" that HIV/AIDs is a gay male disease related to "promiscuity ... endemic to homosexual behaviour" (P. Verburg, "The Dirty Politics of Homosexual Health," *AR*, 3 June 1996, 37). Information provided elsewhere in the article came from Paul Cameron's Family Research Institute. "Gays have been known to engage in other unhealthy activities, such as inserting 'toys' like bottles, flashlights and even gerbils into the rectum, 'golden showers' (drinking or being splashed with urine) and eating and wallowing in feces" (36). It is worth noting that Cameron was expelled from the American Psychological Association in 1983 (C. Rusnell, "Report on Gay Parenting Cites Discredited Doctor," *EJ*, 18 October 1997, B4). He had been censured by other bodies – like the American Sociological Association and the American Psychiatric Association – as well as by an American judge for making misrepresentative statements about homosexuals in court. The work produced by Cameron's Family Research Institute is organized and disseminated primarily by one man – Paul Cameron.

Elsewhere an extensive and sensationalized account of anal intercourse as "a mixing bowl of semen, germs or infections on the penis" is juxtaposed with "normal sex," in which a more sanitized, medicalized language is used to describe how "the multi-layered and more flexible vaginal wall keeps viruses from entering the blood stream" (P. Verburg, "The Dirty Politics of Homosexual Health," *AR*, 3 June 1996, 36). A bar graph was included, in which the bars were indicated by tombstones designating lifestyle and lifespans. According to this graph, married males die at seventy-four; divorced and single males die at fifty-seven; while homosexual males die at forty-two, and those with AIDS die, on average, at thirty-nine. These statistics were provided courtesy of Cameron's Family Research Institute. Married, divorced, and single males were not identified as heterosexual: their heterosexuality was presumed and required no label on the tombstone.

When I think of gays I don't think of sex. I think of people like W.H. Auden, Tchaikovsky, James Dean, Shakespeare: I think of intelligence and accomplishment. Why do others insist on thinking of sex when they think about us? Do they want sex with us? Is that their problem? (Oscar, 1998)

In this special feature *AR* discredited the 1948 Kinsey Report, with its estimate that 10 percent of the population is homosexual, while elsewhere using these same numbers to support whatever argument it proposed. Even though *AR* thought the number of homosexuals was very small, it still believed that these people consituted a significant and powerful horde of social deviants who engaged in horrible sins and crimes. It was difficult enough for *AR* to contemplate individual homosexual deviants without having to contend with a group with legal group status. *AR* focused on gay male sex in its efforts to pathologize homosexuality, yet it also wanted to deny lesbians human rights protection based on its depictions of the "unhealthy lifestyle" of gays. AR linked both gay men and lesbians to death because of their apparent inability to reproduce and, therefore, "cheat" death.

In the same issue, a special report on "dirty politics" reiterated the *AR* worldview that married heterosexuals and "family values" were under attack from deviants. Sin and punishment figure strongly as the backdrop to the "dirty politics" article as well as in an advertisement that drew a link between abortion and breast cancer (Alberta Prolife/Edmonton, "There Is a Link between Abortion and Breast Cancer" (advertisement), *AR*, 3 June 1996, 44).

Given this barrage of representations of homosexuality, what mainstream Albertan would be happy at the idea of any queer person being in close proximity to her/him or to her/his children? Queer and questioning youth were especially vulnerable. They bore the full brunt of this weekly onslaught, which was delivered to their "safe and caring" schools, was seemingly available on every shelf and table top, and was readily accessible to all those around them.

I know exactly how they would react if they knew I was gay. My mom would be sorta okay with it, maybe not as okay on the inside as she would appear on the outside. My dad would be a bit upset and would put both feet in his mouth. He'd probably try to blame someone, maybe Oscar, because he has been calling me a lot. I think my parents suspect he's gay and might be "recruiting" me or something. Maybe they'd blame Ellen Degeneres. (Rudolf, 1998)

The Ugly Canadian: Ottawa's Delegation to a UN Conference Preaches an Extreme Anti-Family Crusade That Enrages the Third World (*AR* cover, 1 July 1996)

Canadians Go Home: At UN Conference in Turkey, Ottawa's Strident Homo-Feminist Agenda Provokes an Angry Counter-Attack from the Third World (T. McFeely, *AR*, 1 July 1996, 28-33)

The Treason of the Clerics: Gay Apostasy Subverts and Paralyzes the Canadian Catholic Church (J. Woodard, *AR*, 8 July 1996, 28-31)

See No Evil: Canada's Somnolent Catholic Bishops Capitulate on Gay Rights to Cover up a Same-Sex Spousal Benefits Deal with the Victims of Their Homosexual Priests (*AR* cover, 8 July 1996)

The Natural Family Is Alive and Threatened: Statscan Fires Another Numbers Barrage to Screen the Advance of Gay Rights (P. Verberg, *AR*, 8 July 1996, 37)

Homosex for the Masses: The Showcase Channel Airs a Celebration of Gay Porn (K. Anderson, *AR*, 15 July 1996, 29)

The Mouse Trap: A Backlash Brews against Disney's Sugar-Coated Revisionism and Omnipotent Cultural Power (*AR* cover, 22 July 1996)

Maybe They Don't Want a Cure: Ugly AIDS Conference Protests Overshadow Reports of Progress (D. Sheremeta, *AR*, 22 July 1996, 30-2)

Alberta Report cover, 8 July 1996

Intensifications: The Calgary Board of Education

Unsurprisingly to *AR*, feminists were busy assaulting the natural family at UN conferences, and even Disney and the Roman Catholic Church were implicated as pro-gay in the magazine's battle against queer Albertans. Disney had become a huge threat, with its extension of spousal benefits to homosexual employees. As a result of this, "[at] the Southern Baptist Convention's annual meeting in June, 13,000 delegates representing some 16 million members voted to threaten a boycott against Disney for 'promoting homosexuality'" (P. Verburg, "In the Maw of the Mouse: Disney's Pervasive Empire is Corrupting Our Cultural Heritage," *AR*, 22 July 1996, 26). The Anglican and United Churches, unlike the Baptist Church or the church of the Byfields, had endorsed gay pride parades (Ted and Virginia Byfield, "Of Course There Can Be a "Gay Theology," also a Pedophile or a Con Man's Theology," *AR*, 8 July 1996). However, according to *AR*, the sinister threat of homosexuality was poised to strike close to home as the gay agenda prepared to hit Alberta schools.

On 11 June 1996 the Calgary Board of Education (CBE) heard a report on counselling support for homosexual youth safety and adopted a series of motions to develop an information package to ensure the safety of sexual minority youth in their school district. Pat Boyle, advisor on gender issues for the CBE, was a member of a committee that developed an action plan that was to be considered by the superintendents' council. It is worthwhile directly quoting the recommendations adopted, in principle, by the CBE at the September meeting because they stand in such stark contrast to the wasteland of positive initiatives for queer youth in Alberta schools.

(a) An Advisory Group to be established to assist the Advisor on Gender Issues with further planning and the implementation of the following actions. The Advisory Group to include representation from schools, departments, Calgary Health Services and Calgary Police Services (SRO Unit).

(b) The Professional Resource Centre to put together a Staff Resource Package that will include several articles on the safety needs of gay/lesbian youth. The Professional Resource Centre will also continue to make this matter part of its collection development.

(c) The Video Loan Pool to look into purchasing video material on this matter.

(d) The Evaluation/Selection Group of Research and System Development to evaluate material, non-fiction and fiction, for suitability in school libraries.

(e) Workshops on homophobia and homosexuality to be held for Principals, Assistant Principals, Counselors, CALM Teachers, and other Teaching Staff.

(f) Harassment workshops will include information about the safety and well-being of gay/lesbian students and staff.

(g) The Advisor on Gender Issues will attend meetings of the Calgary Police Service's Gay and Lesbian Community Police Liaison Committee. The Calgary Police Service will be providing workshops on homophobia and homosexuality for all School Resource Officers in the next year.

(h) The Advisor on Gender Issues will conduct a workshop on gay/lesbian youth at Teachers' Convention in February 1997.

(i) Gender Attitude and Achievement Promotion (GAAP) will have a session on gay/lesbian youth issues in December 1996 for junior high teachers who are interested in gender issues (Calgary Board of Education 1996).

The willingness of the CBE to include all staff, in particular teachers, was testimony to its interest in the well-being of all its constituent members and goes beyond the Alberta Teachers' Association initiatives for the new millennium. The resultant backlash placed the action plan in a defensive position, with every action and purchase in support of lesbian and gay youth coming under intense public scrutiny.

Ever since I remember, like in Grade 1, they would call me "sissy" and "girl" and stuff. It wasn't until junior high that they actually called me "faggot." (Rupaul, 1998)

It is very, very hard to go against the grain when you are small. When you don't have any power and you have no voice. Having the school board put into place a safety plan helps. You know that we are going to institute a new policy and you cannot say this kind of thing, that you can't discriminate because of sexual orientation in the schools, that is part of it. It will not make everything better because there is no reinforcement, but it is a step in the right direction. (Virginia, 1998)

Because of the political make-up of its board, the CBE initiated an action plan when others did not. It was the largest school board in the province and was often embroiled in controversy with the provincial government. Unlike the CBE, the Edmonton Public School Board did not include controversial issues in its plans, even though Edmonton was considered to be a holdout against the Progressive Conservative domination of Alberta (C. Ruttan, "Three Cheers for Calgary School Board," *EJ*, 10 May 1997, H2). Individual members of the CBE had "snatched victory from a right-leaning slate of candidates who wanted to take over the board" (A. Mitchell, *Globe and Mail*, 7 March 1997, A2). It is significant with regard to what transpired that this savvy and progressive school board had a contingent of strong women members.

I quit school last March because of the homophobic harassment at my high
school. No one at the school took me seriously and the teacher tried to claim
I had shoved her when I escaped from the class. Even though we had a plan
[safety action plan] in our school area – see, this lady from the central office
came out to the school – I had to quit because my school wouldn't do
anything. (Michel, 1998)

According to the *Edmonton Journal*'s S. Ruttan, "the Klein government
hates the Calgary Board of Education. It is the epitome of everything the
government wants to stamp out – rebellious, female-dominated, liberal, big-
spending" ("Three Cheers for Calgary School Board," 10 May 1997, H2).
The CBE, led by Chair Jennifer Pollock with the support of all the other
board members as well as Deputy Superintendent Donna Michael, was willing to fight for adequate funding of schools, for less provincial control, and
for social justice issues.

The CBE led the country with such initiatives as appointing a gender
equity officer, Pat Boyle. School boards across Canada relied on Boyle as a
consultant, and a considerable part of her part-time position was spent as-
sisting other boards. Boyle did an incredible amount of work over the two-
year period leading up to the 25 February 1997 meeting to prepare the board
for all the issues involved in the action plan. This included having queer
youth, parents, and other adults – including community leaders – attend
the meeting and talk about their lives. Boyle knew that discussions about
queer lives needed to include queer people rather than those who hated
them – an idea that was unintelligible to *AR*. In addition, the CBE spent
time addressing the possibility of a backlash from organized religious fundamentalists. As Boyle reported later, neither she nor the board had begun
to imagine the viciousness of the backlash (P. Boyle, personal communication, 14 May 1997).

The 25 February 1997 meeting was the showdown for final approval of
the Guidelines for the Implementation of the Action Plan on Gay/Lesbian/
Bisexual Youth and Staff Safety. Referring to it as a "showdown" cannot
begin to capture the fractiousness of the events leading up to, and the shrill
tone of, this meeting. In its "Fighting Back" column, *AR* lent support to the
resistance to the action plan:

12 February all concerned Calgary Public School Board parents and taxpayers are asked to attend a public meeting at 7:30 p.m. at the Calgary Convention Centre, Macleod Salon D, 120 - 9 Avenue SE. The purpose of the meeting
is to discuss the school board's Action Plan to adopt a policy on "Homosexual Youth Safety." The board has had very little input from parents regarding this policy (see story, page 32). Come and be informed of the effects

and ramifications, and give your input. Call 403-288-5332 or 403-239-8765 for further information. (*AR*, 10 February 1997, 39)

Throughout the city, churches affiliated with AR organized gatherings. At these meetings parents were provided with testimonials from a "recovering homosexual," with graphic details of his deadly gay sexual practices. This, of course, was generalized to all other homosexuals, as was the message that if he could beat such a depraved lifestyle so could anyone. Other information about the depravity of homosexuality was also made available. Parents and other concerned people were warned to attend the February board meeting and to make their voices heard; if they did not, then the gay agenda would take over their schools, and their children would be recruited and/or preyed upon.

> *As soon as I sat down at my desk, kids were like, throwing pencils. They were throwing them at me and saying, "Fucking homo faggot." This was in CALM [Career and Life Management]. (Michel, 1998)*

> *My teachers never had anything to do with it. Like, they never stopped anything. They downplayed the name calling and stuff. It was ignored. I realized that if something was going to happen, I would have to do it myself. (Greg, 1998)*

> In late August, over 100 Christians from 16 churches met at the Centre Street Church in Calgary, to discuss a recent public school board resolution to legitimize homosexuality in the curriculum. These parents decided to form a Calgary chapter of Citizens United for Responsible Education (CURE), a Toronto-based network founded in 1992. (J. Woodard, "Back into the Bedrooms of the Nation," *AR*, 16 September 1996, 32)

Reading the minutes for the "regular meeting of the Board" renders the chaotic and acrimonious struggle that ensued into a dry-sounding event, something it most definitely was not (P. Boyle, personal communication, 1997). Concerned citizens packed the meeting, and the police were in attendance should things get completely out of hand. In the *Globe and Mail*, A. Mitchell wrote: "by all accounts, it was a noisy meeting" ("School Trustees Create Storm over Gay Rights," March 1997, A2). Shouting and screaming made it difficult for the board to proceed with business. In spite of intense resistance from members of the audience, the motion to adopt the action plan passed unanimously.

In the weeks that followed, attempts to intimidate board members and staff necessitated all visitors to the CBE building going through a security check point. I was one such visitor. Pat Boyle was singled out because she was a "gender consultant" and, therefore, an automatic enemy (CURE founder Dave Butler quoted in J. Woodard, "The Protestants Tackle Another Reformation," *AR*, 16 September 1996, 32). Phone calls to the CBE, and especially to Boyle, were screened because so many of them were hate calls. Boyle reported that friends of hers who attended meetings in the Calgary area organized by her opponents told her that she was so completely vilified that they were aghast. Indeed, they became very worried about her safety and well-being. During their meetings, religious fundamentalists made similar verbal attacks against other CBE members. *AR* assisted the fundamentalist cause by reproducing an excerpt presented to the CBE on 14 September 1996 by concerned parent and medical doctor L. Macphail, listing the deadliness of "the lifestyle." This, of course, added a further fright factor to CURE's resistances to the action plan (L. Macphail, "The Adverse Health Effects of Homosexuality Should Be Taught," *AR*, 14 October 1996, 33).

> *There was this teacher there and she was a lesbian. She was really awesome to be around and stuff. She taught me not to pass judgment on people because of their orientation and stuff. I would see her around here and there and she is really cool. I respect her. (Michel, 1998)*

A fear of the queer predator taking innocent children and youth was turned into a fear of the predator state operating in the interests of a powerful homosexual lobby. The provision of a safety action plan, which would include counselling for queer youth, produced both a tacit recognition that queer youth might exist and fears that the state was taking children from their parents. Thus, this latest battle against homosexuality involved organizing against state education (J. Woodard, "Now They're The School's Children," *AR*, 14 October 1996, 32). Tom Crites, head of Parents for Choice Association, opined, "Whose kids are they anyway? We know what's best for our kids" (A. Mitchell, "School Trustees Create Storm over Gay Rights," *Globe and Mail*, 7 March 1997, A2).

The ownership of other human beings, especially children or youth, was central to these adult narratives that masqueraded as family values. Parents for Choice could countenance neither the notion that children and youth might have sexual identities nor the possibility that traditional families might contain queer members. Concerned parents were represented as those who resisted the action plan and who managed the sexuality of their offspring through intimidation, psychotherapy, and ostracism. Those, especially feminists, who supported queer rights were by definition anti-family. The vilification of feminism – in the form of the CBE and its contingent of strong women

– was consistent with fundamentalist religious values regarding father-headed traditional families, in which women are homemakers and both women and children are under patriarchal control.

Whereas *AR* cast the struggle over the action plan as an issue about homosexual content in the curriculum, the action plan itself was based on tenets of the Canadian Charter of Rights and Freedoms and the Human Rights Act. Both the charter and the Human Rights Act are concerned with obligations of public institutions, such as schools, to all their constituent members, including queer youth and teachers. As Boyle stated, "We have a legal obligation to make sure students are safe in our schools" (A. Mitchell, "School Trustees Create Storm over Gay Rights," *Globe and Mail*, 7 March 1997, A2). Yet pressure on the CBE continued long after the plan had passed, making change difficult if not, at times, impossible. For example, with the inclusion of lesbian and gay materials in libraries, Tom Crites and his group called for book banning – a call with which school board chief superintendent Donna Michaels agreed (A. Mitchell and B. Laghi, "Books Banned after 'Gay Agenda' Complaints," *Globe and Mail*, 20 November 1997, A1).

Pat Boyle kept making suggestions, and they said they couldn't do some but would do other things if anything else happened. The school just didn't care, or they were stupid, or they were afraid of getting into trouble from parents and stuff. Well, a few days later, the same thing happened in CALM class, and so I said fuck it and I was out of there. Teachers said, "Why are you leaving? You are doing so well academically." And I said, "I can't handle the shit and no one will do anything. And also my safety is an issue, so I'm going home." (Michel, 1998)

G Is for Gay – and Gullible: Calgary Public Believes 13% of Its Students May Be Homosexual (J. Woodard, *AR*, 1 July 1996, 34-5)

Equality, but Not If It Costs: A Well-To-Do Lesbian Refuses to Pay Support to Her Rejected Ex-Lover (C. Champion, *AR*, 26 August 1996, 32)

Condom Education Is Not Sex Education: Saskatchewan Decides There Will Be Mandatory Copulation Instruction after All (S. Parker, *AR*, 1 July 1996, 34-5)

The Protestants Tackle Another Reformation: Calgary Evangelicals Gather against the Advance of the Gay Curriculum (J. Woodard, *AR*, 16 September 1996, 32)

Back into the Bedrooms of the Nation: As the World Recoils from Pedophilia, the UN Gay Lobby Stops Opposing It (J. Woodard, *AR*, 16 September 1996, 35)

Who Should Pay for Self-Inflicted Ailments? As Demands Grow for Free AIDS Treatment Klein Muses about Personal Responsibility for Sickness (C. Champion, *AR*, 23 September 1996, 11)

Fatal Fear of the Gay Lobby: Testimony in a Toronto Lawsuit May Complete Krever's Obstructed Inquiry into Red Cross Blood Contamination (C. Champion, *AR*, 23 September 1996, 23-4)

One Not-So-Gay CBC Employee: Mothercorp Is Sued for Withholding Pension Benefits (C. Champion, *AR*, 23 September 1996, 24)

The Pedophile Charge That Stunned BC: Few Parents Knew about the Other Life of Their Popular Gay School Principal (R. Brunet, *AR*, 23 September 1996, 28)

Chris P. Carrot Comes to Alberta: The Animal Rights Mascot Finds Little Sympathy in Cattle Country (C. Champion, *AR*, 30 September 1996, 19)

How Feminists Dominate the Courts: When They Mount Charter Challenges, They Usually Win (C. Champion, *AR*, 30 September 1996, 24-5)

Fast-Track to Discrimination: Young Female Judges Seek Better Compensation Than Male Benchers (C. Champion, *AR*, 30 September 1996, 24-5)

Deconstructing the Arts Faculty: Doctrinaire Feminism Tightens Its Grasp on the U of A's Biggest Department (P. Verburg, *AR*, 30 September 1996, 32-7)

The Devil in Disguise: Angels in America (*AR* cover, 7 October 1996, 1)

The Other Victims of the U of A's Deconstructionists: Teachers (L. Craig, *AR*, 7 October 1996)

Now They're the School's Children: Calgary Parents Are Stonewalled on Unmonitored Homosexual Counselling (J. Woodard, *AR*, 14 October 1996, 32)

The Adverse Health Effects of Homosexuality Should Be Taught (L. Macphail, *AR*, 14 October 1996, 33)

Keep Those Redneck Moms and Dads in the Dark: Calgary's Public School Board Wants the Right to Send Teens to Gay Activists for Counselling. (L. Sillars, *AR*, 10 February 1997, 32)

School Trustees Create Storm over Gay Rights (A. Mitchell, *Globe and Mail*, 7 March 1997, A2)

Gays Get in the Door: Calgary Public Proceeds with Its Acceptance Promotion (L. Sillars, *AR*, 17 March 1997, 30)

Parents Learn to Fight the Gay Agenda: BC's Battle against Anti-Family Propaganda Gains Momentum (J. Collins, *AR*, 5 May 1997, 34-5)

Books Banned after "Gay Agenda" Complaints: Move by Calgary Public School Board Called Part of the Explosion of Antihomosexual Sentiment. (A. Mitchell and B. Laghi, *Globe and Mail*, 20 November 1997, A1 and A8)

Gay Culture Comes to Calgary Public Schools: The CBE Ungraciously Bans Some Sexually-Explicit Homosexual Fiction (L. Sillars, *AR*, 15 December 1997, 58)

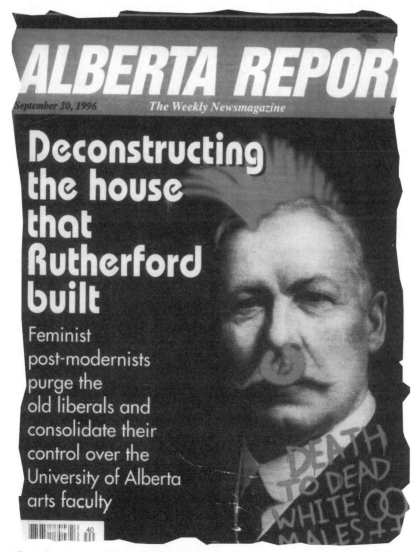

Alberta Report cover, 30 September 1996

Angels in Alberta: *AR* Devils in Disguise?

AR's fears mushroomed due to its belief that attacks on the traditional family had become global (H. Dykxhoorn, "The Fight for Family Goes Global," *AR*, 21 April 1997, 42) and were being mounted from a number of directions. These attacks included: homosexual porn as art (K. Torrance, "Hold Your Nose and Pay," *AR*, 15 September 1997, 10-13); a takeover of Disney (P. Verburg, "In the Maw of the Mouse: Disney's Pervasive Empire Is Corrupting Our Cultural Heritage," *AR*, 22 July 1996, 26-30; D. Di Sabatino, "Disney versus Christendom," *AR*, 18 August 1997, 33-4); mainstream religions, including the Roman Catholic, United, and Anglican Churches ("See No Evil," *AR* cover, 8 July 1996; J. Woodard, "The Protestants Tackle Another Reformation," *AR*, 16 September 1996, 32-7); and the universities via feminism and women's studies (L. Craig, "The Other Victims of U of A's Deconstructionist Teachers," *AR*, 7 October 1996, 32-3). It was clear to *AR* that "collectively feminists adhere to a 'post-modern' ideology that rejects the intellectual and cultural heritage of Western civilization" – an ideology that, much like that of strident homosexuals, rejects traditional values (P. Verburg, "Deconstructing the Arts Faculty," *AR*, 30 September 1996, 32).

Meanwhile, "the powerful gay lobby" was blamed for the Canadian Red Cross's tainted blood scandal (C. Champion, "Who Should Pay for Self-Inflicted Ailments?" *AR*, 23 September 1996, 23-4). According to *AR*, senior administrators at the Red Cross were so afraid of this powerful group and their advocates that they made poor management decisions, with deadly repercussions for their clients. Even though "no one really knows how many homosexuals there are" (K. Avram, "The Most Deadly Lifestyle," *AR*, 25 November 1996, 26), there were enough to bring down the Canadian blood system.

While *AR* admonished sexual minorities to stay private, it outed two lesbians in a highly public way (P. Verburg, "Deconstructing the Arts Faculty," *AR*, 30 September 1996, 33), and a spectral figure – the pedophile – began to emerge as the magazine's major preoccupation. As the theatre of war widened, the play *Angels in America* arrived in Alberta. The *AR* cover of 7 October 1996 openly declares war, with the caption "Controversy Rages over the Arrival of a Play that Casts AIDS-Afflicted Homosexuals as Martyrs in the War against Western Civilization" juxtaposed with the words "Angels in Alberta" and a replica of the poster used for the theatre production in Calgary. In short, *AR* thought *Angels* to be thoroughly disgusting.

> The devil in disguise: *Angels in America*, which opened in Alberta last month, is the most celebrated play of recent memory. In Alberta, however, it has been one of the most reviled. Its admirers see it as a moving depiction of the pain suffered by AIDS victims. But it has at its core a revolutionary

hatred for restraint of any kind. While its critics demand an end to govern-ment sponsorship of such productions, others propose a more radical solu-tion: empowering audiences to take back the theatres. ("The Devil in Disguise," *AR*, 7 October 1996, 1)

A flurry of editorials and articles appeared in Edmonton and Calgary, spearheaded by the *Calgary Herald*'s Peter Stockland. The *AR* indicated that Stockland accused *Angels* of "obscenity, anti-religious hatred, and of being a demonstration of the urgent need to overhaul the province's arts funding

Alberta Report cover, 7 October 1996

process" (K. Grace, "When All Else Fails, Boo," 7 October 1996, 36). *AR* also reported a survey conducted by another newspaper, the *Sun*, which surveyed Alberta MLAs for their opinions on *Angels in America* (ibid.). Five MLAs called for the Alberta Foundation for the Arts (AFA) to withdraw funding for Alberta theatre projects. The producer-director of *Angels* condemned those who were hypercritical of a play they had not seen.

> *Like Roy Cohen has that speech in* Angels in America, Part 1. *It's who I am, not who I sleep with or what I am not. I am not only who I sleep with or what I do in bed. (Virginia, 1998)*

One MLA, Jon Havelock, reversed his opinion after seeing the play. In a statement from her office, Shirley McLellan, minister of community development, said that she was "'not inclined to set herself up as judge and jury' on any AFA funded project" (K. Grace, "When All Else Fails, Boo," *AR*, 7 October 1996, 37). While the review by reporter Grace was itself somewhat subdued, at least by *AR* standards, the theme of a war on Western civilization had spread, gaining a new theatre: heaven.

> [*Angels*] is an artistic failure but it bears a powerful revolutionary message. While it elevates the belief current in the "AIDS community" that victims of the disease are holy martyrs, homosexuals and AIDS victims are only one division of Mr. Kushner's vaster army: one that seeks to destroy the very concepts of the law – on earth and in heaven. (K. Grace, "The Lawless Millennium," *AR*, 7 October 1996, 34)

In yet another article in the same edition of *AR*, the Marquis de Sade as well as "radical deconstructionist" Michel Foucault and structuralist Roland Barthes were put forth as evidence of the folly of multiculturalism. These multicultural intellectuals were progenitors and, therefore, promoters of the "AIDS cult," in which the "object is to break down the moral barriers erected against perversity, not for the sake of the perverse, but to destroy the civilization those barriers protect" (K. Grace, "De Sade the Prophet," *AR*, 7 October 1996, 39). The link between multiculturalism and homosexuality was forged on the notion that traditional Western culture was under extreme threat from foreign ideas embodied in those hordes of people who did not belong in Alberta. "Deadly, infected, and contaminating homosexual bodies" was the metaphor that tied all these threatening ideas and people together.

In keeping with the theme of the demise and death of Western civilization, the following week *AR* linked the "hipness" of baldness – which it saw as a "sign of aging, death, debilitation, illness" – with homosexuality in "an instance of mass culture devouring 'alternative' forbidden fruit" ("Naked," *AR* cover, 14 October 1996; C. Cosh, "The Shape of Things to Come," *AR*, 14 October 1996, 26-9). The bald head of "radical deconstructionist" Michel Foucault was pictured alongside the bald heads of other famous and less famous people, all of whom were implicated in homosexuality and taking Alberta down a slippery slope leading to the death of the traditional family, Western civilization, law and order, and (now) heaven.

Alberta Report cover, 14 October 1996

Comparing Alcoholism and Homosexuality: A Yale Psychiatrist Pursues an Incendiary, but Compassionate, Analogy (C. McGovern, *AR*, 11 November 1996, 40)

A Judge Rewrites Alberta's Marriage Law: He Decides the Legislature Will Give Marital Rights to Unmarried Couples (C. Champion, *AR*, 18 November 1996, 28-9)

They'd Rather Go to the Bar: A Red Deer Homosexual Organization Wilts from Lack of Interest (D. Sheremeta, *AR*, 19 November 1996, 36)

A Monument to Political Correctness: Board Members Set Aside Their Hurried Approval of a Vancouver AIDS Memorial (J. Collins, *AR*, 25 November 1996, 36)

The Most Deadly Lifestyle: Roughly One in Six Male Homosexuals Has HIV or AIDS (K. Avram, *AR*, 5 November 1996, 26)

Grease for the Squeakiest Wheel: AIDS Drugs Get Twice as Many New Dollars as Cancer (J. Champion, *AR*, 2 December 1996, 11)

Freedom to Spread Disease: A BC Court Rules That Transmitting HIV Is Not a Crime (R. Brunet, *AR*, 2 December 1996, 29)

Men of Their Word: Promise Keepers Aim to "Re-Civilize" Men – and Salvage Civilization (T. O'Neill with R. Hiebert, *EJ*, 2 December 1996, 36-7)

More Bad News on Single Motherhood: A Statscan Child Health Survey Shows the Strength of Traditional Families (J. Woodard, *AR*, 9 December 1996, 38-9)

Vancouver's Depraved New World: The City Plumbs New Depths of Prostitution, Pornography, and Perversion (R. Brunet, *AR*, 10 March 1997, 16-19)

Diesel Dykes and a Devil Worshipper Named Louise: A Key Witness Said the Lady's Week-Long Visit Might Have Slipped His Mind (L. Sillars, *AR*, 17 March 1997, 24-5)

Abuse Made Me Gay, Now I Have AIDS (C. Champion, *AR*, 23 December 1996, 40-1)

Federal Favours for "Queer Culture": Minister Hedy Fry Says Homosexuals Qualify for Multicult Grants (M. Jenkinson, *AR*, 23 December 1996, 8-9)

The Battle over Gay Sexuality: As Scriptural Belief Dwindles, the Anglicans – and Others – Succumb to Politics (J. Woodard, *AR*, 30 December 1996, 32-3)

If You've Got 'Em, Flaunt 'Em: An Estrogen-Laden Convict Wants a Taxpayer-Funded Sex Change (L. Sillars, *AR*, 6 January 1997, 22-3)

Just Whack 'Em Around – They Love It: A Teacher Charges That Schools Are Overtly Hostile to Young Men (C. Cosh, *AR*, 6 January 1997, 41)

A Costly and Temporary Fix for Reckless Sex: Though AIDS Drug Treatments Are Extending Lives, the Battle Remains Far from Won (J. Woodard, *AR*, 27 January 1996, 33)

Manning Goes Recruiting in Vancouver: A Gay Magazine Tries a Little Straight-Baiting, But the Reform Leader Doesn't Bite (J. Power, *AR*, 3 February 1997, 9)

Legislated Male-Bashing, Tory Style: Alberta will Copy Saskatchewan's Prove-Your-Innocence Domestic Abuse Law (L. Sillars, *AR*, 3 February 1997, 28)

What Odd Messages We'll Hear from the *Globe*, If Its Editor's Expectations Come True (T. Byfield, *AR*, 24 March 1997, 44)

Sexy, Sophisticated, or Smutty? Naked Lesbian Kissing Is Deemed Acceptable for Suppertime TV (D. Sheremata, *AR*, 28 April 1997, 25)

Predatory Pedophiles Enter the War

While the homosexual agenda continued to assault Western civilization, the heavens, and traditional families, according to the *AR*, Promise Keepers, an organization of like-minded men, were bringing salvation to the "rubble of a destroyed Western civilization" by "espousing a high-powered combination of Christianity, commitment to – and leadership of – wife and children, sexual purity, and fellowship with other men" (T. O'Neill with R. Hiebert, "'Especially' No White Males," *EJ*, 2 December 1996, 36). Heterosexual masculinity, Alberta style, would save the world. Women continued to be a large threat, especially single mothers. *AR* writers had uncovered that single mothers, especially young ones, were devastating to traditional family values (J. Woodard, "More Bad News on Single Motherhood," *AR*, 9 December 1996, 38). Ethnic minorities in Alberta who supported the political right were on the rise. This was fine by *AR*, because, even though these people weren't real Albertans, they were at least politically astute (L. Sillars, "The Rise of the Ethnic Right," *AR*, 16 December 1996, 13-14). *AR* discovered that the conspiracy against Western men and boys was worse than could be summed up in the phrase "no white men need apply." More than any other social group, white males were bashed in an overtly hostile world created by radical, powerful, and power-hungry feminists who, of course, were linked to the strident homosexual lobby (L. Sillars, "Legislated Male Bashing," *AR*, 3 February 1997, 28).

These assaults against men were manifest in phobias against a "triune male-referenced God" and, worse, were also perpetrated by other males seduced by the feminist agenda, like United Church theologian Chris Levan of Edmonton (J. Woodard, "From United to Unitarian in One Easy Step," *AR*, 13 January 1997, 34). Male bashing was also evidenced in domestic abuse legislation, which worked against fathers (L. Sillars, "Legislated Male Bashing," *AR*, 3 February 1997, 28). Classrooms were hostile towards males, with "whacking around" being the most common discipline used against male students in kindergarten through to Grade 12 (C. Cosh, "Just Whack 'Em Around – They Love It: A Teacher Charges That Schools Are Overtly Hostile to Young Men," *AR*, 6 January 1997, 41).

> *I think I still live in a traditional masculine role and it's tough for me to have to live in a role like that. It's part of the reason I am going to therapy, so that I do not have to be that kind of mainstream male who dominates women [and] children and cannot show or even have emotions. (Oscar, 1998)*

Lesbians involved in sports also constituted an attack on traditional heterosexual masculinity as these women had "characteristics traditionally taken as male: strength, speed, endurance and aggressiveness" (L. Sillars, "Hockey Pays the Price for Gay Tolerance," *AR*, 20 January 1997, 33). One special *AR* magazine exposing the assault on males included a cover with a butch-femme couple entwined in each other's arms and facing into the shadows. The cover had the following headline: "From Dyke to Diva: Lesbianism Has Become a Sexy and Sophisticated Refuge for Women Who Have Given up on Men," and the issue also contained a feature article on this topic (*AR* cover, 12 May 1996; J. Woodard, "Lesbianism Gets a Makeover," *AR*, 12 May 1997). That lesbians might have sexual desires outside the heterosexual matrix, which did not preclude other kinds of relationships with boys and men, was not countenanced by *AR* reporters (in spite of the earlier *AR* coverage of the lesbian sex show performed by Kiss and Tell).

Further evidence of the spread of male-bashing was found in popular culture, such as the sitcom *Ellen*, starring a lesbian character played by lesbian actor, Ellen Degeneres (J. Woodard, "Lesbianism Gets a Makeover," *AR*, 12 May 1997, 28). Meanwhile "sodomy was salubrious" for gay men because "celibate homos were shown to be five times likelier to attempt suicide than sexually active homos"; therefore, if you're homosexual, then you should "f– as if your life depends on it" (K. Grace, "Salubrious Sodomy," *AR*, 27 January 1997, 15). Strangely, this *AR* imperative to "f–" was considered to be a healthy response for all homosexuals, including lesbians, even though *AR* writers were unclear about whether lesbians could actually "f–."

Other dangers loomed. Witches on the Queen Charlotte Islands in British Columbia terrified normal Christians (R. Skelly, "Cursed by Wiccans," *AR*,

Alberta Report cover, 12 May 1997

11 November 1996, 42-3), and devil-worshipping diesel dykes skulked in Calgary, Alberta (L. Sillars, "Gays Get the Door," *AR*, 17 March 1997, 24-5). Most of the province had become unsafe, as had most of the country. Vancouver, British Columbia, was a modern-day Sodom and Gomorrah rife with "prostitution, pornography, and perversion" (R. Brunet, "Vancouver's Depraved New World," *AR*, 10 March 1997, 16-19). Right-thinking Lethbridge, Alberta, however, knew how to limit moral pollution of the sort that had taken over Vancouver (L. Sillars, "How to Limit Moral Pollution,"

AR, 10 March 1997, 19). Federal MP Svend Robinson of Vancouver was especially vile because he supported the "normalizing of buggery" through lowering the age of consent from eighteen to fourteen (J. Woodard, "The Sex Crime That Disappeared: Today's Laws Permit Most of the Child Abuse Alleged at Maple Leaf Gardens," *AR*, 17 March 1997, 38), while even Reform leader Preston Manning was "recruiting" in that Sodom-like city (J. Power, "Manning Goes Recruiting in Vancouver," *AR*, 3 February 1997, 9), giving the religious right further pause in their support for him and the Reform party. Orphans in Newfoundland had been abused by priests; this had turned them gay, and now they were further victimized because they had AIDS (C. Champion, "Cashing in on Victimhood," *AR*, 23 December 1996, 40). And pedophile Protestant priests were responsible for the "wash-out" lives of boys who were now grown men (L. Sillars, *AR*, 3 February 1997, 36).

Hockey Pays the Price for Gay Tolerance: Thanks to the Courage of NHLer Sheldon Kennedy, the Ugly Truth about Predatory Homosexual Coaches Finally Comes Out (L. Sillars, *AR*, 20 January 1997, 30-4)

Homosexual Predation Afflicts Women's Sports Too. (L. Sillars, *AR*, 20 January 1997, 33)

The National Game Gets Slashed: Critics Conclude the Problem Is Hockey, Not Homosexual Predators (J. Woodard, *AR*, 3 February 1997, 42-3)

The CHA versus the Chicken-Hawks: A New Hockey Policy Shoots Wide on Barring Homosexual Predators (E. Kalbfleisch, *AR*, 16 June 1997, 35)

One small city in Saskatchewan was a particularly vile place as it spawned a scandal that rocked the very foundations of Canadian national identity by assaulting the dignity of hockey and heterosexual manliness. Swift Current, Saskatchewan, became a horror for young males because it made it possible for "homosexual predators, emboldened by a permissive society," to invade the macho world of Canadian ice-hockey via the dressing rooms of junior hockey ("Out of the Closet: Into the Dressing Room," *AR* cover, 20 January 1997). "Over the past decade, Canadians have been scandalized time and again by stories of men groping and sodomizing young males in residential schools, orphanages and boys' clubs. The one place no one expected such abuse to occur was in that last, great bastion of macho culture in Canada: hockey" (L. Sillars, "Hockey Pays the Price for Gay Tolerance," *AR*, 20 January 1997, 30).

The cover of *AR* featuring the above articles shows the figure of a coach with his arm around a young hockey player as they sit on a bench in a dressing room. Both have their backs to the reader. The photo is dark and

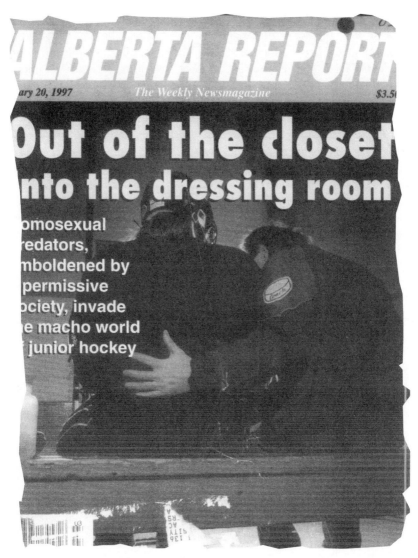

Alberta Report cover, 20 January 1997

shadowy and, when read in relation to the caption about homosexual predators, forecasts abuse in every hockey dressing room across the land. Parents
and other adults must be on guard against this previously unknown danger
to the sexual well-being of their male children. Not only were classrooms
and churches hostile places for males but now even ice-hockey – the most
revered of Canadian sports, typified by the fabled images of fathers bonding

with sons in makeshift ice-rinks all over suburban backyards and homesteads – had become unsafe. *AR* demanded answers as to how the "ravenous homosexual predator ... continued unchecked for so long in the virile, unreconstructed world of hockey" (L. Sillars, "Hockey Pays the Price for Gay Tolerance," *AR*, 20 January 1997, 30). Worse, other incidences of such abuse surfaced closer to home in Alberta, as disclosures were made about Brian Shaw, former head coach of the World Hockey Association's Edmonton Oilers.

AR used its special report to explore what it had long claimed to know was responsible for the battle against Western civilization, the celestial world, law and order, the traditional father-headed family, and now young, straight masculinity. Not surprisingly, *AR* found that "the homosexual issue has blurred the boundaries of sexual behavior and morality" (L. Sillars, "Hockey Pays the Price for Gay Tolerance," *AR*, 20 January 1997, 31). One of its "experts," Gwen Landolt of REAL Women, warned readers that this was just the beginning of an epidemic of such disclosures. She opined that, "given the growing social acceptance of homosexuality, Canadians should brace themselves for more deviants to pop up behind the benches of young hockey players" (31).

As further evidence of the link between human rights for homosexuals and a burgeoning world of homosexual pedophilia, *AR* reported that "Toronto homosexual Gerald Hannon," a former journalism instructor and vocal advocate of so-called "intergenerational sex ... thought it strange that a society which willingly grants legal rights to homosexuals would react in disgust to the image of Graham James pressing his naked body against a ... 14-year old" (L. Sillars, "Hockey Pays the Price for Gay Tolerance," *AR*, 20 January 1997, 31). *AR* exploited the hockey scandal by conflating sexual abuse of children with the sexual abuse of a fourteen-year-old youth. The idea that youth may be sexually active was not countenanced, in spite of evidence about sexually transmitted disease and teenage pregnancy, which certainly indicate otherwise. By relying on the shadowy spectral figure of the homosexual pedophile to explain coach Graham James, *AR* again attempted to achieve its goal of boosting sales through "gutsy" and controversial reporting.

Strangulation by the Charter: Only a Lucky Few Have Benefited from 15 Years of Judicial Supremacy (J. Woodard, *AR*, 5 May 1997, 20-1)

Lesbianism Gets a Makeover: ABC and Disney Approve a Prime-Time Homosexual, While the Media Applauds (J. Woodard, *AR*, 12 May 1997, 28-31)

Rubbing Out Rubbers: Alberta Health Abandons Condom Advocacy, as Homosexuals Abandon "Safe Sex" (J. Woodard, *AR*, 19 May 1997, 42-3)

In Search of the Rural Gay: Alberta Planned Parenthood Pushes Teenaged Homosexuality (J. Woodard, *AR*, 26 May 1997, 33)

A Few of His Favourite Things: Edmonton's Gay Councillor Decries – and Confirms – a Stereotype (M. Milke, *AR*, 16 June 1997, 15)

Embracing Diversity – with Tiny Plastic Arms: Popular New Dolls Range from the Disabled to the Depraved (D. Sheremeta, *AR*, 7 July 1997, 42)

Smart Homosexuals Vote Conservative: A Prominent Canadian Tory Makes the Oxymoronic Case for Gaycons (E. Kalbfleisch, *AR*, 28 July 1997, 31)

No Censors Here! Submissions May Be Parodies, Askew Retellings, Dark Versions or Modern Adaptations but, Most Importantly, Must Be Explicitly EROTIC. Preference Will Be Given to Gay, Lesbian, Transgendered, Multi-Gendered, and Radical Sexualities (such as S/M) (K. Grace, *AR*, 11 August 1997, 17)

The West's Gay-Friendly "Conservative" Parties Had Better Wake Up (L. Byfield, *AR*, 11 August 1997, 2)

Disney versus Christendom: As a Church Boycott Spreads, the Family Entertainment Conglomerate Finds out It's a Small World after All (D. Di Sabatino, *AR*, 18 August 1997, 33-4)

Sex and the Single Priest (J. Woodard, *AR*, 18 August 1997, 34)

A Head-Tax on Orientals: Alberta's Asians Suffer a Growing Addiction to Gambling (D. Di Sabatino, *AR*, 25 August 1997, 30)

How to Make Men into Mice: The Noble Sport of Hunting Is Vanishing from Our Increasingly Feminized, Fractured, Futile Culture (L. Sillars, *AR*, 8 September 1997, 28-30)

Les bums de Banff: The Resort Copes with a Plague of Quebecois Tramps (L. Sillars, *AR*, 15 September 1997, 16)

Proud to Escape Homosexuality: But in BC, Ex-Gays Were Not Allowed in a "Pride Parade" (S. Parker Jr., *AR*, 22 September 1997, 38)

Of Drag Queens and Doctors' Wives: Two New Memoirs by Edmontonians Are Diversely Countercultural (P. Bunner, *AR*, 1 December 1997, 43)

The War for the Children: An International Child Abductor Sues for Custody (L. Sillars, *AR*, 17 November 1997, 32)

Furious Debate over Foreskins: A Medical Ethicist Challenges Parents' Rights to Authorize Circumcision (L. Sillars, *AR*, 17 November 1997, 34-5)

An Epidemic of Shortsightedness: Most Popular AIDS "Solutions" Only Reinforce Destructive Behaviours (R. Hudson, *AR*, 17 November 1997, 35-6)

Punishment for BC's Pedophile Principal: A Homosexual School Official Is Fired amid New Accusations of Sex with Students (S. Parker Jr., *AR*, 24 November 1997, 24-5)

The Simpson Phenomenon: A Family-Values Firebrand Is Shaking up BC (D. Cunningham, *AR*, 24 November 1997, 34-5)

The Feminization of the Liberal Arts: UBC's Equity Shrugs off News of a Huge Pro-Female Gender Gap (T. O'Neill, *AR*, 24 November 1997, 36-7)

Vancouver's Growing HIV Epidemic: The Gay Aversion to Condoms Puzzles Experts (R. Brunet, *AR*, 13 October 1997, 44-5)

Compulsive Permissivism: Vancouver's Liberal Drug-Addict AIDS Strategy Is Being Pushed toward "an Unprecedented Catastrophe" (R. Brunet, *AR*, 20 October 1997, 31-2)

The High Price of Gay Sensitivity: The Red Cross Is Found Financially Liable for Helping Infect Canadians with HIV (P. Donnelly, *AR*, 27 October 1997, 26)

Predatory Museums in Red Deer
According to *AR*, new gun control legislation constituted yet another form of male-bashing ("Manhood's Last Stand," *AR* cover, 8 September 1996). Society was becoming "more urbanized, feminized and eco-neurotic" (L. Sillars, "How to Make Men into Mice," *AR*, 8 September 1997, 28). Moreover, according to *AR*, the right of traditional families to own their children was being undermined. These interfering outsiders included medical ethicists who called into question the necessity of circumcising male infants (L. Sillars, "Furious Debate on Foreskins," *AR*, 17 November 1997, 34-5). Given that, to *AR*, gays were suspect males, it was not surprising that, according to the magazine, unlike real men "gays felt they had been cheated" by the removal of their foreskins (34). A further assault on masculinity was manifest in the dismissal of fathers' rights as mothers abducted children (32). As if this were not bad enough, toys could no longer be counted on to either produce gender appropriate behaviours or to reveal those who were deviant. "Popular new dolls range from disabled to the depraved ... The doll world is becoming not only multicultural, but more raunchy ... Big Dyke Barbie shows off her pierced nose, while Hooker Barbie wears a negligee and carries a condom. Drag Queen Barbie is actually Barbie companion Malibu Ken acting out in wig and gown" (D. Sheremeta, "Embracing Diversity – with Tiny Plastic Arms," *AR*, 7 July 1997, 42).

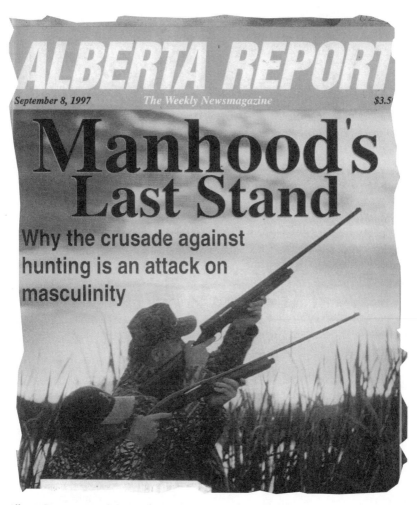

Alberta Report cover, 8 September 1997

Against this sinister backdrop, in August 1997 the provincial government was "caught" funding a project to collect reminiscences from local gay men and lesbians in Red Deer. A moral mini-panic erupted and continued for a month, with letters and articles in local and national newspapers as well as statements made by provincial and federal politicians. MLA Stockwell Day opened fire by declaring that "a museum ... was not the appropriate place to champion the cause of gay rights" (D. Frum, "Politician Caught Red-Handed Speaking Up for Moral Views: Stockwell Day's Courage under Fire," *Financial Post*, 26 August 1997, 17). The *Financial Post*'s David Frum para-phrased Day's concerns that "the people of Red Deer would be offended by this use of public money and a public facility – especially since one of the missions of this facility is the education of the young" (ibid.). Day stated further that the grant "legitimizes a lifestyle choice that doesn't deserve this kind of attention" (F. McNair, "Reform MP Supports Stand on Gay Grant," *EJ*, 25 August 1997, A7).

> *People tell me that I'm a very enjoyable kind of person, very happy, and I think it is just my natural way. I came from a family, you know, my mother's side especially, where storytelling is a big thing, and my granny is a very good storyteller. I kind of picked up her talent, and now its finally coming out, especially with friends. (Jack, 1998)*

Stockwell Day and fellow Red Deer MLA Victor Doerksen demanded, on behalf of their constituents, that the museum return the money and that Community Development Minister Shirley McClellan cancel the grant ("Treasurer Wants Gay Study Grant Money Returned," *EJ*, 16 August 1997, A1). Both claimed that "the gay-history project offends the city's traditional values" (L. Goyette, "Albertans Think for Themselves, Thanks," 20 August 1997, A14). MP for Yellowhead, Cliff Breitkreuz, declared: "as you know, only 30 years ago it [homosexuality] was in the Criminal Code, and people were prosecuted if they were caught sodomizing ... it is strange to go from one extreme to another in such a short time" (F. McNair, "Reform MP Supports Stand on Gay Grant," *EJ*, 25 August 1997, A7). No one pressed Breitkreuz as to why he thought people telling their stories should be equated with sodomy.

An *Edmonton Journal* editorial indicated that "gay Albertans pay taxes, vote, even buy lottery tickets," and it charged Day with "gay-bashing" and "catering to some narrow-minded constituents and his own prejudices" ("Stockwell Day Goes Gay-Bashing Again," 19 August 1997, A12). Day responded in a letter to the editor, saying that the *Edmonton Journal* had engaged in name-calling when it described his actions (*EJ*, 25 August 1997, A9).

If the Red Deer museum was going to go forward with such a project, then Link Byfield would offer his advice on more provocative titles for exhibits.

> Suppose it wanted to demonstrate the evils of homosexuality, and all the compulsive and revolting things homosexuals do with urine and feces, and explain in graphs and diagrams why they carry such an astonishing array of intestinal parasites and venereal diseases. Would she [McClellan] grant that too? Would we have fun-loving "Homo on the Range" in Red Deer, but up in Lacombe "The Perils of Perversion" – both sponsored and endorsed by the Alberta government? ... If Wild Pansies of Red Deer catches the public

fancy, fine. ("If Red Deer Wants to Study Gays, That's Their Business – Not the Taxpayer's," *AR*, 8 September 1997, 2)

Given the government's opposition to including sexual orientation in the Alberta Individual Rights Protection Act, it was disingenuous of *AR* to suggest that homosexuality was sponsored and endorsed by the Alberta government. A consequence of the attention given to the Red Deer and District history project was a boost in visitors to both Red Deer and the museum (M. Sadava, "Klein Won't Pull Grant for Gay History Study," *EJ*, 26 August 1997, A6). This points to one of the ironies of *AR*'s ongoing coverage of sexual minorities in the province: by taking up homosexuality in the way it did, it produced a very public profile for issues that would not otherwise have arisen. In fact, one could easily argue that *AR*'s high-profile coverage constituted "endorsement," and a weird form of sponsorship, of homosexuality.

Pedophilia Is Dragged from the Closet: A Rash of Arrests Highlights a Perversion Little Understood, Except That It's Disproportionately Homosexual (J. Woodard, *AR*, 6 January 1997, 34-5)

The Sin Is to Talk about It: *Maclean's* Drops an Accomplished Homosexual from Its Annual Honour Roll (R. Owen, *AR*, 6 January 1997, 28)

Gay Foster Parent to Fight Gov't Policy: Lesbian Foster Mom Angry about Ban on "Non-Traditional" Families (C. Gillis, *AR*, 18 March 1997, A6)

Insistence on "Tradition" No favor to Foster Kids: Gay, Lesbian Foster Parents Need Not Apply (L. Goyette, *EJ*, 18 March 1997, A13)

Lesbian Mom Appeals Provincial Ruling (C. Gillis, *EJ*, 21 March 1997, A6)

Virtually Normal Isn't Normal Enough: Alberta Will Maintain Its No-Homosexual Foster Care Policy (R. Daniel, *AR*, 7 April 1997, 9)

The Fight for the Family Goes Global (H. Dykxhoorn, *AR*, 21 April 1997, 42)

The Unnatural Law Party: Alberta's Conservatives Waver in Their Stand against Homosexual Foster Care, and the Consequence May Be Far-Reaching (J. Avram, *AR*, 5 May 1997, 11)

Telegraphing a Retreat? Alberta May No Longer Oppose Gay Foster Parents (K. Torrance, *AR*, 23 June 1997, 12)

Gay Foster Mom Vows Court Battle: Barred from Caring for Kids (M. MacKinnon, *EJ*, 15 July 1997, B1)

Protect Foster Kids from Gay Discrimination – Oberg (T. Arnold, *EJ*, 16 July 1997, A1)

Drop Anti-Gay Fight, Province Urged (T. Arnold, *EJ*, 17 July 1997, B3)

Oberg's Twisted Logic on Gay Parenting: Perverse Gov't Bias Still Lurking in the Closet (M. Lisac, *EJ*, 17 July 1997, A10)

Doublespeak by Minister on Gay Issue (G. Filax, *EJ*, 20 July 1997, A9)

Gay Foster Parents Can Provide Excellent Care (A. Williams, *EJ*, 22 July 1997, A7)

Klein Blacklist Includes Most Albertans (A. Dashtgard, *EJ*, 24 July 1997, A11)

If Gays, Lesbians Want Kids, Let Them Make Their Own: Discrimination Isn't the Same as Bigotry (P. Menzies, *AR*, 25 July 1997, A 17)

Province Has No Policy on Gay Fostering, Says Klein (T. Arnold, *EJ*, 25 July 1997, A6)

The Tale of the Blue-Eyed Albertans (L. Goyette, *EJ*, 26 July 1997, G1)

Double Disadvantage: Discrimination against Them Described as "Alberta's Double Disadvantage" (Jean Forest, *EJ*, 28 July 1997, A7)

Questions Can Find Who's a Fit Foster Parent (C. Malmo, *EJ*, 1 August 1997, A15)

Opening the Door to Gay Parents: Klein Approves Homosexual Foster Families While the Hard-Liners in His Caucus Run for Cover (*AR* cover, 11 August 1997)

Silence of the Lambs (*AR*, 11 August 1997, 1)

Alberta's New Family Policy: Klein Capitulates on Homosexual Foster Parenting and Most Right-Wing MLAs Remain Obediently Mute (K. Torrance, *AR*, 11 August 1997, 10-15)

Welcome to Super Unnatural BC: Thus Neutered, the Law against Gay Adoption Was Repealed Four Months Later (C. Cosh and D. DeCloet, *AR*, 11 August 1997, 12-13)

Oberg Hasn't Changed Mind on Gays (L. Johnsrude, *EJ*, 3 October 1997, B7)

Dr. Oberg Gets His Answer: Activists Trot out Bogus "Evidence" to Support Homosexual Fostering (J. Woodard, *AR*, 6 October 1997, 12)

Report on Gay Parenting Cites Discredited Doctor: Conclusions Strongly Negative towards Gays, Critics Say (C. Rusnell, *EJ*, 18 October 1997, B4)

The Judges Will Decide: Oberg Can't Make up His Mind on Gay Foster Parenting (K. Torrance, *AR*, 20 October 1997, 13)

Political Agenda behind Study: Assess Gay Parents as Individuals (Editorial, *EJ*, 21 October 1997, A14)

The Trouble with Ms. T: Incompetent Media Coverage Aside, Fatherless Foster-Parenting Is Second Rate (J. Woodard, *AR*, 3 November 1997, 31)

Gay Mom Loses Battle for More Foster Children (L. Johnsrud, *EJ*, 19 November 1997, A6)

Lesbian Foster Mom Fears Fallout from Publicity (J. Danylchuk, *EJ*, 1 April 1998, A5)

Judge Decides Gay Foster Mom May Be Named (R. Henderson, *EJ*, 7 April 1998, A6)

Open Letter to an Albertan Named Ms. T: Foster Mother Is a Victim of Alberta's Toxic Homophobia (L. Goyette, *EJ*, 8 April 1998, A14)

The T Stands for Teresa – Teresa O'Riordan: A Morinville, Alta., Lesbian Foster Mother Loses Her Plea to Overturn Public Policy Anonymously (P. Donnelly, *AR*, 20 April 1998, 29)

Ministerial Review of Same-Sex Foster Families "Fear-Mongering": Oberg Not Qualified to Overrule Professional Staff, Opposition Says (A. Jeffs, *EJ*, 25 March 1999, A8)

Predatory Parents

Throughout 1997 yet another battle regarding sexual minorities in Alberta emerged. Ms. T, a foster parent, made public a new ban on "non-traditional" families fostering children and youth – a ban directed by Social Services Minister Stockwell Day. Beginning in 1996 the government, under the auspices of Day, had been tinkering with ideas like the "natural family" (L. Goyette, "Insistence on 'Tradition' No Favor to Foster Kids," *EJ*, 18 March 1997, A14). The *Edmonton Journal* reported on a 13 January 1997 letter sent by Day to an advocacy group representing foster parents. In this letter Day wrote: "In those instances where non-traditional families have had children placed with them in the past, we will not be placing more children in these homes ... however the children currently in these homes will not be removed" (C. Gillis, "Lesbian Mom Appeals Provincial Ruling," *EJ*, 21 March 1997, A6).

Day did not provide a definition of non-traditional families, but it soon became clear that Ms. T, who, over a seventeen-year period, had been the "mother of several birth children and foster mother to over 70 foster children" was not part of a traditional family when she was denied foster children in January 1997. Ms. T decided to contest the decision through the government's appeal process, arguing that "it's discriminating on the basis of sexual orientation and denying children access to potentially stable foster homes" (C. Gillis, "Lesbian Mom Appeals Provincial Ruling," *EJ*, 21 March 1997, A6). Yet another home-grown moral panic was under way in Alberta. In an astonishing admission, made on 16 July 1997, new social services minister Lyle Oberg stated that the reason for "disallowing gays and lesbians from being foster parents" was "discrimination" (T. Arnold, "Protect Foster Kids from Gay Discrimination – Oberg," *EJ*, 16 July 1997, A1). According to Oberg, since gay and lesbian communities indicated that they were discriminated against, he did not want to subject children in their care to this sort of thing. He failed to note that his government's policy on special treatment for sexual minorities was one of the constitutive features of that discrimination.

Editorials and letters to the editor filled both daily papers in Calgary and Edmonton, Alberta's two largest cities. Taking up the idea pulsing through the gay foster parents debate, Mark Lisac noted in his 17 July 1997 article in the *Edmonton Journal* that the "suggestive link of sexual orientation to child molesting takes us into the rough territory of slanderous bullying" and is part of the "perverse gov't bias still lurking in the closet" ("Oberg's Twisted Logic on Gay Parenting," 17 July 1997, A10). In a commentary of 25 July 1997, Peter Menzies wrote that "if gays, lesbians want kids, let them make their own" (*EJ*, A17). Menzies, like so many others, did not seem to realize that many lesbians and gays do have children and that heterosexual parents "make" sexual minority children and youth.

> *The one thing my mom mourns – well, because I am queer – is that she would never be a grandmother. I told her that lesbians were having children all the time now and I would as well when I find the right lesbian and have my career up and going. (Chastity, 1998)*

On 11 August 1997 *AR* devoted a "special" issue, complete with magazine cover, to Ms. T ("Opening the Door to Gay Parents"). The cover, like its murky-looking predecessors "Dyke to Diva" (12 May 1997) and hockey coach predator "Out of the Closet, into the Dressing Room: Homosexual Predators, Emboldened by a Permissive Society, Invade the Macho World of Junior Hockey" (20 January 1997), featured a shadowy pair of gay men facing forward yet lurking in a doorway. They are entwined with one another while their free arms are extended, offering an invitation to a small child who is in the forefront of the picture. The child is poised in hesitation at the threshold, uncertain as to whether he/she should enter. *AR* represented the two adults as male, even though the foster parent who brought this issue to the

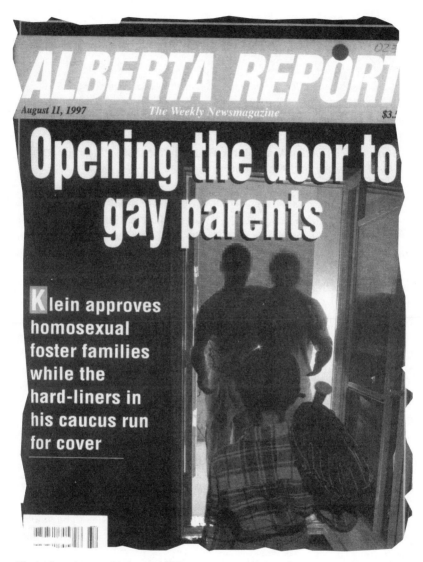

Alberta Report cover, 11 August1997

public eye was a woman. Since lesbian predators do not have the same cultural resonance within homophobic discourse as do gay male predators, *AR* elided lesbians with gay men. With the words, "Klein Approves Homosexual Foster Families While the Hard-Liners in His Caucus Run for Cover," *AR* assigned blame to both the premier and homosexuals ("Opening the Door to Gay Parents," *AR* cover, 11 August 1997). Inside, the caption "Silence of the Lambs" greeted the reader, alongside a mini-copy of the cover. Invoking both the Bible and a popular film, the message suggested that innocent children are going to be slaughtered in this latest homosexual war against traditional families in Alberta.

> *Like, TV sets you up for failure. Like, look at these picture-perfect families, and look how they got their lives together after somebody got out of the Betty Ford Center or after somebody died. Well, that is not true. You can go years, if somebody dies you are close to, or whatever. You go through years of heartache and heartbreak. Like* Little House on the Prairie. *Well, it's little joke on the prairie. (Michel, 1998)*

On 20 April 1998 *AR*, along with other media, released Ms. T's name and the name of the town in which she lived, publicly outing her. Given their 1993 (T. Byfield, "Fie upon that Dastardly Tory Who Won't Come Out of the Closet," *AR*, 14 June 1993, 52) and 1997 (R. Owen, "The Sin Is to Talk about It," *AR*, 6 January 1997, 28) stand on keeping sexual orientation a private matter, this contradiction revealed the punitive manner in which *AR* was willing to treat sexual minorities. In her "Open Letter to an Albertan Named Ms T," in which she refused to out Ms. T, *Edmonton Journal* writer Linda Goyette summarized how this woman had been treated by *AR*, commenting, "bigotry is a chosen lifestyle" ("Open Letter to an Albertan Named Ms T," *EJ*, 8 April 1998, A14). One effect of this bigotry was that, even with the shortage of adequate foster care homes, needy children and youth were denied the care of one excellent foster parent – Ms. T – for the years 1997 and 1998.

> *I heard about the foster parent. She had been a foster parent for eighteen years and raised twenty-four kids and now all of a sudden she can't. It's like going through the whole foster care system, and I have first-hand knowledge, of how much it [homosexuality of foster parent] is not even an issue. It is not even something that needs to be considered. That really gets to me. (Virginia, 1998)*

Predatory Teachers, Supreme Judgments, and a Seismic Moral Panic
Each of the moral panics about homosexuality cultivated by *AR* and facilitated by elected provincial government members occurred within the context of the decade-long *Vriend* case *(Vriend v. Alberta)*. In an exceptional move on 2 April 1998 the Supreme Court of Canada altered the Alberta human rights code by reading in sexual orientation as a protected category, thus disallowing the provincial government the opportunity to continue opposition to equality rights enshrined in the Charter of Rights and Freedoms by dragging out revisions to its human rights legislation.

Alberta Report cover, 17 November 1997

On 17 November 1997 *AR* did a special feature on *Vriend* entitled, "Winners and Losers," which turned homosexuals into the ultimate predators as now even the unborn had become prey to homosexual rights. The caption underneath the headline stated, "Why do Canada's courts invent charter rights for gays and not for babies?" This was inserted between a picture of Vriend and his partner and a classic picture of a fetus. Inside the magazine, articles included, "The Chosen and the Choosers: Once Again the Supreme Court Embraces Gays and Abandons Babies"; "From Perverse to Macabre";

"When Vriend Wins, So Does Graham James"; "The Slavery-Abortion Parallel"; and "A Supreme Display of Judicial Prejudice."

Given the negative national attention accorded to the Province of Alberta during the Supreme Court hearing of *Vriend, AR* had work to do in its war against homosexuality in advance of the Court's decision. On 15 December 1997 *AR* featured an advertisement entitled "Gay 101 in Our Schools?" It was addressed to concerned Christians, asking them if they knew what their children were being taught about homosexuality in schools and whether these innocents knew how to protect themselves (back inside cover). A wide-eyed little girl stares out at readers and unknown dangers – an image clearly meant to raise parental fears. For a small donation readers could join the Christian Heritage Party of Canada and receive a book entitled *Homosexuality and the Politics of Truth*. A similar add appeared on 9 February 1998, this one entitled "Guess Why Trouble-Makers Like Delwin Vriend Always Win in Court?" This time readers were being asked to support Alberta Federation for Women United for Families, headed by Hermina Dykxhoorn. Dykxhoorn's Family Federation is "against easy divorce, permissive sex-ed, radical gender feminism, the normalization of homosexuality and any other issue that threatens families," and it wanted donations (Alberta Federation of Women United for Families, *AR*, 9 February 1998, 21).

Gay Rights Grind Ever-Onward: The Crown Surrenders a Key Point on "Spousal Benefits." (J. Woodard, *AR*, 10 November 1997, 26)

Truth Becomes a Hate Crime (J. Woodard, *AR*, 10 November 1997, 26)

How Did It Happen That We Have No Right to Life, But Do Have a Right to Sodomy? (L. Byfield, *AR*, 17 November 1997, 2)

The *Vriend* Case Isn't Simply about Rights, But about Who Really Runs the Country (L. Byfield, *AR*, 15 December 1997, 52)

Rumblings of a Counter-Revolution: Alberta's Justice Minister Blames Politicians for the Rising Tide of Judicial Activism (J. Woodard, *AR*, 19 January 1998, 10-14)

Hold Hands or Flunk: A UVic Grad Fights Being Labelled a Homophobe (S. Parker Jr., *AR*, 19 January 1998, 42-3)

Scapegoating the Indian Residential Schools: The Noble Legacy of Hundreds of Christian Missionaries Is Sacrificed to Political Correctness (P. Donnelly, *AR*, 26 January 1998, 6-11)

On 19 January 1998 *AR* featured an article concerning "judicial activism," along with a photograph of a stern-looking Jon Havelock, provincial justice minister. *AR* fretted over appointments made in backrooms with input from "an array of feminist, aboriginal, Jewish, gay and criminal-rights activists" (J. Woodard, "Rumblings of a Counter-Revolution! Alberta's Justice Minister Blames Politicians for the Rising Tide of Judicial Activism," *AR*, 19 January 1998, 10). The problem of judicial activism, according to Havelock and *AR*, was that the Supreme Court was made up of the wrong kind of people.

AR spelled out the remedy for its readership should the Supreme Court rule in favour of *Vriend:* that remedy was to pressure MLAs to invoke Section 33 of the Charter of Rights and Freedoms – the notwithstanding clause. Not only would this remove the threat of *Vriend*, the individual homosexual who stood for all homosexuals, but it would also, according to federal

---

28 January 1991
Vriend is fired from King's College for being a homosexual.

27 November 1993
Vriend takes his case to the Alberta Court of Queen's Bench.

13 April 1994
Justice Anne Russell rules that Alberta's human rights law is inconsistent with the Canadian Charter of Rights and Freedoms and that the Individual Rights Protection Act must include sexual orientation.

5 May 1994
Alberta government decides to appeal Vriend.

23 February 1996
Alberta Court of Appeal rules in favour of the government in a deicison by Justice John McClung.

6 March 1996
Vriend decides to appeal to the Supreme Court of Canada, which agrees to hear the case.

4 November 1997
Supreme Court hearings on *Vriend* begin. Court hears from seventeen intervenors, including religious and civil liberties groups.

2 April 1998
Supreme Court rules that Alberta's human rights law is unconstitutional and must protect people from discrimination based on their sexual orientation.

Reform MP Jason Kenney and *AR*, "[begin] the recovery of democracy" (J. Woodard, *AR*, 19 January 1998, 14). Provincial treasurer Stockwell Day indicated that the province might use the notwithstanding clause (A. Jeffs, "Religious Groups Urge Government to Defy Ruling," *EJ*, 31 March 1998, A1), and Premier Ralph Klein mused that the Supreme Court decision could have a financial impact on the Alberta government (A. Jeffs and L. Johnsrude, "Gay Rights Could Cost, Says Treasurer," *EJ*, 1 April 1998, A6). Both these warnings indicate that the Alberta government sensed it was going to lose at the Supreme Court.

> Here's to You, Mr. Robinson: It Turns out the Homosexual MP's Young Cuban Playmate Has Been Allowed to Travel Free as His "Spouse" (T. Bloedow, *AR*, 2 February 1998, 11)

> Human Rights Is One of BC's Few Growth Industries (D. DeCloet, *AR*, 2 February 1998, 50)

> So Much for Graphic, How-To Sex Education: A Long-Term Rise in Teen Pregnancy Leaves More Girls in Misery and Conservatives Feeling Vindicated (P. Hansard, *AR*, 16 February 1998, 25)

> Experts in Their Fields: Ottawa Pays a Gay Lobbyist to Survey Gay Bashing (D. Cunningham, *AR*, 23 February 1998, 7)

> Cupid Is a Homophobe: Langara College Is Ridiculed for Banning a Valentine's Day Poster (K. Torrance, *AR*, 2 March 1998, 34-5)

> Apart from Gambling and Balanced Budgets, What Exactly Does Ralph Klein Believe In? (L. Byfield, *AR*, 23 March 1998, 2)

> So What about Opting out on *Vriend*? (P. Donnelly, *AR*, 30 March 1998, 12)

> Oh, Those Wily Coyotes: Farmers Suffer a Reign of Terror in Smoky Lake Thanks to a Warm Winter (D. Sheremeta, *AR*, 30 March 1998, 23)

> Opting out an Option if Public Consents, Day Says (A. Jeffs, *AR*, 31 March 1998, A1)

In April 1998, in a stunning 8-1 decision, the Supreme Court of Canada ruled in favour of Delwin Vriend and against the Province of Alberta.

> The Supreme Court of Canada has rebuked the Alberta government for evading its democratic duty to prevent discrimination against all Albertans, including gays and lesbians. In a unanimous decision released Thursday, the court ruled that legal protections must immediately be made available to the province's homosexual community. It ended a seven-year battle by con-

cluding that sexual orientation must be "read in," or assumed to be part of, the Individual's Rights Protection Act as a prohibited ground of discrimination ... the deliberate exclusion was not an oversight. The denial of equal rights reinforces stereotypes that gays and lesbians are less deserving and less worthy, he [Cory] said. It "sends a strong and sinister message ... It could well be said that it is tantamount to condoning or even encouraging discrimination against lesbians and gay men. (N. Ovenden, "Supreme Court Delivers Rebuke," *EJ*, 3 April 1998, A3)

Hunt J.A. concluded that "[g]iven these considerations and the context here, it is my opinion that the failure to extend protection to homosexuals under the *IRPA* can be seen as a form of government action that is tantamount to approving ongoing discrimination against homosexuals. Thus, in this case, legislative silence results in the drawing of a distinction" (Hunt J.A. in *Vriend v. Alberta*, 17/47, 2 April 1998).

I was dressed in drag but had to take the bus to my party. This guy started harassing me, calling me a faggot and homo, and he was going to kick my fucking butt, and he said, "You're my fucking bitch," so I moved to the front of the bus. The driver's, like, "This person, guy, this human being has rights. Just as many rights as you do. Just read the Charter of Rights and Freedoms Act. Just because he is dressed like this does not mean that you have the right to pick on him. People are allowed to express themselves any way they wish." I still know the bus driver's name and number, and I am going to phone the transit commission and tell them what a wonderful guy he is. (Michel, 1998)

The Supreme Court clearly stated that the Alberta government's action constituted state-produced and state-sanctioned discrimination and that, in fact, provincial "silence" on the part of elected representatives had resulted in the drawing of a distinction, the creation of a special status. Victory for sexual minority Albertans was short-lived, however, as Premier Ralph Klein decided to wait a week, consulting with his caucus, who were to hear from their constituents regarding whether or not to invoke the notwithstanding clause.

The week exploded with homophobic diatribes against sexual minority Albertans. The proliferation of hateful discourse that followed the Supreme Court ruling was the culmination of years of government resistance together with that of organized anti-gay lobbies, including the Canada Family Action Coalition headed by Roy Beyer; Calgary's Parents Rights Association; the Medicine Hat Citizens' Impact Coalition; Alberta Pro-Life; the Alberta Federation of Women United for the Family led by Hermina Dykxhoorn, feminist watcher; and University of Calgary professor Ted Morton and his tiny Alberta Civil Society Association;[1] and, of course, *AR* (J. Woodard, "A Rich, Educated, Unpersecuted Elite," *AR*, 20 April 1998, 13). Beyer cited fears that "the ruling could be used to protect polygamy, bestiality and pedophilia," and a local Alberta Federation of Women United for the Family president, Cory Morcos believed that "accepting the ruling [would] erode family values." Both called for Albertans to flood MLA offices with demands to invoke the notwithstanding clause (A. Jeffs, "Religious Groups Urge Government to Defy Ruling," *EJ*, 3 April 1998, A3).

Elected representatives made public statements. For example, Lac La Biche-St. Paul MLA Paul Langevin said: "People know where I stand on the gay rights issue, I believe it's a moral issue and I'm not prepared to support gay rights this time" (L. Johnsrude, "Gay Rights Upheld," *EJ*, 3 April 1998, A9). Environment Minister Ty Lund commented, "My constituency is very, very upset that unelected judges are telling elected politicians what to do," and he added that his constituents believed in law and order (R. Pedersen, "Gay Rights Ruling Sparks Rural Uproar," *EJ*, 5 April 1998, A1). Unprecedented displays of hatred and vitriol were unleashed in the province. Members of the provincial government were particularly culpable with regard to placing queer Albertans at risk in such a public way.[2]

The moral panic in the wake of *Vriend* went beyond even Premier Klein's wildest imaginings. He referred to the volume of hate as "appalling faxes and phone calls," along with form and handwritten letters that, "quite frankly make your stomach churn" (L. Johnsrude, "No 'Special Rights': Klein," *EJ*, 8 April 1998, A1, 20). Thousands of calls and letters arrived in the premier's office and the offices of MLAs. Opponents of the ruling launched a newspaper and television ad campaign, which argued that inclusion of sexual orientation in the IRPA would promote homosexuality and weaken the family. Talk show hosts entertained the spewing of hate from anyone with an opinion.

"'I don't want to see them, I don't want to smell them, I don't want anything to do with them,'" the caller said of gays, the disgust palatable in his voice" (J. Geiger, "Anti-Gay Tirades Spew Hatred Most Foul," *EJ*, 12 April 1998, F4).

A week later, Klein, flanked by cabinet ministers McClellan and Havelock, declared that the province would *not* invoke the notwithstanding clause. It would, however, place "fences" against the pursuit of gay rights beyond those pertaining to housing and employment issues. The Alberta government placed an advertisement entitled "Facts about Alberta's Human Rights Laws and the *Vriend* Decision" in all daily newspapers around the province in an attempt to explain the limitations of the decision and, it hoped, to allay fears (Government of Alberta, *EJ*, 15 April 1998, A7). *AR* objected that Albertans were opposed to the premier's position; it was as though queer

Albertans were not Albertans. The 20 April 1998 issue featured a special report and a cover entitled "Ralph's New Friends," featuring Delwin Vriend and his partner smiling in front of the legislative building in Edmonton.

In the same *AR* issue, 20 April 1998, there was another call for donations and action, this time from Roy Beyer's Canada Family Action Coalition (CFAC). The advertisement, which was entitled "It's Not Too Late! – If Vriend Wins ... Who Loses?" stated that "the natural family, the fabric of our society, will be seriously undermined" (36). The ad disingenuously charged that Vriend was fired for violating the college's policy regarding sex outside of marriage. CFAC, like the Alberta Federation of Women United for the Family (AFWUF), continued to deny that queer people like Vriend came from families much like their own.

AR patriarch, founder, and president Ted Byfield denounced Klein's decision to not invoke the notwithstanding clause in *Vriend* as "probably his most grievous decision ever" (*AR*, 20 April 1998, 44).

> Why is this issue so divisive? I think it's because this particular activity, among males anyway, revolts and offends many people. The spectacle of men coupling, while certainly absurd and the subject of snickers and jokes from the Greeks onward, many also find repulsive. They see it as a perversion of nature, like garbage in a river of toxic blight on a forest, as something unnatural, something not intended to be (T. Byfield, "If Klein Has Managed to Split The Right in Alberta, This Is Not Inconsequential," *AR*, 20 April 1998, 44)

Significantly, 20 April's issue was the same one in which the *AR* outed Ms. T.

On 4 May 1998 there was yet another CFAC advertisement in *AR*, this time calling for a "public rally for the family," at which Kari Simpson was to advise concerned Albertans about "the Vriend decision: what it means – what we must do" (Public Rally for the Family," 32). The list of potential dangers included threats to education, children and youth, and the traditional family as well as the likelihood of gay adoption, gay public exhibitionism, and even the curtailment of traditional free speech. The next page contained a CFAC petition calling on Premier Klein to use the "notwithstanding clause" (33). In the same issue, the *AR*'s token queer voice, John Mckellar of Homosexuals Opposed to Pride Extremism (HOPE), declared his group to be pro-civilization and anti-special rights for gays (J. Woodard, "Gays for Family Values," *AR*, 4 May 1998, 14).

In her public rally (read: rant), anti-gay activist Kari Simpson summarized the aftermath of the years during which the *Vriend* decision worked its way through the courts: "Make no mistake, people ... it's a war" (K. Steel, "A Firebrand from BC," *AR*, 25 May 1998, 10). Readers of "radical deconstructionist"

Michel Foucault (1980b, 14) may recall this statement: "the history which bears and determines us has the form of *war* rather than that of a language: relations of power, not relations of meaning."

Gay Rights Upheld: Alberta Won't Challenge the Supreme Court Ruling (L. Johnsrude, *EJ*, 13 April 1998, A1)

Our Once Gutsy Premier Ralph Klein Now Quails and Cowers under the Ottawa Whip (T. Byfield, *AR*, 13 April 1998, 52)

Ralph's New Friends: Klein Sides with Gays, the Supreme Court, Ottawa and the Media in Defiance of the Will of Albertans (*AR* cover, 20 April 1998)

If Klein Has Managed to Split the Right in Alberta, This Is Not Inconsequential (T. Byfield, *AR*, 20 April 1998, 44)

Ralph Gets Moral, and Alberta Gets Gay Rights: How Klein Snookered Public Opinion to Satisfy Homosexuals, the Supreme Court and the Media (J. Woodard, *AR*, 20 April 1998, 12-17)

A Rich, Educated, Unpersecuted Elite: "This Isn't an Oppressed Minority; This Is a Decadent Elite" (J. Woodard, *AR*, 20 April 1998, 13)

The Strategy of a Human-Rights Ambush (J. Woodard, *AR*, 20 April 1998, 14)

What Use Are Grizzlies? They Look Nice, but They Aren't Ecologically Crucial (L. Sillars, *AR*, 20 April 1998, 25)

The Media's Inquisitional Court Has Handed Down Another Denunciation of Inquisitions (T. Byfield, *AR*, 27 April 1998, 44)

Albertans Have to Tell Ralph to Give Them a Direct Vote of Gay Rights (L. Byfield, *AR*, 27 April 1998, 2)

Until We Regain Control over Our Own Laws, We Can't Call Ourselves a Democracy (L. Byfield, *AR*, 4 May 1998, 2)

One Surrender Too Many: Klein's Capitulation on Vriend – and Much Else Prompts Talk of an Alternative Conservative Party (K. Steel, *AR*, 4 May 1998, 10-12)

Ralph's Line in the Sand on a Slippery Slope: Recent History Demonstrates the Futility of Talking about "Fences" against Gay Rights (J. Woodard, *AR*, 4 May 1998, 13-14)

Gays for Family Values: A Toronto Homosexual Campaigns against Special Rights (J. Woodard, *AR*, 4 May 1998, 14-15)

Rally "Round the Family" Sceptical of Klein's Promised "Fences," CFAC Keeps the Heat on with Rallies and a Petition (K. Steel, *AR*, 25 May 1998, 9)

A Firebrand from BC: CFAC Brings in Kari Simpson to Rouse Opposition to Gay Rights (K. Steel, *AR*, 15 May 1998, 10)

So Where Are Those "Fences"? Klein Dithers While the Gay Agenda Gathers Momentum (J. Woodard, *AR*, 15 June 1998, 16-17)

In a 13 August 1998 interview with *Outlooks*, a Calgary magazine for Alberta's queer communities, Klein made the following statement: "What matters most to me is whether or not somebody is a good person. Are they hard-working? Honest? Sincere? Responsible? Are they good and decent human beings? Those are the important things" (T. Arnold, "Consenting Adults Fine with Klein," 13 August 1998, A5). It is unlikely that Klein had a sudden epiphany in the wake of the Supreme Court ruling in *Vriend*. If he had done the right thing much earlier, then he would have saved thousands of taxpayer dollars, which were spent on a series of legal battles in the service of a minority group made up of religious fundamentalists who wanted special rights for themselves. By not taking this position earlier, Klein aided and abetted Christian fundamentalists in their war against homosexuality.

And you know, after I am bleeding, after I have my stitches, after my broken ribs mend and I am sitting somewhere, anywhere. I am still gay. No one has gotten rid of me. You can't physically brutalize someone, or terrorize someone to change what they are. You have to change your own ignorance. You have to learn, you have to be educated. (Virginia, 1998)

Will the Real Predators Please Stand Up?

The moral panic over homosexuality reached a crescendo with the culmination of the Supreme Court reading in the *Vriend* case. Central to producing the moral panic in Alberta were sensationalized accounts of homosexuality published in *AR*. Significantly, in the seeming absence of real queer Albertans, provincially elected politicians took *AR* accounts seriously. For many other Albertans, queer and otherwise, it appeared that the only information available about homosexuality was that provided by *AR*.

AR utilized moral-theological, medico-moral, and human rights discourses to denounce homosexuality, and this had the effect of keeping the more moderate elected representatives in the province off balance and on the defensive. *AR* was able to utilize homophobic discourse for its own purposes because many elected members of the Alberta legislature, and others in the province, already believed much of what the magazine said about homosexuality. Fundamentalist Christian discourse, which was an ally of the publishers of *AR*, informed the values of some members of the Legislative Assembly. Within this brand of Christian fundamentalism the patriarchal family is the only tolerable form of family.

Alberta Report cover, 20 April 1998

Believing that humans are born into sin, *AR*-style fundamentalist Christians saw themselves and their children as constantly tempted by the pleasures of the flesh and as particularly vulnerable to the sins of any form of
sexuality outside of procreative heterosexual marital relations. The "sins"
of homosexuality, of pleasurable and non-procreative sexuality, were especially vexing. Stockwell Day explicitly used his position as MLA to turn his
form of Christianity into provincial policy, thus imposing an even more
rigid hierarchy of sexuality on all Albertans. Premier Ralph Klein tried to
balance politics between the pole of "severely normal" Albertans and the
pole of "abnormal" Albertans like homosexuals, feminists, and environ-

mentalists, thus successfully avoiding the unpopularity that might have arisen had he aligned provincial human rights protections for gays and lesbians with that set out in the federal Charter of Rights and Freedoms. "Klein tried to create the impression that he was caught between two extreme points of view, and managed to orchestrate the spectacle, which was like a boxing match with himself as the beleaguered referee in the middle" (Dumas 1998, 28).

One of the many myths regarding homosexuality, and gay men in particular, is that such people are sexual predators who prey upon innocent children and youth. Yet, in their war against homosexuality, *AR* and their supporters were themselves exposed as predators. They preyed on people's fears and anxieties. Relying on discourses of sin, crime, deviance, pathology, and human rights as special rights in order to set homosexuals apart as a separate species whose lives embraced a culture of death, *AR* voyeuristically produced a false identity as it obsessed over homosexuality, especially homosex. Its intention was to eliminate a specific group of people from public consciousness and to maintain a narrow notion of who was to be accepted as a proper, normal Albertan. The irony is that its mission failed, in part, because of the intense public profile *AR* obsessively gave to queer issues.

This is like a gender war, kind of thing, but this is also a war about orientation. (Virginia, 1998)

I demanded that my library carry The Advocate, *for balance, if they were going to carry the* Alberta Report *and all its fucking shit ... but the librarian said she could not do that but would not tell me why. (Oscar, 1998)*

This brings me to the end of the objectives I have for this book. I wanted to demonstrate the heaviness of expert, legal, and popular discourses about sexuality, gender, and youth that queer youth had to negotiate while living in Alberta in the 1990s. While many of these discourses shaped how young people elsewhere understood their lives, sexual minority people in Alberta also had to contend with a provincial government that still, in this new century, actively works to deny sexual minority rights. In the 1990s this state-sanctioned homophobia was reflected and fuelled by a provincial magazine, *Alberta Report,* which was widely distributed throughout Alberta and was engaged by prominent and "ordinary" citizens alike.

Dominant discourses from both academics and the popular press concerning gender, sexuality, and youth attempt to fix the limits of how young people can negotiate their identities. Still, as the voices of the young people in *Queer Youth* show, despite the heaviness of these discourses, some youth in Alberta were willing to speak back. Most were aware of *Alberta Report,* prominent as it was in their schools and often used in social studies courses. All were critical of the demands of conventional notions of gender and were aware that at least some part of their negotiations with gender did not cohere with the dominant imperative that behaviour, sexual desire, and sexual practice line up with their bodies. While some did, many did not fit into stereotypical notions of youth as dependent and innocent. Some had been forced onto the street or into foster care by unforgiving parents. All had realized that they could be punished for not conforming to gender norms. While not all the youth in this book spoke of legal discourses affecting their lives, many of them did. These young people were painfully aware of the impact that debates about their civil rights had on them. Yet, as I emphasize throughout, the queer youth represented here cannot be reduced to painful stories. In fact, the voices of these queer youth disrupt the seemingly fixed categories produced by dominant discourses of "gender," "youth," and "sexuality." Even though they faced common difficulties as queer youth, they all differed from one another. And all refused to be consumed by discourses that purported to know who they are.

Notes

()　　　()

Introduction

1　With federal government initiatives to expand the legal definition of marriage to same sex partners, Alberta politicians have publicly announced that Alberta may invoke the not-withstanding clause as a way of opting out of legalizing same sex marriage. Legal experts note this is not possible since the federal government has jurisdiction and is responsible for legal definition and regulation of marriage. In response, the province has indicated that it will refuse to provide licences to gays and lesbians seeking to marry within the province. Elsewhere, the provinces of Ontario and British Columbia have performed numerous same sex marriages. Within queer communities the idea of marriage remains a contentious is-sue; however, in the face of homophobia across the country – especially in Alberta – com-munity members have been compelled to support the cause.

2　"Severely normal" was first coined in relation to the claim that "normal" students were disrupted by the integration of special needs students into Alberta classrooms. Klein took up this phrase to describe Albertans in relation to "outsiders" who would disrupt Alberta's conservative ways. *Edmonton Journal* writer, Paula Simons, wrote about Klein's "imaginary, prototypical, 'severely normal' Albertan" as recently as 20 May 2003 ("Alberta's Real Marthas, Henrys Have Plenty to Tell Premier Klein," B1, B2).

3　The Social Credit party was first headed by Premier William Aberhart from 1935 to 1943, then by Premier Ernest C. Manning from 1943 to 1968. Taking over at Manning's death, Premier Harry Strom served from 12 December 1968 to 10 September 1971. This amounted to a total of thirty-five years in power (1932-68) for the Social Credit party. The political impulse underpinning Social Credit had early ties to the idea of "social credit" espoused by Colonel C.H. Douglas, who theorized that the discrepancy between costs of production and the purchasing power of individuals required government supplement in the form of a social credit that would eliminate poverty. Efforts to incorporate "social credit" into Alberta's economy as well as to change the administration of banks and newspapers, both of which Douglas identified as problems, were blocked by the federal government. In time, with Alberta's growing wealth, social credit was deemed unnecessary and, therefore, was never realized. Alberta's Social Credit was a fiscal and socially conservative political party with strong support within the province and even stronger roots in fundamentalist Chris-tianity. Colonel Douglas quit his advisory position early in his Social Credit tenure, leaving the province because of disputes with Premier William Aberhart over the application of his theory. Books discussing Alberta's Social Credit history include Hesketh (1997) and Elliot and Miller (1987). Taking over after Aberhart's sudden death, Premier Ernest Manning, during his tenure as premier, broadcast his "Back to the Bible Hour" series every Sunday. Alberta's social conservative ethos extended in other directions as well. From the 1940s onward, Alberta, like most other provinces, actively embraced the eugenics movement. However, Alberta is unique for the length of time it adhered to this project and for its refusal to acknowledge any responsibility or obligation to those who were harmed. For example, Albertans deemed mentally unfit were sterilized well into the 1980s. Just prior to the federal Supreme Court decision in *Vriend*, Alberta's justice minister Jon Havelock created an enormous public outcry when he tried to limit settlement to those who were wrongfully sterilized during Alberta's eugenics period.

4 The Progressive Conservatives have been in power from 10 September 1971 to the present. These thirty-two plus years attest to a newer, dominant form of Alberta identity. Even though the name is the same, arguably the Progressive Conservative party under the leadership of Premiers Peter Lougheed (1971-85) and Don Getty (1985-92) was a different entity from the Progressive Conservative party under Ralph Klein. The difference reflects a shift to the right – a shift present in all Canadian political parties.

5 The National Energy Program under Prime Minister Pierre Trudeau was viewed by Alberta as a federal tax grab focused on the province's oil revenues. More recently, changes to Alberta Health Care under Premier Ralph Klein have given rise to federal threats to cut off transfer payments to fund provincial health care. Alberta's resistance to the ratification of the Kyoto Accord in 2003, its refusal to endorse the UN Rights of the Child, and its continued opposition to federal gun registry legislation are other examples of provincial-federal tensions.

6 *Alberta Report* "ended its 30-year run as a fervent voice for conservatism in Alberta and the West on Monday, finally shutting down operations after years of financial troubles" (J. Markusoff, "Report Ends Controversial 30-Year Run," *EJ*, 24 June 2003, A6).

Chapter 2: Production and Consumption of Youth Identity

1 While it is not possible to take up all the works that encompass the term "youth studies," my argument is directed at literature that assumes the category is "natural" and that proceeds to research or theorize from that point.

2 My location as both adult and researcher presented interesting dilemmas. My research is implicated in the authority of a body of expert knowledge from which it is not possible to escape. Taking up the category while destabilizing it shifts the expertness of my knowledge to what Linda Hutcheon (1989) calls a "complicitous critique."

3 This is not a definitive history of the category "youth" but, rather, an indication of some conditions that came together to make possible contemporary subjectivities. How persons aged thirteen to twenty-one actually lived their lives is an important question.

4 Arnett (2000) and Rice (1999) have written introductory readers for youth studies, and the assumption of heterosexual, nuclear families permeates both. For example, the dysfunctional family is often related to heterosexual, nuclear family breakdown.

5 The idea of moratorium, or period of delay, is from Erikson (1950, 1968).

6 Media coverage of what happened to Virk, as well as that of what occurred in Taber, Alberta, and Littleton, Colorado, is replete with adult concerns about youth violence. Yet there is little attention paid to the gender and sexuality policing that occurs among youth.

7 Heterosexism and homophobia produce a diasporic-like migration to queer meccas in large urban centres like Vancouver, Canada; Sydney, Australia; and San Francisco, United States, as well as the creation of gay ghettos. Sexual minorities are underrepresented in rural areas and overrepresented in large urban centres. The longing for family is manifest in this quest for and migration to urban gay communities. Even where sexual minorities do not physically migrate far from home, their sense of self as valued and desired members of a family is gravely disturbed by a heterosexist and homophobic culture. These are significant themes throughout the life histories of each queer youth in this book. Their longing for home, family, belonging, and a sense of place is a poignant and sorrowful part of their life journey.

8 The statistics within other minority groups tell a similar story. Aboriginal youth, for example, have the highest rates of suicide in the United States (National Centre for Health Statistics 1999).

9 A telling indictment of the cultural imperative that youth should live at home is manifest in the lack of funding for youth emergency services such as the Youth Emergency Shelter (YES) in Edmonton. The YES director reported that the shelter obtains over 60 percent of its budget through fundraising and that it must beg and borrow many needed items. I

attended a one-day workshop for youth crisis workers, where we learned that there are fewer than twenty shelter-beds in the greater Edmonton area designated for youth.

Chapter 3: Social/Legal Production of Sexual Minorities in Canada

1 During the course of an RCMP investigation into a case of arson, Klippert was interviewed and charged after he told police that he "had been a homosexual for twenty-four years and admitted to certain sexual acts with males. He was charged with four counts of 'gross indecency.'" All acts were consensual and not "public'" (Kinsman 1996, 258).
2 A vibrant gay liberation movement facilitated a public face for lesbians and gays in Canada. *Queer Youth* does not go into the gay liberation movement, but I do wish to acknowledge the invaluable contribution made by those involved. See Miriam Smith (1999) for a detailed analysis of this movement.
3 Wilson's case, as presented here, is drawn from Herman 1994; Yogis, Duplak, and Trainor 1996; Kinsman 1996; and MacDougall, 2000.
4 In September 2000 the BC Supreme Court overturned a BC Court of Appeal ruling that struck down the Surrey School Board's decision to ban three books about children living with gay or lesbian parents. The appeal court said that the December 1998 decision was flawed because it wrongly determined that the board had been influenced by the religious beliefs of some trustees when it decided that the three books – *Asha's Mums; One Dad, Two Dads, Brown Dads, Blue Dads;* and *Belinda's Bouquet* – would not be approved as learning resources. But Justice Kenneth MacKenzie, who wrote the appeal court decision, also said that the three books met the board's criteria for school library use and that, therefore, teachers could take them into kindergarten and Grade 1 classes for story time and discussion.
5 Named for Ellen Degeneres, actor and comedian.
6 Named for Michel Foucault, French intellectual.
7 Named for Oscar Wilde, playwright.
8 Our interviews began half way through the school year, just as anti-gay harassment against Oscar was increasing.

Chapter 4: Queer Identities and Strange Representations in the Province of the Severely Normal

1 All of the organizations and persons listed here appear as experts in the "war" and in pages of *AR* throughout the 1990s.
2 Incidents of queer bashing increased around the province, as documented by various community centres. The pall of hatred cast over queer Albertans was substantial.

References

Adam, B. 1995. *The Rise of a Gay and Lesbian Movement*. Rev. ed. London: Prentice Hall.
–. 1996. "Structural Foundations of the Gay World." In S. Seidman, ed., *Queer Theory/ Sociology*, 111-26. Cambridge: Blackwell.
Adams, G.R., T.P. Gulotta, and R. Montemayor, eds. 1992. *Adolescent Identity Formation*. Newbury Park, CA: Sage.
Adams, M.L. 1997. *The Trouble with Normal: Postwar Youth and the Making of Heterosexuality*. Toronto: University of Toronto Press.
American Psychiatric Association. 1994. *Diagnostic Criteria from DSM-IV*. Washington, DC: American Psychiatric Association.
Aries, Phillipe. 1962. *Centuries of Childhood*. New York: Knopf.
Aristotle. 1954. *Rhetoric*. Trans. W. Rhys Roberts. New York: Modern Library.
Arnett, J.J. 1999. "Adolescent Storm and Stress, Reconsidered." *American Psychologist* 54: 317-26.
–. 2000. *Adolescence and Emerging Adulthood: A Cultural Approach*. Upper Saddle River, NJ: Prentice Hall.
Arnett, J.J., and S. Taber. 1994. "Adolescence Terminable and Interminable: When Does Adolescence End?" *Journal of Youth and Adolescence* 23: 517-37.
Bagley, C., and P. Tremblay. 1997. "The Great Taboo: Gay Youth and Suicide." *Times.10* 4: 5-6.
Barber, B., J. Olsen, and S. Shagle. 1994. "Associations between Parental Psychological and Behavioral Control and Youth Internalized and Externalized Behaviors." *Child Development* 62: 1120-36.
Bar-Joseph, H., and D. Tzuriel. 1990. "Suicidal Tendencies and Ego Identity in Adolescence. *Adolescence* 25: 215-23.
Bartky, S.L. 1990. *Femininity and Domination: Studies in the Phenomenology of Oppression*. New York: Routledge.
Baumrind, Diana. 1991. "Parenting Styles and Adolescent Development." In J. Brooks-Gunn, R. Lerner, and A.C. Petersen, eds., *The Encyclopedia on Adolescence*, 746-58. New York: Garland.
Bianchi, S.M., and D. Spain. 1996. Women, Work, and Family in America. *Population Bulletin* 51: 1-48.
Bleys, R. 1995. *The Geography of Perversion: Male-to-Male Sexual Behaviour outside the West and the Ethnographic Imagination, 1750-1918*. New York: New York University Press.
Board of Governors of the University of Saskatchewan, Kirkpatrick, and Stinson v. *Saskatchewan Human Rights Commission*, [1976] 3 W.W.R. 385 (Sask. QB).
Boyer, C.B., and S.M. Kegeles. 1991. "Aids Risk and Prevention amongst Adolescents. *Social Science and Medicine* 33: 11-23.
Boyle, P. 1996a. *An Action Plan for Gay/Lesbian/Bisexual Youth and Staff Safety*. Calgary, AB: Calgary Board of Education.

–. 1996b, 24 September. "Introduction." In *An Action Plan for Gay/Lesbian/Bisexual Youth and Staff Safety*, 1-7. Calgary, AB: Calgary Board of Education.

–. 1996c. *Report on Counselling Support for Homosexual Youth Safety*. Calgary, AB: Calgary Board of Education.

Britzman, D. 1995. "What Is This Thing Called Love?" *Taboo: The Journal of Culture and Education* 1: 65-93.

Brownworth, V. 1992. "November: America's Worst-Kept Secret." *The Advocate*, 38-46.

–. 1996. "No Place Like Home." In V. Brownworth, ed., *Too Queer: Essays from a Radical Life*, 67-73. Ithaca, NY: Firebrand.

Buhrmester, D., and J. Carbery. 1992. "Daily Patterns of Self-Disclosure and Adolescent Adjustment." Paper presented at the biennial meeting of the Society for Research on Adolescence (March), Washington, DC.

Bull, C., and J. Gallagher. 1996. *Perfect Enemies, the Gay Movement, and the Politics of the 1990s*. New York: Crown Publishers.

Burke, P. 1996. *Gender Shock: Exploding the Myths of Male and Female*. New York: Doubleday.

Butler, J. 1990. *Gender Trouble: Feminism and the Subversion of Identity*. New York and London: Routledge.

–. 1993. *Bodies That Matter: On the Discursive Limits of "Sex."* New York and London: Routledge.

–. 1997. *The Psychic Life of Power*. Stanford, CA: Stanford University Press.

Calgary Board of Education. 1996. *Report to the Regular Meeting of the Board: An Action Plan for Gay/Lesbian/Bisexual Youth and Staff Safety*, 24 September. Calgary, AB: Calgary Board of Education.

Chakkalakal, T. 2000. "Reckless Eyeballing: Being Reena in Canada." In R. Walcott, ed., *Rude: Contemporary Black Canadian Cultural Criticism*, 160-71. Toronto: Insomniac.

Chamberlain v. *Surrey District School Board No. 36*, [2002] 4 S.C.R. 710, S.C.C. 86 (Can L11).

Cole, D.E., H.O. Protinsky, and L.H. Cross. 1992. "An Empirical Investigation of Adolescent Suicidal Ideation." *Adolescence*, 27: 813-18.

Coleman, E. 1989. "The Development of Male Prostitution Activity among Gay and Bisexual Adolescents." In G. Herdt, ed., *Gay and Lesbian Youth*, 131-50. New York: Harrington Park Press.

Connell, R. 1995. *Masculinities*. Berkeley: University of California Press.

Cornell, D. 1992. *The Philosophy of the Limit*. New York: Routledge.

Corrigan, P. 1987. "Race/Ethnicity/Gender/Culture: Embodying Differences Educationally: An Argument." In J. Young, ed., *Breaking the Mosaic*, 20-30. Toronto: Garamond.

Cote, J.E., and A.L. Allahar. 1994. *Generation on Hold: Coming of Age in the Late Twentieth Century*. Toronto: Stoddart.

DeBaryshe, B.D., G.R. Patterson, and D.M. Capaldi. 1993. "A Performance Model for Academic Achievement in Early Adolescent Boys." *Developmental Psychology* 29: 795-804.

De Beauvoir, S. 1973. *The Second Sex*. Trans. H.M. Parshley. New York: Knopf.

Dereske, J. 2001. *Miss Zukas Shelves the Evidence*. New York: Avon.

Dinshaw, C., and D. Halperin. 1993. "From the Editors." *Gay and Lesbian Quarterly* 1 (1): iii-iv.

Dornbusch, S.M., P.L. Ritter, R. Mont-Reynaud, and Z. Chen. 1990. "Family Decision Making and Academic Performance in a Diverse High School Population." *Journal of Adolescent Research* 5: 143-60.

Dreyfus, H., and D. Rabinow. 1983. *Michel Foucault: Beyond Structuralism and Hermeneutics*. Chicago: University of Chicago Press.

Dukes, R.L., and B.C. Lorch. 1989. "The Effects of School, Family, Self-Concept, and Deviant Behaviour on Adolescent Suicide Ideation." *Journal of Adolescence* 12: 239-51.

Dumas, J. 1998. "V Day." *Other Voices* 11 (1): 23-38.

Egan and Nesbit v. *Canada* (1995) 124 D.L.R. (4th) 609.

Elliott, D.R., and I. Miller. 1987. *Bible Bill: A Biography of William Aberhart*. Edmonton: Reidmore Books.

Erikson, E.H. 1950. *Childhood and Society*. New York: W.W. Norton.

–. 1968. *Identity: Youth and Crisis*. New York: W.W. Norton.

Feldman, S.S., and G.R. Elliott. 1990. *At the Threshold: The Developing Adolescent.* Cambridge: MA: Harvard University Press.

Filax, G.E., and D.A. Shogan. 2003. "Sexual Minorities in Canada." In J. Brodie and L. Trimble, eds., *Reinventing Canada: Politics of the 21st Century*, 164-74. Toronto: Prentice Hall.

Foucault, M. 1979. *Discipline and Punish: The Birth of the Prison.* Trans. A. Sheridan. New York: Vintage.

–. 1980a. *The History of Sexuality.* Vol. 1: *An Introduction.* New York: Vintage.

–. 1980b. *Two Lectures.* In C. Gordon, ed., *Power/Knowledge: Selected Interviews and Other Writings, 1972-1977*, 78-108. New York; Pantheon.

–. 1980c. *Truth or Power.* In C. Gordon, ed., *Power/Knowledge: Selected Interviews and Other Writings, 1972-1977*, 109-33. New York: Pantheon.

Frankfurt, K. 1999. "Countering a Climate Hostile to Gay Students." *High School Magazine* May/June: 25-29.

Freud, A. 1958. "Adolescence." *Psychoanalytic Study of the Child* 15: 255-78.

–. 1969. "Adolescence." In A.E. Winder and D. Angus, eds., *Adolescence: Contemporary Studies*, 13-24. New York: America Books.

Freud, S. 1959 [1917]. "Mourning and Melancholia." In *Sigmund Freud Collected Papers,* Vol. 4, 152-70. Authorized trans. under supervision of Joan Riviere. New York: Basic Books.

–. 1964 [1940]. *An Outline of Psychoanalysis.* Standard ed. London: Hogarth.

–. 1972. "The Sexual Life of Human Beings." In *Introductory Lectures on Psychoanalysis*, 303-38. Harmondsworth: Penguin.

Frum, D. 1997. "Politician Caught Red-Handed Speaking Up for Moral Views: Stockwell Day's Courage under Fire. *Financial Post*, 26 August, 17.

Frye, M. 1983. *The Politics of Reality: Essays in Feminist Theory.* Trumansburg, NY: Crossing Press.

Fuligni, A., and J. Eccles. 1992. "The Effects of Early Adolescent Peer Orientation on Academic Achievement and Deviant Behaviour in High School." Paper presented at the biennial meeting of the Society for Research on Adolescence (March), Washington, DC.

Gallup, G., Jr. 1990. *America's Youth in the 1990s.* Princeton, NJ: Author.

Garber, M. 1989. "Spare Parts: The Surgical Construction of Gender." *Differences* 1 (3): 137-59.

Gibson, P. 1989. "Gay Male and Lesbian Youth Suicide." In *Report of the Secretary's Task Force on Youth Suicide: Prevention and Intervention in Youth Suicide*, 110-42. Rockville, MD: US Department of Health and Human Services.

Gottfredson, M., and T. Hirschi. 1990. *A General Theory of Crime.* Stanford, CA: Stanford University Press.

Green, R. 1987. *The "Sissy Boy Syndrome" and the Development of Homosexuality.* New Haven: Yale University Press.

Greer, A., H. Barbaree, and C. Brown. 1997. "Canada." In D. West and R. Green, eds., *Sociolegal Control of Homosexuality: A Multi-Nation Comparison*, 169-77. New York: Plenum Press.

Griffin, C. 1993. *Representations of Youth: The Study of Youth and Adolescence in Britain and America.* Oxford: Polity.

Griffin, P. 1993-94. "Homophobia in Sport: Addressing the Needs of Lesbians and Gay High School Athletes." *High School Journal* 77: 80-7.

Grotevant, H.D. 1987. "Toward a Process of Identity Formation." *Journal of Adolescent Research* 2: 202-22.

Haber, C. 1991. "The Psychoanalytic Treatment of a Preschool Boy with a Gender Identity Disorder." *Journal of the American Psychoanalytic Association* 39 (1): 107-29.

Halberstam, J. 1998. *Female Masculinity.* Durham: Duke University Press.

Hall, G.S. 1904. *Adolescence: Its Psychology and Its Relation to Physiology, Anthropology, Sociology, Sex, Crime, Religion and Education.* Vols. 1-2. New York: D. Appleton.

Hall, S. 1990. *Cultural Representations and Signifying Practices.* New York: Routledge.

Halperin, D. 1995. *Saint Foucault: Towards a Gay Hagiography.* New York: Oxford University Press.

Hausman, B. 1995. *Changing Sex: Transsexualism, Technology, and the Idea of Gender.* Durham: Duke University Press.

Hazell, P. 1991. "Postvention after Teenage Suicide: An Australian Experience." *Journal of Adolescence* 14: 335-42.

Hemmings, A. 1998. "The Self-Transformations of African American Achievers." *Youth and Society* 29: 330-68.

Henry, C.S., A.L. Stephenson, M.F. Hanson, and W. Hargett. 1993. "Adolescent Suicide in Families: An Ecological Approach." *Adolescence* 28: 291-308.

Herdt, G. 1989. *Gay and Lesbian Youth.* New York: Harrington.

Herman, D. 1994. *Rights of Passage: Struggles for Lesbian and Gay Equality.* Toronto: University of Toronto Press.

Herschberger, S.L., N.W. Pilkington, and A.R. D'augelli. 1997. "Predictors of Suicide Attempts among Gay, Lesbian, and Bisexual Youth." *Journal of Adolescent Research* 12: 477-97.

Hesketh, B. 1997. *Major Douglas and Alberta Social Credit.* Toronto: University of Toronto Press.

Humphreys, A. 1999. "Gay Pastor Sues Police Force for Outing Him." *National Post*, 8 December, A3.

Hunter, J. 1990. "Violence against Lesbian and Gay Male Youths." *Journal of Interpersonal Violence* 5: 295-300.

Hunter, J., and R. Schaecher. 1987. "Stresses on Gay and Lesbian Adolescents in Schools." *Social Work in Education* 9: 180-90.

Hutcheon, L. 1989. *The Politics of Postmodernism.* New York: Routledge.

Jagose, A. 1996. *Queer Theory: An Introduction.* New York: Oxford University Press.

Jesuit Centre for Social Faith and Justice. 1995. "In Search of Safety: The Lives of Lesbian and Gay Youth." In *The Moment*, 1-13. Toronto: Jesuit Centre for Social Faith and Justice.

Kessler, S. 1998. *Lessons from the Intersexed.* New Jersey: Rutgers University Press.

Kessler, S., and W. McKenna. 1978. *Gender: An Ethnomethodological Approach.* New York: John Wiley and Sons.

Kett, J. 1977. *Rites of Passage: Adolescence in America, 1790 to the Present.* New York: Basic.

Khayatt, D. 1994. "Surviving School as a Lesbian Student." *Gender and Education* 6: 47-61.

Kielwasser, A., and M. Wolf. 1993-94. "Silence, Difference, and Annihilation: Understanding the Impact of Mediated Heterosexism on High School Students." *High School Journal* 77: 58-79.

Kinsman, G. 1996. *The Regulation of Desire: Homo and Hetero Sexualities.* Montreal: Black Rose.

Kiss and Tell. 1994. *Her Tongue on My Theory.* Vancouver, BC: Press Gang Publishers.

Koopmans, M. 1995. "A Case of Family Dysfunction and Teenage Suicide Attempt: Applicability of a Family Systems Paradigm." *Adolescence* 30 (117): 87-94.

Kourany, R.F. 1987. "Suicide among Homosexual Adolescents." *Journal of Homosexuality* 13: 111-17.

Kruks, G. 1991. Gay and Lesbian Homeless/Street Youth: Special Issues and Concerns. *Journal of Adolescent Health* 2: 515-18.

Kuttler, A.F., A.M. La Greca, and M.J. Prinstein. 1999. "Friendship Qualities and Social-Emotional Functioning of Adolescents with Close, Cross-Sex Friendships." *Journal of Research on Adolescence* 9: 339-66.

Larson, R., and M.H. Richards. 1994. *Divergent Realities: The Emotional Lives of Mothers, Fathers, and Adolescents.* New York: Basic.

Lester, D. 1987. "A Sub-Cultural Theory of Teenage Suicide." *Aolescence* 22: 317-20.

–. 1988. Youth Suicide: A Cross-Culture Perspective." *Aolescence* 23: 955-58.

–. 1991. "Social Correlates of Youth Suicide Rates in the United States." *Adolescence* 26: 55-58.

Levi-Strauss, C. 1969. *The Elementary Structures of Kinship.* Trans. J.H. Bell. Ed. J.R. von Sturmer and R. Needom. Boston: Beacon.

Lorber, J. 1994. *Paradoxes of Gender.* New Haven: Yale University Press.

Lorde, A. 1984. *Sister Outsider: Essays and Speeches.* Trumanship, NY: Crossing Press.

MacDougall, B. 2000. *Queer Judgments: Homosexuality, Expression, and the Courts in Canada.* Toronto: University of Toronto Press.

MacKenzie, G.O. 1994. *Transgender Nation.* Bowling Green, OH: Bowling Green State University Press.

Marcia, J.E. 1966. "Development and Validation of Ego Identity Status." *Journal of Personality and Social Psychology* 3: 551-58.

–. 1980. "Identity in Adolescence." In J. Adelson, ed., *Handbook of Adolescent Psychology,* 159-87. New York: Wiley.

–. 1989. "Identity and Intervention." *Journal of Adolescence* 12: 401-10.

–. 1993. "The Relational Roots of Identity." In J. Kroger, ed., *Discussions on Ego Identity,* 101-20. Hillside, NJ: Erlbaum.

–. 1994. "The Empirical Study of Ego Identity." In H.A. Bosma and L.G. Tobi, eds., *Identity and Development: An Interdisciplinary Approach,* 391-414. Mahwah, NJ: Erlbaum.

–. 1999. "Representational Thought in Ego Identity, Psychotherapy, and Psychosocial Developmental Theory." In I.E. Siegel, ed., *Development of Mental Representation: Theories and Applications,* 391-414. Mahwah, NJ: Erlbaum.

Marcus, G., and M. Fischer. 1986. *Anthropology as Cultural Critique: An Experimental Moment in the Human Sciences.* Chicago: University of Chicago Press.

Martin, A.D. 1982. "Learning to Hide: The Socialization of the Gay Adolescent." *Adolescent Psychiatry: Development and Clinical Studies* 10: 52-65.

Martin, A.D., and E.S. Hetrick. 1988. "The Stigmatization of the Gay and Lesbian Adolescent." *Journal of Homosexuality* 15 (1-2): 163-85.

McClintock, A. 1995. *Imperial Leather: Race, Gender and Sexuality in the Colonial Context.* New York: Routledge.

McCue, P. 1991. "Addressing the Invisible Minority: Facing Homophobia." *Teacher* 3: 9.

Mead, M. 1982 [1961]. *Coming of Age in Samoa.* New York: Morrow Quill.

Melby, J.N., and R.D. Conger. 1996. "Parental Behaviours and Adolescent Academic Performance: A Longitudinal Analysis." *Journal of Research on Adolescence* 6: 113-37.

Midgely, C., and T. Urdan. 1995. "Predictors of Middle School Students' Use of Self-Handicapping Strategies." *Journal of Early Adolescence* 15: 389-411.

Miller, B.C., and B. Benson. 1999. "Romantic and Sexual Relationship Development during Adolescence." In W. Furman, B.B. Brown, and C. Feiring, eds., *The Development of Romantic Relationships in Adolescence,* 99-121. New York: Cambridge University Press.

Miller, K.E. 1990. "Adolescents' Same-Sex and Opposite-Sex Peer Relations: Sex Differences in Popularity, Perceived Social Competence, and Social Cognitive Skills." *Journal of Adolescent Research* 5: 222-41.

Mitchell, A. 1997. "School Trustees Create Storm over Gay Rights." *Globe and Mail,* 7 March, A2.

Money, J. 1994 [1968]. *Sex Errors of the Body: Dilemmas, Education, Counselling.* Baltimore: Johns Hopkins University Press.

Money, J., and A.A. Erhardt. 1972. *Man and Woman, Boy and Girl.* Baltimore: Johns Hopkins University Press.

Moore, S., and D. Rosenthal. 1993. *Sexuality in Adolescence.* New York: Routledge.

Moran, J.P. 2000. *Teaching Sex: The Shaping of Adolescence in the 20th Century.* Cambridge, MA: Harvard University Press.

Morano, C.D., R.A. Cisler, and J. Lemerond. 1992. "Risk Factors for Adolescent Suicidal Behaviour: Loss, Insufficient Family Support, and Hopelessness." *Adolescence* 28: 851-65.

Moynihan, D. 1965. *The Negro Family: The Case for National Action.* Washington, DC: Office of Planning and Research Universities, Department of Labor.

Muska, S., and G. Olafsdottir. 1998. *The Brandon Teena Story.* Zeitgeist Films.

Newton, E. 2000. *Margaret Mead Made Me Gay: Personal Essays, Public Ideas.* Durham: Duke University Press.

Nicolosi, J. 1991. *Reparative Therapy of Male Homosexuality: A New Clinical Approach.* Northvale, NJ: J. Aronson.

O'Byrne, S., and J. McGinnis. 1996. "Case Comment: *Vriend* v. *Alberta, Plessy* Revisited: Lesbian and Gay Rights in the Province of Alberta." *Alberta Law Review* 34 (4): 892-924.

O'Connor, A. 1993-94. "Who Gets Called Queer in School? Lesbian, Gay and Bisexual Teenagers, Homophobia, and High School." *High School Journal* 77: 7-12.

Paikoff, R.L., and J. Brokkes-Gunn. 1991. "Do Parent-Child Relationships Change during Puberty?" *Psychological Bulletin* 110: 47-66.

Paluszny, M., C. Davenport, and W.J. Kim. 1991. "Suicide Attempts and Ideation: Adolescents Evaluated on a Pediatric Ward." *Adolescence* 26: 959-76.

Parsons, T. 1951. *The Social System.* Glencoe, IL: Free Press.

–. 1964. *Essays in Sociological Theory.* Chicago: Free Press.

Patton, C. 1995. "Between Innocence and Safety: Epidemiologic and Popular Constructions of Young People's Need for Safe Sex." In J. Terry and J. Urla, eds., *Deviant Bodies: Critical Perspectives on Difference in Science and Popular Culture*, 338-57. Bloomington: Indiana University Press.

Paul, E.L., and K.M. White. 1990. "The Development of Intimate Relationships in Late Adolescence." *Adolescence* 25: 375-400.

Peck, D.L. 1987. "Social-Psychological Correlates of Adolescent and Youthful Suicide." *Adolescence* 22: 863-78.

Perlman, S.B. 1980. "Pregnancy and Parenting among Runaway Girls." *Journal of Family Issues* 1: 262-73.

Petersen, A.C. 1993. "Creating Adolescents: The Role of Context and Process in Developmental Trajectories." *Journal of Research on Adolescence* 3: 1-18.

Plato. 1956. *Great Dialogues of Plato.* Trans. W.H.D. Rouse. New York: Mentor.

Price, J.N. 1999. "Racialized Masculinities: The Diploma, Teachers, and Peers in the Lives of Young African American Men." *Youth and Society* 31: 224-63.

Quinlivan, K. 1996. "Claiming an Identity They Taught Me to Despise." *Women's Studies Journal* 12: 99-113.

Rekers, G. 1995. *Handbook of Child and Adolescent Sexual Problems.* New York: Lexington Books.

Rekers, G., and O. Lovaas. 1974. "Behavioral Treatment of Deviant Sex-Role Behaviors in a Male Child." *Journal of Applied Behavior Analysis* 7 (2): 173-90.

Rekers, G., and S. Mead. 1979. "Early Intervention for Sexual Identity Disturbances: Self-monitoring of Play Behaviour." *Journal of Abnormal Child Psychology* 7 (4): 405-23.

Rekers, G., and S. Morey. 1990. "The Relationship of Measures of Sex-Typed Play with Clinician Ratings of Degree of Gender Disturbance." *Journal of Clinical Psychology* 46 (1): 28-34.

Rekers, G., A. Rosen, and S. Morey. 1992. "Projective Test Findings for Boys with Gender Disturbance: Draw-a-Person Test, IT Scale, and Make-a-Picture Story Test." *Perceptual and Motor Skills* 71 (3): 771-9.

Rekers, G., J. Sanders, and C. Strauss. 1981. "Developmental Differentiation of Adolescent Body Gestures." *Journal of Genetic Psychology* 138: 123-31.

Remafedi, G. 1991. "Risk Factors for Attempted Suicide in Gay and Bisexual Youth." *Pediatrics* 87: 869-75.

–. 1994. "Introduction: The State of Knowledge on Gay, Lesbian, and Bisexual Youth Suicide." In G. Remafedi, ed., *Death by Denial: Studies of Suicide in Gay and Lesbian Teenagers*, 7-14. Boston: Alyson.

Rice, F.P. 1999. *The Adolescent: Development, Relationships, and Culture.* 9th ed. Boston: Allyn and Bacon.

Rich, C.L., M. Sherman, and R.C. Fowler. 1990. "San Diego Suicide Study: The Adolescents." *Adolescence* 27: 73-86.

Rivers, I. 1997."Violence against Lesbian and Gay Youth and Its Impact. In M. Schneider, ed., *Pride and Prejudice: Working with Lesbian, Gay and Bisexual Youth*, 31-48. Toronto: Central Toronto Youth Services.

Roberts, G. 1999. *Adam and Evil.* New York: Fawcett.

Rofes, E. 1983a. *I Thought People Like That Killed Themselves: Lesbians, Gay Men and Suicide.* San Francisco: Grey Fox Press.

–. 1983b. "Opening up the Classroom Closet: Responding to the Educational Needs of Gay and Lesbian Youth." *Harvard Educational Review* 59: 444-53.

Rostow, A. 1999. "Hostile Hallways." *Girlfriends* 40 (June): 28-32.

Rotheram-Borus, M.J., and C. Koopman. 1991. "Sexual Risk Behaviour, AIDS Knowledge, and Beliefs about AIDS among Predominantly Minority Gay and Bisexual Male Adolescents. *AIDS Education and Prevention* 3: 305-12.

Saint Augustine. 1961 [1950]. *Confessions.* Trans. with an introduction by R.S. Pine-Coffin. Harmondsworth: Penguin.

Savin-Williams, R.C. 1994. "Verbal and Physical Abuse as Stressors in the Lives of Lesbian, Gay Male, and Bisexual Youths: Associations with School Problems, Running Away, Substance Abuse, Prostitution, and Suicide." *Journal of Consulting and Clinical Psychology* 62: 261-9.

Sayer, D. 1991. *Capitalism and Modernity: An Excursus on Marx and Weber.* New York: Routledge.

Schneider, A.G., N.L. Faberow, and G.N. Kruks. 1989. "Suicidal Behaviour in Adolescent and Young Adult Gay Men." *Suicide and Life Threatening Behaviour* 19: 381-94.

Scholinski, D. 1997. *The Last Time I Wore a Dress.* New York: Riverhead.

Sedgwick, E. 1990. *Epistemology of the Closet.* Berkeley: University of California Press.

–. 1993. "How to Bring Your Kids Up Gay: The War on Effeminate Boys." In E. Sedgwick, *Tendencies,* 154-64. Durham, NC: Duke University Press.

Seidman, S., ed. 1996. *Queer Theory/Sociology.* Oxford: Blackwell.

Sethna, C. 2000. "High-School Confidential: RCMP Surveillance of Secondary School Student Activists." In G. Kinsman, D. Buse, and M. Steedman, eds., *Whose National Security? Canadian State Surveillance and the Creation of Enemies,* 121-30. Toronto: Between the Lines.

Shafer, D., and P. Fisher. 1996. "Sexual Orientation in Adolescents Who Commit Suicide." *Suicide and Life Threatening Behaviour* 26: 218.

Shapiro, J. 1991. "Gender and the Mutability of Sex. In J. Epstein and K. Strands, eds., *Body Guards,* 248-79. New York: Routledge.

Shogan, D. 1999. *The Making of High-Performance Athletes: Discipline, Diversity, and Ethics.* Toronto: University of Toronto Press.

Silin, J. 1995. *Sex, Death and the Education of Children: Our Passion for Ignorance in the Age of AIDS.* New York: Teachers College Press.

Singer, L. 1993. *Erotic Welfare: Sexual Theory and Politics in the Age of Epidemic.* Ed. and introduced for publication by J. Butler. New York: Routledge.

Smith, G.W. 1993. "Homophobic Schools: Factories of Violence." *Orbit: Ideas about Teaching and Learning* 24: 18-19.

–. 1998. "The Ideology of 'Fag': The School Experience of Gay Students." Ed. for publication by D.E. Smith. *Sociological Quarterly* 39: 309-35.

Smith, K. 1999. *Mental Hygiene: Classroom Films, 1945-1970: Sex, Drugs, Dating, Driver Safety.* New York: Blast.

Sommers, B.H. 1984. "The Troubled Teen: Suicide, Drug Use, and Running Away." *Women's Health* 9: 117-41.

Sommerville, J. 1982. *The Rise and Fall of Childhood.* Beverly Hills, CA: Sage.

Spradley, J. 1979. *The Ethnographic Interview.* New York: Harcourt Brace Jovanovich.

Stack, S.M. 1985. "The Effect of Domestic/Religious Individualism in Suicide, 1954-1978." *Journal of Marriage and the Family* 47: 431-7.

Steinberg, L., in collaboration with B. Brown and S. Dornbusch. 1996. *Beyond the Classroom: Why School Reform Has Failed and What Parents Need to Do.* New York: Simon and Schuster.

Steinberg, L., S.D. Lamborn, S.M. Dornbusch, and N. Darling. 1992. "Impact of Parenting Practices on Adolescent Achievement: Authoritative Parenting, School Involvement, and Encouragement to Succeed." *Child Development* 63: 1288-88.

Stivers, C. 1988. Parent-Adolescent Communication and Its Relationship to Adolescent Depression and Suicide Proneness. *Adolescence* 23: 291-5.

Strommen, E.F. 1989. "You're a What? Family Member Reactions to the Disclosure of Homosexuality." *Journal of Homosexuality* 19: 37-58.

Stychin, C. 1995. *Law's Desire: Sexuality and the Limits of Justice.* London: Routledge.

Terry, J., and J. Urla, eds. 1995. *Deviant Bodies.* Bloomington: Indiana University Press.

Tishler, C.L. 1992. "Adolescent Suicide: Assessment of Risk, Prevention, and Treatment." *Adolescent Medicine* 3: 51-60.

Tyack, D.B. 1990. *The One Best System: A History of American Urban Education.* Cambridge, MA: Harvard University Press.

US Department of Health and Human Services. 1989. *Report of the Secretary's Task Force on Youth Suicide.* Vol. 3: *Prevention and Interventions in Youth Suicide.* Rockville, MD: US Department of Health and Human Services.

Vriend v. Alberta, [1994] 6 W.W.R. 414 (Alta. QB); appeal allowed (1996) 132 D.L.R. (4th) 595 (Alta. CA); reversed (1998), 156 D.L.R. (4th) 385 (S.C.C.).

Wade, N.L. 1987. "Suicide as a Resolution of Separation-Individuation among Adolescent Girls." *Adolescence* 22: 169-77.

Warner, M., ed. 1994a. *Fear of a Queer Planet: Queer Politics and Social Theory.* Minneapolis: University of Minnesota Press.

–. 1994b. "Introduction." In M. Warner, ed., *Fear of a Queer Planet: Queer Politics and Social Theory,* vii-xxxi. Minneapolis: University of Minnesota Press.

Waterman, A.S. 1992. "Identity as an Aspect of Optimal Functioning." In G.R. Adams, T.P. Gullotta, and R. Montemayor, eds., *Adolescent Identity Formation.* Newbury Park, CA: Sage.

Weeks, J. 1985. *Sexuality and Its Discontents: Meanings, Myths and Modern Sexualities.* New York: Routledge.

Whatley, M.H. 1988. "Raging Hormones and Powerful Cars: The Construction of Men's Sexuality in School Education and Popular Adolescent Film." *Journal of Education* 170 (3): 100-21.

Williams, A.F. 1998. "Risky Driving Behaviour among Adolescents." In R. Jessor, ed., *New Perspectives on Adolescent Risk Behaviour,* 221-40. New York: Cambridge University Press.

Wilson, A. 1996. "How We Find Ourselves: Identity Development and Two-Spirit People." *Harvard Educational Review* 66: 303-17.

Yogis, J., K. Duplak, J.R. Trainor. 1996. *Sexual Orientation and Canadian Law: An Assessment of the Law Affecting Lesbian and Gay Persons.* Toronto: Emond Montgomery Publications.

Youniss, J., J.A. McLellan, and M. Yates. 1985. *Adolescent Relations with Mothers, Fathers, and Friends.* Chicago: University of Chicago Press.

Zucker, K., and S. Bradley. 1995. *Gender Identity Disorder and Psychosexual Problems in Children and Adolescents.* New York: Guilford Press.

Index